For my patient wife Carla
and my two little monkeys…
Mhairi and Rhian

- more than the world -

The people and events have been changed to protect the innocent, and any similarities to actual persons, either living or dead, are merely coincidental.

First Edition
Text copyright © Michael Kelly, 2010

Hotel Life

A Survivor's Guide to Food and Beverage

Foreword

In order to reach the heights of the Food and Beverage Manager position you must be committed, love variety, cope well under pressure, and have a great sense of humor. My own pilgrimage towards this goal was spurred on by an inspirational sight many years ago by the Manager of the Ellwyn Hotel in Portobello, Alex.

It was a cold and wet winter evening when I made my way to the bar in the hotel to watch the big match: Liverpool versus Manchester United. The bar was packed as everyone clamored for a spot close to the TV. This was difficult as Alex had placed the eighteen inch TV at just above head height on the wall. Unless you were in the first row or stood at six foot three, you danced back and forth all night trying to catch a glimpse through a sea of elbows and shoulders.

As kick-off time approached, the referee called the game off due to the monsoon-like rain on the field. The disappointed crowd in the bar slowly started to file out as they finished their pints. An unusually quick-thinking Alex, sensing the urgency of the situation, needed a plan to keep the crowd drinking in the bar. With only his t-shirt on, he squeezed through the crowd and across the street to his apartment. Four minutes later, a soaking wet Alex slid back through the crowd to the TV and inserted his favorite video: Escape to Victory.

For those unfamiliar with this war-time Stallone classic, the story pits the Germans against a group of POW's in a soccer match. The POW's try to use the match as a vehicle to escape from the POW camp.

Great bursts of laughter greeted Alex's strange choice of film, but within a few minutes, he had half the pub buying tickets in the draw for the first and last goal scorer in the movie. Most of the crowd now had to stay for the entire movie to see if they had won.

Large cheers went up every time the POW's scored (the Germans not being overly popular in the UK since the 1940's). I marveled at Alex's ability to problem solve with such radical thinking.

This was a turning point in my own thinking too. I knew at that moment that if Alex could run a hotel, so could I! All I had to do was figure out how to get there.

Food and Beverage is not an easy job, and it is certainly not for everyone. The hours are long, it is physically demanding and the pay is notoriously low when you are starting out.

It is also not without its pitfalls. There are plenty of managers and co-workers who are competing for promotions, targets, bonuses and the incredibly short-term adoration of their managers. There are guests looking for freebies and owners looking to cut costs any way they can. It can be cut-throat! As I keep telling any of the staff that still listen to me: "Remember: this is a business." Sometimes this is brought back to me like a brick in the face.

Over time, I realized that each department in a hotel is a completely different animal, and that there are certain rules of engagement the Food and Beverage Pilgrim must stick to when dealing with them…or else! It's like playing fifteen games of poker at one time: it's difficult to remember what cards you're holding in every game.

This book will give the reader an insight into which cards to play in each game and when to play them, without breaking the rules of engagement. Hopefully, you will also gain an insight as to what kind of pitfalls may be in store for you…and how to avoid them. However, the most valuable thing to take away from this book is the importance of retaining your sense of humor if you are to have any chance of survival in the Food and Beverage world.

Chapter One – The Nocturnal Mafia

"Jesus Christ! Not again!" Carla leaped out of bed like a salmon at the sound of the first ring. I had no desire to answer the phone, but I knew it was hopeless to ignore it. These bastards gave up at nothing. I managed to open one eye enough to peek at the seldom-required alarm clock. 4:00am, not bad. Five and a half hours sleep. Not a personal best, but around the average for a busy weekend at work.

The phone had rung out at least three times as I trudged the death march to the hallway to await the next series of rings. I no longer keep a phone closer than eight feet to where I sleep. The shock I get when it goes off during the night results in a racing heartbeat that a two hour marathon couldn't achieve. It can take me over an hour to recover enough to get back to sleep. Carla on the other hand, is the deepest sleeper I have ever known.

Should something accidentally awake her before her eight hours are officially up however…look out! I had thought about putting a measuring tape at the side of her bed. I have no doubt she could clear two feet above bed height while still horizontal. It might take a B-52 bomber to wake her however. So eight feet away, the phone usually posed no problem…for her at least.

I cringed as I picked up the phone halfway through its first ring. "Slurp, slurp." Diego. My heart sank. Until proven otherwise, I always hold out the faintest hope that it really could be a wrong number.

I dreaded calls from Diego. Everything was a trauma. I could tell from his long, drawn out slurping that this was going to be a good one. He reveled in the dramatic. He was obviously eating something too; he usually was. If I had to guess, I'd have gone for the chocolate and pistachio ice cream.

The pastry chefs were so fed up about running out of ice cream when he was on the night before, that they got a new set of keys made for the Pastry room. Of course, as Night Manager, Diego had access to every key in the house! His huge bowls of ice cream through the night were legendary. One pastry chef used to swear he could tell us the hotel occupancy from the number of scoops of ice cream that were missing. He was never far away either! I held my breath until he'd inhaled another shovelful.

"Barbara just called in sick.'

"Fucking bitch, what is it this time?" I had been through enough HR courses even at this early point in my career to know that this was not the HR-recommended response I should have delivered. However; "Thank you for bringing this to my attention. That is indeed unfortunate," certainly did not pop out at me.

I had not been at enough HR courses at this point to realize that some people know what your triggers are, and that they can't wait to bait you into a reaction.

I didn't need a lot of baiting on this one though. Barbara called in sick a lot. Diego knew how this drove me crazy. No doubt that was why he was enjoying this call. I could picture him sitting in the back office, feet up on the desk, with a Jurassic sized bowl of ice cream…probably with two extra pint-sized scoops for this particular call. We both knew I was hooked though.

"What's wrong with her this time?"

"She said she was throwing up all night." Of course! What else? This was Barbara's sickness of choice. Unless there was something in it specifically for Barbara, she was always sick when you most counted on her. A psychological nut job with behavioral issues that her two year old son Ryan (aka sickness excuse number 2…but only by a wheeze) would have been hard pressed to emulate. She had been the Room Service Supervisor for as long as I could remember.

This was a big weekend for us and her shift started in less than two hours. I guestimated rather quickly that my odds of getting someone to cover by 6:00am on this Sunday morning were somewhere between zero and fuck all. There was silence (apart from the occasional slurp) on the line as I weighed my options. Diego would not interrupt this silence. This was top entertainment when you held a job in which trying to resist the pastry room was your toughest task.

Feebly, I threw it out there: "How many breakfast pre-orders do we have?"

"Slurp, slurp. Forty six at the last walkround,"

"Fuck it! Send me a cab at five thirty." Click.

I was now wide awake. I checked the clock again. 4:10am. Although I had been in semi-denial about balding for a number of years, I would have had to admit that I could not spend anywhere near eighty minutes getting ready for work. Pissed off at Barbara; always letting everyone down. Pissed off at Human Resources; they never help me do anything about Barbara. Pissed off at Diego; why the hell do Nights always call you before the problem is even close to a crisis? Pissed off at just about everyone. "I bet the Director of Sales doesn't get a call at 4am when someone calls in sick!" I murmured to myself.

5:30am: my cab arrives. Diego is standing at Reception as I walk in, grinning. I've had a while to think about my approach. "Diego, you know I'll come in, why didn't you call me around 5am so I could get a bit more sleep?" As I get closer, I realize he isn't grinning. Ice cream stains around his lips had widened his smile. I was right…chocolate.

His shoulders shrugged up as high as the Andes, as he prepared himself for the Diego mantra. In his long, drawn out, high-pitched Argentine accent, he replied: "But Mike, what could I do?"

I swear that phrase will follow me to my grave.

There was really no point in playing the scenario out any further with him. You see, the Night staff are the Semi-Untouchables in the Hotel hierarchy. They know it, and everyone that has thirty days hard labor in a hotel knows it too. The Night Manager reports to the Front Office Manager, so you have to pass on your carefully re-worded comments and recommendations regarding a member of the Night team to the Front Office Manager.

Try to do this in person, and not by phone or e-mail. This way, you can get close enough to stick a finger in one of their ears. I have never actually tried this myself, but I can think of nothing else that may successfully result in the information not going in one ear and straight out the other. They may smile, pretend to take notes and in some extreme cases, even feign interest. Do not be fooled by these cunning tactics. This is a natural reflex that occurs in all Front Office Managers. Rest assured that no exchange between the Front Office Manager and the Night team member will take place.

At first, I assumed this was because the Front Office Manager wouldn't actually recognize their staff member in order to discipline them. Although this is true in most cases (Front Office Managers generally arriving at 9:01am and departing certainly no later than 4:59pm), there is a more simple reason the exchange will not occur: all managers of Night staff live in constant fear that they will quit. The thought of working these unsociable hours themselves would strike fear into the Grinch-sized hearts of even the most committed Front Office Manager.

From the Front Office Manager's point of view, there are plenty of excuses to help them avoid a discussion with, and (deep breath) action against, the Night staff.

For an appetizer, who is going to corroborate any alleged misdemeanor against them? There are generally very few guests or staff wandering around a hotel after 11:00pm. Witnesses are scarcer than foie gras in a vegan's fridge

For an entrée, the Night team is, among other things, a team. Even though they may report to different departments, they all have at least one thing in common: they are in this job for life. Therefore not many internal witnesses are going to support any evidence you may have.

For dessert, Human Resources usually need a week in therapy after spending months interviewing some of the top entertainers from a police line-up in order to find the one person with a somewhat reasonable excuse for wanting to work these hours. So Human Resources is not likely to pursue any disciplinary action for misdemeanors up to, and I am sure including, manslaughter against the Semi-Untouchables.

The reason so many strange candidates apply for this position? They know a) there are not a lot of guests or staff about in a hotel after 11pm, so witnesses to any of their petty thefts will be hard to find; and b) any internal witnesses would never support any evidence against them, so they are in a job for life.

Actually, they are kind of like a Nocturnal Mafia in the hotel, and they have their own punishments for breaking 'the code.' Grassing for personal gain is without a doubt the most heinous of crimes against the Nocturnal Mafia. This only happens for one reason: the promotion. Therefore the punishment meted out by the Mafia to those not under the direct protection of Human Resources is cruel and unusual: irony.

Once the 'grass' is promoted to day shift, they too now have to live with the constant and terrifying fear of the Night team. Suddenly on days off, Night staff start calling in sick. 'The grass' (he can no longer be called by the name on his new badge) is called in to cover Night shifts because nobody else knows how to cover the shift.

The grass finds he is drawn back into the dark world again, except living with the enemy now. Every time their guard is down and their basic instinct returns, witnesses appear over their shoulders. If only they had just kept quiet. The stress builds. Combined with the switching back and forth from days to nights, they have to call in sick themselves. Their manager then questions their commitment; and before you can say 'turncoat,' HR is upon them. Except now, no longer under the protection of the Night team...they are sacked.

Through trial and error I have concluded that there are two basic types of Night Manager: the Spineless Jellyfish and the Classic Brown-Nose.

Less deadly than its Australian namesake, the Spineless Jellyfish is readily identified by their heat-of-the-moment e-mails. When you come across these e-mails for the first time, it is important not to panic. The Jellyfish is as scared of you as you are of them at this point. However, any sudden movements can cause a sting that you may never recover from. Take two deep breaths and check the details of the e-mail.

To the Spineless Jellyfish, timing is everything. Like a terrorist's bomb, their fingerprint is the timing of the explosion. If they sent the e-mail within thirty minutes of starting or ending their shift, you have a SJ. Congratulations! These are usually harmless so you can relax. No matter who was copied in on this e-mail, its main purpose was to vent, and not to maim.

At this point, you have three options:

a) Delete the e-mail without reading it. It is hardly essential reading after all.

b) Forward the e-mail to their superiors and copy in Human Resources. This is suicidal. The superiors and HR will avoid you at all costs until they feel confident that it has blown over. Shunned and alone, you will second guess your every decision for the next month. Therefore this course of action is only recommended once you have secured another position in another continent, preferably in a different line of work.

c) File the e-mail away in a sub-folder and do not respond or react to the sender in any way. Pretend you never saw it. This is the highly recommended course of action for two reasons:

1. Control. Within forty five seconds of sending any such e-mail, the sender will have told the entire Night Mafia of their e-mail; why it will offend you, and how it will land you in the HR office. The Mafia will be positively drooling whilst watching you for signs of anger and frustration. Therefore if you can completely disregard any issue mentioned in the e-mail, the rest of the Night team will question whether any such e-mail was actually sent; thereby upsetting the Mafia's confidence in The Don.

2. Control. The Don will know his word is now under scrutiny. He also knows you have the Ace of Spades filed away in a sub-folder if required at any time. Watch for a change of attitude towards you. Give nothing away. Fearing a lack of confidence from within, The Don will most likely lash out at an easier target now, perhaps Reservations for over-booking rooms. You can now afford to be smug in the knowledge that you have upset the balance of power at Night. It may take several weeks before the natural order is restored. Should any of your staff call in sick during this time, rest assured you will get the extra hour's sleep.

As you can see from reasons one and two, it is advantageous to be in control when dealing with the Night Mafia. Any pest controller will tell you that the key to controlling unwanted pests is to catch them. Identification is crucial in determining how you are going to get rid of your pests.

Diego was a Jellyfish. I had discovered this through a series of e-mails that had left me sleepless for four nights. I did manage to regain control, but not via the normal route of disregarding e-mails.

Everyone had something on Diego. But they all knew it had to be really big to bring down this Don. For example, I had known for years that Diego spent an hour on the phone to his family and friends in Argentina every night. Exactly 3:00am to 4:00am sharp. I had verified it many times just for a laugh.

I'd asked him for help with something one night prior to leaving. He e-mailed back twenty-five minutes before his shift ended to say that he'd been too busy to get to it…sorry! The pastry chef verified that we had only been at fifty-three percent occupancy that night. I checked the phone log next. Sure enough, someone had made a call to area code 51 from precisely 3-4 am.

The fact that the phone log in this hotel was accessible to all was unusual. What was even more unusual was that Diego continued to make these calls, in spite of this. If I knew of these phone calls, IT certainly would; which meant that the General Manager and Human Resources knew too. I decided not to e-mail HR with this info.

One particularly busy night in the lounge, I had just closed the bar when two very drunk guests walked in. I explained that the bar was now closed and I would call the Night Porter to serve them. The last thing these two needed was another drink, but this routine is normally so predictable: They get another drink. They are so tired that they fall asleep, normally without taking more than one sip. The events that unfolded on this occasion however, were anything but predictable.

The standard procedure for closing a hotel bar is as follows: 'last orders' must be called at the scheduled closing time. Non-residents cannot buy another drink and must leave the premises after finishing their last drink, unless accompanied by a resident. The Night Porter is then responsible for any beverage service.

This is where the fun and games begin.

If a resident is present, he may buy drinks for non-residents, but he must sign the drinks to his room. A room key with ID is always required as proof of residency. Cash and credit card are usually not permitted. If a resident is seen taking cash for these, service may be refused to all. This can be very difficult to catch, never mind prove. However it is much easier when tipsy non-residents suddenly spot residents from half way across the room and stagger over to offer him drinks and cash if he will sign for another round. It is also easier when the Night Porter is in the bar scouting out who is paying cash and who is signing to a room when last orders are called.

The Night Manager is then tracked down to be informed that the bar is closed. The rough sequence of events after delivering this message can be heard at every hotel in every city, every night: The Night Manager will drop everything he is doing and stare you down to ensure he has heard correctly. "Did you call last orders?"

"Yes."

"How many residents are in the bar?" Crunch time. Too many and he says they can't cope…you have to stay. Too little and you are dragged into HR at your next earliest inconvenience to be asked why you left the night staff with a lounge full of residents. You can feel the tension as you watch a single bead of sweat appear on his upper lip…definitely not ice cream.

"Six."

"Okay."

Now it is a race against time. Like a gunfight in a Clint Eastwood movie, you both try to remain calm as you nervously, and almost too slowly, walk away from each other. Out of sight of the other, the Night Manager waddles as quickly as possible to the bar to count the number of residents; while you race, heart pounding, to the changing rooms to make a quick exit. At this point there is no worse feeling as you open your locker and hear the dull 'bang' of the door crashing behind you. Diego, in full sweat now: "A group of fifteen residents just walked in."

Bastard!

I used to wonder how it was possible that this slug could outrace me three nights out of four, every week! I had read somewhere that under great duress, people can have superhuman strength for short periods of time; but this was once a night, three nights a week, every week!

If you work with a Night Manager like this, I recommend hiding in the shower stall for ten minutes, until he checks elsewhere for you. Do not hide in the toilet cubicle, although there is no danger of them using the staff bathrooms (they only use the public ones), they are trained to look for you there.

Should you try to cash out quickly and get changed out of your prisoner's stripes before informing the Night Manager that the bar is closed…be prepared. You may get out faster, but the Nocturnal Mafia now has the high moral ground. You can expect an e-mail from The Don and very likely an invitation to join Human Resources for a documented refresher in bar closing policies and procedures.

If you do manage to sneak out, and the bar is officially declared closed, there is no re-opening. Any further orders for drinks must be directed to the Night Porter. For the Night Porter, this is Testosterone Time. The Night Porter is a low rank in the Nocturnal Mafia family tree. Therefore they do not miss an opportunity to stamp this little bit of authority on their weakest prey: the inebriated.

I don't know why Night Porters hate serving guests. I mean really, what did they think the job entailed? I suppose it is possible that after forty-seven years of doing it, they may have forgotten what the job description stated word for word. However, I would have thought that the repetitive nature of 'see guest…serve guest' would have stayed with them for life.

It's also not like they are being pulled away from another particularly pleasant part of their job. But hate it they do. They have devised some clever tactics to avoid it too!

Their favorite tactic involves an intense, cat and mouse game of 'delay and annoy.'

'Delay' involves, obviously, avoiding serving the guest for as long as possible. This has two main goals:

1. Hope that the guest is very drunk and actually falls asleep; or

2. Annoy the guest so much that they just go to bed.

Needless to say, both can backfire tremendously. If a guest has had so much alcohol that they can fall asleep on a chair or sofa in your lounge, it is entirely possible that they could lose control of a bodily function or two. I have personally witnessed countless hundreds of such inebriated, but valuable, hotel guests in my lounges. I have also had a couple of them urinate on my chairs. This is entirely acceptable from the Mafia's point of view.

They know that when questioned as to why they didn't clean the mess up; the 'we simply did not see the stain when we helped the poor, unfortunate gentleman to his bedroom' excuse will be more than enough to placate any ears that matter.

Should you ever have occasion to remove inebriated, sleeping guests from your hotel or home; do so from behind, with the guest's mouth facing away from you. I have witnessed several spectacular vomits on my lounge furniture. I am actually convinced this is quite a skill, requiring a good deal of technique and practice. I'm not sure if it's an art form or a sport, but I was lucky to have a couple of Gold medalist contenders in my lounge on the same evening several years ago.

A young English gentleman who had 'never tasted whisky before' took the Gold; clearing three chairs with his outstanding effort. The Silver went to the slightly older Irish gentleman who did clear the sofa opposite him when prodded, but lost points for catching his friend on the shoulder. On a positive note, most of the other residents left very quickly after this and we got to close the bar earlier than usual.

Vomiting is definitely not the sought after reaction from a Nocturnal Mafia point of view. They can hardly get away with the 'I honestly did not see or smell that when we moved him' excuse for not cleaning it up.

If you happen to be a hotel resident enjoying a late night drink one evening, keep your eyes peeled for the 'sleepers.' Sit at least three tables away if possible. You will usually get a split-second warning when someone is about to vomit. Just before the first chunk is expelled, the Night Porter will very clearly signal with a shout of: "I'm not cleaning that." Unless you have Porter-like reflexes however, it may be too late to react.

The 'annoy' is mainly achieved through the 'delay' routine, however some other tactics commonly employed include:

a) 'And you are…?' It must be stressed that this is a particularly difficult technique and is not for the rookie Night Porter. To excel at this skill takes guts. To be bothered to want to go toe-to-toe with several guests at a time, sometimes even remaining calm, takes a desire to antagonize guests that can only take years to perfect; because it would be much faster and easier to serve them.

When called to the bar for Night Porter service, the Porter must first explain the Night Rules...one at a time...as the guest breaks each rule. This has the added annoyance of the guest believing that they are one step from service each time, only to be cruelly confronted with another obstacle after each hurdle.

The Night Rules are simple. They have to be! Rule one: residents must show the room card holder (a small envelope) that has their name and room number on it. No room card holder, no service. I am convinced that guests throw this piece of ID away within 2.5 seconds of checking in. The first guest I ever come across that actually carries this will definitely get a free drink from me!

Guests always carry the room key. Unfortunately, this has no proof of ownership. So for 'the guest's protection,' the Night Porter cannot accept this as proof of residency. Guest annoyance factor = 5.

"What if I tell you my name and room number, can you check that?" a guest may ask.

"Certainly sir. I'll just go and print off a rooming list to check." Estimated Time of Return (ETR) is approximately ten minutes for this. Guest annoyance factor = 6.5

When the Porter returns with the list, and the guest can correctly match the room number and their name, they are ready for Rule Two: Identification. "Now if you have some ID sir? After all, you could have overheard anyone state their name and room number at check-in or in the bar."

It is imperative that the Porter uses the word 'sir' as often as possible at this point. This will not only heighten the tension, but also ensure the guest does not skip a step in the proceedings; thereby cheating the Night Porter out of any entertainment value. Raging, the guest goes to his bedroom for his ID. ETR approx 5 minutes; annoyance factor = 9.

Upon his return, and proof of photo ID, he is greeted with Rule Three: "No problem sir, I will just go and get the keys." ETR 8 minutes; annoyance factor = 11.

Dougie Mains at The Grosvenor Hotel deserves a special mention here. I was fortunate enough to witness his dazzling skills of service-avoidance on several occasions. It was a very small hotel; perhaps that was why he excelled at this particular skill. Unless there was an empty bedroom he could hole up in for an hour, he simply could not use the 'catch me if you can' technique to any great advantage. I am forever indebted to Mr. Mains for an education that can thankfully never be bought.

Dougie was also extremely difficult to control from another point of view: he had his own way of getting revenge. Every time I brought Dougie in for questioning, I had some bizarre incident occur within twenty four hours, that led directly back to him. Like the first case of 'Porn Pictionary' I ever came across:

It was Brian on the phone from Reception: "The group in meeting room A wants to see you."

As I approached the room, I could see through the large glass window. It struck me as odd that a set of male genitals had been boldly sketched on their flip chart. Anatomically correct I thought; but not to scale…unless it was a horse's. As the attendees were all wearing suits, I guessed it wasn't the organizer's idea of an ice breaker to kick off their meeting.

"What do you call this?" the red face screamed at me.

I was speechless. Although I felt confident I knew the answer, my acute F&B Manager senses told me it could be rhetorical. When pushed of course, I could not explain how it had appeared on the fourth page of their flip chart…that was the Night team's responsibility.

"Yep, there were a lot of people wandering around the hotel last night," Dougie replied under oath. "It could have been anybody." Indeed!

I hoped Dougie's written warning would teach him a lesson or two, but it didn't. In fact, when a similar drawing was found in another meeting room the night after issuing the warning, it was I that learned the lesson. I didn't issue Dougie a second written warning, and it never happened again!

b) 'Catch me if you can.' Depending on the layout of your hotel, this can be highly effective. The Night Porter's bar is almost always in a back of house area where the guest can't see it. Some hotels are like rabbit warrens. The idea is to throw the guest off your trail. You go in one door, peek out another, and then return via yet another one. Do this several times and the guest will have no idea where you were coming from or how to find you when they are sober, never mind after a night out!

If you can 'prepare the drinks' out of sight for fifteen minutes or so, the guest may become angered to the point of action. They may go to seek assistance from the Night Manager at Reception. However, it is very likely that The Don will not hear someone banging the bell at Reception as he is on a very important long-distance call; or perhaps by the time he has scraped the ice cream from his tie and chins, the guest has given up and decided to check if the Night Porter has returned with the drinks after all. When he returns to the bar to find the drinks (and Porter) are still MIA, he will be more determined than ever to show them who they are dealing with.

The guest may even venture to look for the Porter through the door that saw him go through to get the drinks. This is unfortunate. Perhaps a drink or two less that evening and they would have seen the trap being set.

Wandering in back of house areas in a hotel is bad for guests. There are only two possible outcomes:

1. Guest gets lost. Back of house areas are remarkably quiet, apart from the Night Chef's ghetto blaster screeching somewhere off in the distance. It is eerie. Should anyone in this unfamiliar territory proceed more than six feet, they will be wandering from locked corridor to locked corridor. I have personally rescued several guests from the Room Service area when arriving for work at 6am.

One lady was missing a shoe, clutching a piece of stale bread to her chest. Frothing at the mouth, she could only keep repeating: "looking for the Night Porter." I'll never forget the look of shock on her face when I told her that the Porter had finished his shift and gone home thirty minutes ago. She didn't realize it, but a day-employee finding her three hours after entering the Forbidden Zone was her best possible outcome.

2. Guest stumbles upon the Night Porter. If this is your fate, the Night Porter will no doubt have an impossibly wide grin on his face. In a rage, you may ask what the delay is all about. This is child's play to the Porter. He has an encyclopedic knowledge of excuses that range from the simple: "I couldn't find the keys," or "I had to change the keg;" to the twisted and impressive: "I heard someone ringing the bell at Reception, but must have just missed them by the time I got there."

This last one is a momentum turner. It insinuates that the guest was actually to blame for the delay. Sensing the initiative, the Night Porter lunges onto the offensive. "What are you doing back of house? This is a restricted area." The guest notes that the 'sir' has been dropped.

Should you ever find yourself in this position as a slightly intoxicated guest, I recommend the following course of action: apologize; clamp mouth shut; about face; return to public area as fast as possible (un-clamp mouth only for directions if more than six feet from the door that you entered Forbidden Zone from).

Do not engage in any conversation. You have no friends back of house. Should you utter anything resembling a threat or complaint about the service, The Don will appear as if by magic over the Night Porter's shoulder. He (and the entire Nocturnal Mafia) has been listening on the walkie-talkie.

The next steps will occur so swiftly they will swirl around your head like your impending hangover. As your hangover rages, you vaguely recall being swarmed and escorted to your room. All the while, The Don informed you that were cut off for wandering about in a Restricted Area and threatening staff. You received an official caution and were threatened with imminent removal from the hotel.

You decide not to visit the lounge for the rest of your stay. You return straight to your room after dinner the next evening. Normal order has been restored.

While the two inebriated gentlemen (I never did get their names) were waiting for the Porter, Diego happened to waltz by (swinging the pastry keys). I called him over. Guest A was sitting on a bar stool just a few feet from us as I informed The Don that these two had been waiting for the Porter for five minutes. Guest B had already assumed the horizontal position on the nearest sofa. Diego took one look at them and was weighing up whether they were too drunk to serve any more. Before he had the opportunity, Guest A decided he had waited long enough. He leered at The Don and demanded action: "How long does it take to get a fucking drink here?"

"Esscuse me? Are you a resident?" Here we go! To be present when the bar was closed and actually witness The Don in a solo performance of the 'and you are?' routine was a rare treat indeed. I settled back against the bar. I was going to enjoy this. I tried desperately, and without total success, to stop from smiling and holding in a snigger.

"Who the fuck are you? Just get me my drinks you spic!" guest A let loose, turning his back on The Don to stare ahead at the empty bar. This guest had obviously not been taught the Night Rules. I had a good idea he was about to learn them. But a racial slur at this point in the proceedings was clearly a breach of etiquette that Diego could not dismiss.

I nearly lost him in the red mist that came down. I followed his highest-pitched, thickest South American accent towards Guest A: "Esscuse me? Wha the fuck did chu say?"

Guest A swiveled on his stool and opened his mouth. But just as he was surely conjuring up another expletive, Diego wound up and punched him, full force, in the stomach. The guest keeled forward slightly, holding his gut. Diego cocked his elbow for another special delivery. My mind raced back to Customer Service 101. No, this was definitely not the 'smile and apologize' response I was taught to deliver at this juncture. "Diego!" I yelled, stunned.

He stopped. He looked at me, horrified; and realized what had just happened. He hadn't just popped a guest in the stomach, risking his career. He had lost his power over me. I now owned The Don!

The Classic Brown Nose (CBN) is by far the most dangerous species of Night Manager. Their lifelong ambition is to win the coveted 'Employee of the Month' award. Although 'Employee of the Year' is too much to even dream about for most Night Managers, some Dons secretly plot the downfall of every other employee in order to win the Holy Grail. Therefore, early identification is crucial to survive the Nocturnal Mafia if your Don is a CBN. The CBN has two main distinguishing features for easy identification:

1. Deadly e-mails. Whereas the Spineless Jellyfish's e-mails are singular in their intent to vent, the CBN's e-mails are designed to injure…and they aim high! Bringing down one manager is the equivalent of fifteen grunts. Their every e-mail brings delusions of being publicly lauded. Any other thoughts when sending an e-mail are a distant second. Ironically, as we will see later, this is also the CBN's Achilles Heel.

If you receive an e-mail with a 'CC' field six times greater than the 'TO' field, you have a Classic Brown Nose. This particular e-mail is usually harmless enough in itself, as it will most likely contain useless information everyone in the CC field knew at least five days prior. They are just letting everyone know that this information has finally sunk in.

If you receive an e-mail that seems absurd or obvious (usually about something you have already discussed with them, and thought you had agreement on) with nobody CC'd, beware. They have 'Blind Copied' (BCC'd) someone else in on it. Whereas the Spineless Jellyfish doesn't know what BCC means, let alone how to use it, the CBN knows all about the BCC. They work the BCC like a potter works his wheel.

When using this tactic, they will always BCC their own manager, Human Resources and occasionally the General Manager. In extreme cases, they may even BCC your manager. However, it must be said that this is a dangerous tactic for them. They will be aware that your manager is going to back you up. Therefore they are pitting their own manager against yours. They will be all too aware that their manager will not be slipping any Employee of the Month votes their way for that.

On rare occasions, you may even receive an e-mail with no 'TO' or 'CC' field. The entire field has been Blind Copied. This can be an effective tactic in the sense that everyone who receives it wastes a lot of time and energy wondering: a) what the actual purpose of it was and b) who else received it. However; it is such an obvious ploy that it must be used extremely sparingly to be effective.

These e-mails are serious, with injurious intent, and must be handled professionally. A timely, but tempered, reply is the order of the day. Be sure to use lots of positive language such as: 'thank you for bringing this to my attention,' or 'I agree that the best thing the company can do is to improve this situation immediately.' Always finish with: 'I will look into this immediately. Thanks and keep up the great work.' That will really frustrate them. You can then delete the e-mail and forget all about its content. They will forget all about the particulars in the ploy anyway, and will already be working on a better plan to catch you out.

If you take the bait and reply with a satisfyingly sarcastic retort; turn yourself in to HR at the nearest opportunity. Explain that you have been under pressure recently (almost any excuse will do…the exorbitant price of gas is good enough) and you replied (uncharacteristically) to an e-mail when you were in the wrong frame of mind and intend to apologize as soon as possible. Time is of the essence. HR will have been forwarded your e-mail within forty three seconds (approximately the time it takes for them to stop rubbing their hands together and hit the 'forward' button.

Watch out for cluster e-mails. The CBN may send numerous e-mails out to every employee in the entire hotel about any number of meaningless topics. Check the calendar. It is probably nearing the end of the month. They are reminding everyone that they are still employed and are technically available for an Employee of the Month vote. Ironically, these have the effect of annoying everyone so much that if even if someone had any intention of casting a 'vote against the system;' they can no longer stomach the thought.

2. The spotless suit. This is perhaps the easiest and quickest way to identify the CBN. If they can wear a single suit (the CBN does not wear a 'uniform') for five straight nights without showing a single crease, you have a Classic Brown-Nose. Where the Spineless Jellyfish is more likely to be unkempt (think ice cream stains and mis-matched socks), the Classic Brown Nose would positively clench their buttocks at the thought of an askew name badge.

The first time I saw Chris he was speaking to our Director of Rooms about fifty feet away, luckily. Any closer and I would have been blinded by the glare from his name badge. I am certain he filled at least an hour of every night with a cloth and a jug of Turtle Wax, polishing every bit of his uniform from his cufflinks to the zipper on his pants.

Chris was an easy diagnosis: CBN. A hand as stiff as a dead rat shot out like a rocket. "Christopher Bueller, Night Manager."

Still squinting, I gave a firm handshake with a weak: "Mike, Director of Food & Beverage."

"A pleasure to meet you Michael." I checked my name badge; it still said 'Mike.' Here is another classic giveaway of the CBN. There is absolutely no slang in their language. They even correct yours.

Even my mother has never called me by my official name. Yet here was this mannequin using it within a split second of meeting me. Any self respecting CBN (and they are all very self-respecting) would never belittle themselves with a shortened name or (heaven forbid) a nickname. You will never see a 'Chris,' 'John' or 'Mike' on a CBN's name badge. It will always be 'Christopher,' 'Jonathon' or 'Michael.' Even if they have to use font size two to fit in. To everyone else's amusement, they probably have more monikers than any other employee among the grunts. As he walked away, the glare from his name badge disappeared, plunging the lobby into darkness

CBN's are a pain the ass. There is no getting around it. The endless e-mails are tiring and frustrating because the subject is always trivial and boring. Therein lies the danger.

I walked into the office after his first night. Six e-mails! I checked the corridor was clear. "Fucking asshole!" I clenched my teeth. "He'll have to do better than that to catch me out on his first night." I got myself a coffee, closed the door and sat down to read.

It was all very standard stuff for a Classic Brown Nose on his first night. Each one: 'just checking what the procedure is for' blah, blah, blah. I knew exactly what his game plan was. The CBN was trying to assess which tasks he could very quickly get out of. He was checking to see if there were written procedures for tasks that my five year old daughter would be able to figure out on her own. Inevitably, in any operation, business picks up, staff change and procedures are altered ever so slightly. The Brown Nose will be onto any procedures that were not updated the night before faster than a bear onto honey. Although not actually responsible for carrying out any of these tasks (this will be done, theoretically, by the Night Porter), the CBN wants to ensure all checklists and written procedures are up to date. This is a double edged sword.

If you choose to ignore the bastard, you are:

a) Technically liable if they get injured trying to carry out a dangerous procedure (like making a sandwich or heating a bowl of soup in the microwave). I say technically because it is far fetched indeed to imagine that they would attempt these tasks even with all the written procedures and training anyway. More likely, it would be brought to your attention in the form of a guest complaint: "The Night Manager informed me that they were 'not comfortable' making my sandwich because they had not been trained in the use of a butter knife."

b) Signaling your intent to ignore him too early. For this slap in the chops, expect double the number of checklists and procedures to update over the next few nights. Leave the ignoring to the Director of Sales. They will have far more experience at this skill, and will just show you up anyway.

I replied to five e-mails with updated checklists and e-mails. No written text. Against all my better judgment however, I did write a reply to one e-mail which asked: "Who is responsible for bringing down any room service trays found on the guest floors during the night?"

I went for a walk. It couldn't be this straight forward. Could it? Then again, it is just possible it could be. In larger hotels, Food and Beverage covers Room Service 24 / 7. However, in this hotel (200 rooms), there were very few room service orders at night, and little else for the Nocturnal Mafia to do. So with a limited menu (sandwiches and microwavables for the culinary-challenged to serve), the Mafia covered Room Service from 11pm-6am. This should be a Food and Beverage Director's wet dream. And it was, when I was dealing with a Spineless Jellyfish. However, this new Classic Brown Nose had thrown a lion among the pigeons.

'What could happen?' I thought as I re- read my prose:

"Christopher, thank you for your enquiry. Please forgive my oversight. Due to the size of the hotel, the Night Team is actually responsible for bringing down any trays found on the floors after 11pm. Please find the updated Nights checklist attached. Thanks again, Michael."

I grinned as I read it back to myself, thoroughly satisfied. The apology was more of a goodwill gesture in case I had missed some angle he was working. After all, F&B was certainly not responsible for the Night Manager's training. Short, sweet and to the point.

I pressed 'send.'

I sat back, relaxed and took a sip of luke-warm coffee. This CBN was already half in my pocket! And then it came to me. Although Chris would not have known Nights were responsible for this task before last night, it is the Night Porter's task to actually bring the trays down. "Oh fuck!" I nearly choked on my coffee as I sat bolt upright and splashed my day timer. "What have I done?" Why would he ask if he didn't even have to do it himself? He was trying to get the Night Porter out of this task. A clear show of strength to the Nocturnal Mafia.

I should have seen the trap. I waited nervously all day, anticipating what type of e-mail the bastard would send back, and who was CC'd (and BCC'd) on it. I didn't have long to wait.

"Hey guy, thank you for the checklist. Is there any way the night room service person can clear the floors before they leave at 11pm? Thanks guy."

Going for the plea bargain. No room to be wishy-washy here. Give an inch and he will be gone a mile with it. "No. They clear what they can, but they are busy with deliveries right until 11pm. Why don't you e-mail me every time you find an unacceptable number of trays on the floors and I'll deal with it?" This was the counter offer. Not much.

He bit. Every morning I walked in to an e-mail in the form of: 'Hey guy, one tray found on the floors last night. Have a great day guy.' When they found ten or more trays, I would forward it to my assistant, Dick. He loved a good laugh at Nights' expense too. I had won the battle, but the electronic war raged on. And who the hell was 'guy?'

No 'Michael.' No 'Mike.' What was this all about? Being a Director of Food and Beverage, I am used to much worse than 'guy.' He would have to do much better than that to offend me. I wondered what it meant though. It could be meant to confuse the entire list of BCC'd recipients. After all, they could all assume the e-mail was meant for them! In the end, I decided it was a smoke screen. Perhaps meant to baffle me into an irate reply to the BCC'd list. No chance.

I did have to update my morning routine checklist though: open office; turn on computer; check all areas fully staffed; pick up reports from Front Office; steal muffin from pastry; pour coffee; delete 'tray update' e-mail from CBN (without reading obviously).

"Andrew, stop. What the fuck are you talking about?" I had been trapped, sitting listening to this buzzing in my ears for a full seven minutes, reading all my e-mails from Chris. No point listening to him. This was like a comedy routine from a broken record. When I'd finished reading, I realized something was blocking my route to the coffee machine for a refill.

"Oh, uhhh, well, okay, well, you see, uhhh, it's funny really, okay, we are missing a check from a transaction last night." Good job I wasn't listening. How on earth he could have been dragging on about that for a full seven minutes was beyond me…but he did. Every morning he could catch me.

"I'll look into it. E-mail me the details." It has always seemed a strange twist of irony to me… the simpler the person, the more complicated the communication.

I usually arrived at work at 6:00am, four days a week, to use the gym. I liked to run at least 5k a day. I found it a great stress reliever and I believe it made me more productive, especially in the first few hours after running, because I felt much more alert.

The hardest part of this routine was trying to get to the gym without being trapped by Andrew. It became more and more like a scene from The Great Escape. The underground Parkade opened at 7am; which meant a Night Porter had to open the Parkade door for me. As I approached the driveway, I'd be counting the number of staff in the area. If there was only one, he was stuck at the door and I had a head start. Two or more, and the race was on.

I would try to park on the lowest level. This gave me the most options for escape routes, and bought me more time to get to them. I had several options, but being a Night Porter he'd probably used most of them in his 'catch me if you can' routine.

My most successful route was: access the laundry room on bottom parking level, hide behind the huge laundry bins in the laundry room for six minutes, take the elevator up to the sixth floor, walk across the corridor to the far fire escape stairs, down to the third level, swipe key to access Health Club, very quick change in change rooms, treadmill…safe. Once I was actually on the treadmill, they would leave me alone. Until then, I was fair game.

There was no more satisfying feeling than hitting the 'quick start' button on the treadmill and seeing Andrew appear in the mirror's reflection, pacing back and forth behind me. I had won. He knew it, and as a matter of honor between gladiators, would let me be…until the next day.

On the one day each week I did not run (a different day each week to keep them guessing), we went through the same ritual. Except that I knew I was trapped in the office, if he saw me drive in. I followed the same ritual: open the office door and close it quietly behind me. Keeping the lights off, I would wait. A tap. Another tap on the door. Shuffle, shuffle. Gone. I turn the lights and computer on only after I am sure the scuffling has faded far enough away.

Except, Andrew just didn't go away. I knew he'd be back. Like a dog waiting at the door for me to come home every day. I half expected him to be outside the door each morning with my slippers and a paper in his mouth. I wasn't sure I had the time it would take to train him up to this though. Instead, I began to wonder how the hell I would get rid of this dog. Should I take him for a walk and abandon him in a park somewhere, or throw a bone off the pool deck on level three?

The Night Mafia are the same in every hotel that I have seen. Human Resources have a never ending line up of these guys…I am sure they come from the carnival. I am convinced that when advertising for the Night Porter position, they use that little sign from kid's fairs: a clown holding a couple of balloons with a ruler that states: 'you must be under this height to enjoy this ride.' Very symbolic.

Christopher used to e-mail me once a week with another security question. This is another CBN trademark: the 'health and safety concern.' They know you can't ignore anything to do with health and safety. When they start you down this line, you do need to communicate with them occasionally. I never really understood this fear though. They all seem to be worried that some crazed lunatic will come wandering into the hotel in the middle of every night looking to kill the Night Team. Apart from in my dreams, this could never happen. All the crazed lunatics are working in hotels through the night, so I never really did much with their requests, but had to appear to do something.

The Don will know you will be reluctant to put anything to do with health and safety in writing. So it is more of an 'annoy' technique designed to get you to bargain down to the real request; perhaps an early finish one morning. Here's how it works:

You receive an e-mail regarding a 'health and safety' issue from The Don. You forward it to whoever is responsible for H&S in your hotel and add: "Dear X, please reply to this asap. I agree with The Don's concern." Then run quickly to 'X' to apologize for the political e-mail: "Sorry X, that bastard dropped me right in it with that e-mail. Can you just bring it up at the next H&S meeting? By the way, nice job putting that 'slippery when wet' sign up by the pool. Good thinking. Here's an 'employee of the month' slip for you." (Remember to hand in the HR copy of this vote!)

Then you have to come in early the next morning, to enquire of The Don if X got back to him on his H&S issue yet. You then inform The Don that, unfortunately, he can't finish early on his birthday, sorry. He will casually mention that he has another H&S concern. You panic. 'Oh, you know what? I will come in early and cover for you that day.' You run off, cursing the bastard.

There is only one way out of this dilemma, but it is such hard work, that you may decide it is easier to cover the bloody shift and be done with it. The only problem with this is that he now knows he can do this whenever he likes; and he will like…often.

I decided to teach a Don of mine a lesson. I became the Health and Safety Chairman. If you want this job in any hotel, it's yours for the asking. Nobody else wants it. Even if the position is not yet vacant…express your desire for control and it will be. You do not require any special training for this position of, on the face of it, power. The job is easy enough:

Call a meeting every four weeks.

Invite the General Manager and one person from each department (only the hourly paid staff will volunteer, mistaking this for a real meeting where important decisions are made).

Print off the thirty 'health and safety' e-mails you have received from Nights since the last meeting and read through them one at a time. Pause for a moment between each one: just long enough for the GM to say 'I will discuss that with the owners and get back to you.'

Wake everyone up with a 'thank you all for coming,' at the end and declare the meeting closed.

Issue minutes from the meeting.

Much to my GM's continual amazement, I had the minutes issued within about five minutes of each meeting finishing. Why they were always amazed I had no idea. I had them written well in advance of each meeting. I would prepare the header: 'Health and Safety Meeting Minutes.' Then each day I would just cut and paste the Nights' 'H&S' e-mails. I added the 'action to be taken' at the side of each entry: 'GM to report back.'

The GM never did report back. So in the end, it's not that much extra work really. At least I maintained control over The Don.

As a footnote, you do not want a representative of the Nocturnal Mafia attending these meetings. They will hijack the meeting and may demand real answers for their concerns. It must be said that it is extremely unlikely they would be seen in daylight for risk of melting; but just in case, the meeting has to be called at short notice and must always start at exactly 2:30pm (right in the middle of their 'night').

In the event that one ever shows up, you have to excuse yourself quickly while they are taking their seats. Call the Director of Sales (on his cell phone – he will be in line at the nearest Starbucks the moment the General Manager goes into a meeting) and ask him to call the GM immediately. The GM can then excuse himself from the meeting immediately, rendering the meeting even more meaningless than before. Remember to amend the 'action to be taken' on each point to 'GM to answer at next meeting' before issuing the minutes.

Christopher continued with his 'health and safety concern' e-mails for quite a few months, but eventually after a painful bout of tendonitis in his wrist (I assumed from furious typing, but could be wrong), decided it was not worth the trouble. I remembered a friend of mine at home in Scotland always used a saying that certainly struck me now: 'it's all fun and games until someone gets hurt…then it's hilarious!'

Christopher turned back to his old tactics.

In fairness, Andrew actually did a fairly half decent job of completing the tasks he was given, but he was such hard work that you just had to switch off when he started talking. He gave all the right details to all the wrong people. And wagging his tail with such enthusiasm! I was sure a higher ranking member of the Mafia was slipping pints of Red Bull into his water bowl for a laugh.

After a while I realized I was never going to get rid of Andrew. So I just accepted the routine. But I soon realized he started coming around a little more each week. It then occurred to me that perhaps Andrew wasn't the real antagonist in this scenario. Perhaps it was Christopher, setting HIS dog on me. All the time I had been thinking it was MY pet, bringing me news each morning. I had been stung. Christopher was good…very good. I had never come across this technique before and as sick and twisted as it was, I had to admit, I was jealous I hadn't thought of it first. It was time to play hardball.

It took a full three weeks for it to come to me, but it was worth waiting for. March 26th. A cluster of meaningless, and in the end mainly unread, e-mails emerge from Christopher. Going for more Employee of the Month votes. Beautiful!

Next morning I came in and did not go for a run. I looked around for something, anything I could use as an excuse to give Chris a coveted Employee of the Month slip. It wasn't easy. Eventually I plumped for the only thing I could see that they had done: taken the newspapers out to the restaurant.

Every hotel has a similar system: forms are available for staff to fill in and give to other staff if they have done any good deeds. The staff member issuing a slip has to write the reason. I have seen everything on these slips from: 'guest was looking for marijuana and Dave sold him some of his own,' to 'I was late so Kate punched in my time card for me.'

Occasionally, some are given for excellent customer service. The forms are usually in duplicate; you give one copy to the staff member you are nominating, and another to HR to count in the voting. I went to find Chris.

He offended my nose before my eyes. Shoe polish. He was in the back office, sweating feverishly with a rag in one hand and his shoe in the other. I felt like I had violated his personal space. He looked at me and then slowly drifted his gaze to my left hand. I nearly got a spit and polish as he drooled and dropped the rag, narrowly missing my foot.

"Christopher, I just wanted to say thank you for putting the papers in the restaurant for breakfast this morning." He held two hands out to catch it, in case it slipped through one.

I waited. Eventually, as he welled up, he got it out: "Thank you so much Michael. I don't know what to say." Sensing an imminent speech that Sally Field would have been proud of, I seized the opportunity to get out quick, while he was still stunned.

I shuffled nervously back to the office, looking over my shoulder. No movement. God only knows how long he sat there staring at it. I got to the office, opened the door and threw a stunning three-pointer into the garbage can across the room. And down it went: HR's copy of Christopher's only vote, never to be seen again.

And that was it; simple really! Once every couple of weeks, he would get one copy of an Employee of the Month vote that would never be seen by anyone else. Note it well: delusions of grandeur…the Achilles Heel of every Classic Brown Nose.

Within weeks, Andrew had been called off me permanently. I used to see him chained to the handle of the Director of Sales' office door each morning thereafter, wagging his tail.

The topper was that I was also on the Executive Committee that counted the votes each month. This was almost too good. What had I done to deserve so much happiness? I writhed with anticipation each time the votes were counted, or not as it were. I could hardly contain my laughter, and very rarely did.

Although the rest of the Executive Committee thought this behavior was a little strange, my assistant would be dying of anticipation; waiting to see my reaction as I walked back to the F&B Office. He would see the Cheshire Cat approach from fifty yards, give me a huge high five and we'd celebrate. "I'll get the lattes," he'd say and run off. I felt total elation. Results like this don't come around every day in F&B. You need to enjoy them.

Of course, they can't all be CBN's or SJ's. There are others who are unique in their own special way…freaks among freaks, if you will. Santa was one such anomaly. 'Jim' to very few, he went by many nicknames. Although Papa Smurf was another of my favorites, he was always Santa to me. Santa wasn't so much of a Don. He was more of a 'Don't.' If there ever was such a thing as a glorified Night Porter, he was it.

On the face of it, I could understand why Human Resources (in their usual desperation), looking at his resume, might interview him. Maybe even e-mail him an offer. On paper, he appeared to be able to count. He also appeared to be able to check guests in and out. However; the interview process should have put an end to any hopes of this unfortunate gaining employment…quickly.

I can only assume that he was never interviewed. He would have been found out after about the first question. Any question. His answer to a simple: 'How are you?' would have been enough for me. You see, what Santa was able to do was overwhelmingly compromised by what he obviously wasn't. His inability to interact was legendary. His inability to multitask had to be seen to be believed. His total lack of health and hygiene was sickening. And Santa was slow…very slow. I had a hunch he was a lost love child from Andre the Giant and a Sloth.

I was the Manager on Duty when he arrived for his first shift. It was 11pm on a Friday night and I was dying to go out to meet my friends for a drink. They had had a good head start, so I ordered a taxi for 11pm on the nose. The taxi pulled up just as Santa waddled in.

At the end of each shift, the Managers on Duty must hand over what has transpired so far that day, business levels and things to be aware of in general. Then they count the hotel's main float and sign over responsibility for it, along with the hotel keys. In some hotels, the float can be several thousand dollars. In this small hotel, it was $1200. Between the day and evening Managers on Duty, the whole handover at 3:00pm would take a maximum of ten minutes.

Mistaking him for a vagrant in search of a room, I said to Vicky on the reception desk: "If this guy's looking for a room, tell him we're full tonight."

"That's our new Night guy," she smirked. Jim had been trained at our sister hotel over the last week. Obviously Vicky had been tipped off.

"Christ!" One look at him and I knew we were in for some fun and games. He stopped outside the entrance to strangle the last few puffs from his cigarette. Casually flicking the butt into the garden area (you can always spot class), he opened the door.

I reluctantly put my hand out: "Mike. Welcome aboard." As he quickly shook my hand, his eyes never left the tiled floor. No doubt looking for butts with a puff still left in them. His sausage fingers all had yellow tips. Something like 'Blimm' mumbled from between the yellow area of his grey beard and moustache set as it continued straight past me. Santa was obviously a casual smoker.

Vicky mouthed the letters 'JIM' to me.

Jim was wrestling with his coat when I returned from washing my hands. When it was finally removed, with Vicky's aid, it revealed a marvelously wrinkled black shirt with a heavy dusting of dandruff along the entire shoulder line. The black tie, stopping just above the enormous navel line, was very Oliver and Hardy-ish and a phenomenal complement to the unique look. However, the most impressive touches belonged to the bottom half.

The enormous trousers could not be completely zipped up, and there was a snowball's chance in hell of the button ever having been buttoned. So the piece de resistance was the half inch thick belt that literally held the entire look together: a rope. Nowhere near heavy duty enough to dangle him on the end of, if required. But just strong enough to keep this set of drapes tied around him with a tidy little knot. Very nouveau. I certainly hadn't seen this in the last edition of GQ, or strangely enough, in the HR Handbook.

On this particular night, the hotel was very quiet. There was absolutely nothing to hand over. Perfect. I could almost hear the music and taste that first pint of Tennents Lager as I opened the safe and pulled out the float. Ten minutes, still counting. Twenty minutes, still counting. My pint was getting warmer. "What are you doing? You've counted it five times!"

"But, but, but, I, I, I, and I've got five different counts," he drew out in a long ramble.

"My taxi!" It was still there alright. I went out to look at the damage. $25 and I hadn't even opened the bloody door. I ran back: "what's the lowest count you've got?"

"Fifty cents short."

"What! You've counted it five times, got five different amounts, but the biggest difference is fifty cents?" I wailed. Thirty minutes. I figured by the time he'd counted the currency correctly, it would have changed in value. I flipped him a dollar and ran for the most expensive taxi ride per mile I have ever had in my life.

This was not the last trouble we would have with Santa's adding issues. He routinely took thirty minutes to count the float. A light shining in the parking lot was enough to throw his concentration. And he would start again. Did I mention he was easily distracted?

Apart from his stunning looks and Einstein-like mathematics skills, Santa had several other talents that were sadly missing from his resume, but really deserved a mention. His long–term memory was one such skill.

Guests would routinely comment to me at breakfast that someone had opened their door briefly around midnight. "Very strange," came out of my mouth. I heard my voice. The guests heard it too. More importantly, I could see they believed me. What I was thinking was more along the lines of: 'Fucking idiot. He's done it again!'

"Let me just investigate this and I'll get back to you."

The successful Food and Beverage Manager must master the art of 'lying through your teeth.' I began learning this skill in a pub when I was nineteen. The other servers told me: "If you forget someone's beer, you tell them the keg is just being changed." It worked, but it was small time stuff.

At the pub level, this is acceptable. For a Food and Beverage Manager, the stakes are much higher than an extra three minutes for a pint. You must believe the garbage that comes out of your mouth at times if you want the listener to. You have to maintain control of your eyes. Let nothing shock you and master the stare. If someone doesn't believe you; admit nothing; ever. Deception is one thing; admitting liability simply does not cut it at F&B Manager level.

My investigation was a two-minute affair: go to office; lock door; kick something; mutter obscenities. A word of advice on the kicking part: ensure that whatever you kick has some give. The fellow F&B Manager at our sister hotel, while in the middle of this routine, put his foot through a door. A broken ankle is top comedy…if it's attached to someone else's foot.

Thoroughly relieved, I returned to the guests with the most empathetic look I could muster, and an explanation: "I am so sorry. It seems that we had a technical issue with our computer system around 11:00pm last night." Technically, this was true; if you count putting an idiot in front of the screen as a 'technical' issue. I mean, NASA put a monkey in a space ship. Of course, NASA didn't let him fly it.

I continued: "The room appeared as 'vacant' in the system." Everyone has had a computer problem at their own home at some time or other, so you can usually get a little bit of sympathy back.

A nod of understanding from the guest followed by my "please, let me take care of your breakfast bill for you," and we close the deal.

"Oh no, that's not necessary, blah, blah, blah."

"Please, I insist. I want to nail the bill to Santa's chest with a hammer, so I really must insist." That last part was barely kept in. Two happy guests; one very unhappy F&B Manager; Santa – none the wiser, but now second on the Death Wish List.

Every F&B Manager must have a Death Wish List. This list is a highly motivational tool. I recommend you start one as soon as you hit the 'Outlet Manager' level. It works like this: whoever is pissing you off the most at any given time, climbs higher up the list. Every time someone takes over the number two spot, you imagine their untimely and ironic demise. You accidentally lock the pastry Chef in his freezer where he freezes to death clutching a profiterole, for example. It can be a wonderful release when you are sitting in meetings or have a spare minute to daydream.

You may choose to post the list in your office (without the title obviously), or just keep it in your head. Posting it can be very effective if you have your own office. Imagine No. 5 on the list visits your office and inquires what the list is all about. You grin and say: 'Oh nothing." They will wonder though. Watch their eyes each day. If they look like they are getting less and less sleep; move them a little higher up the list each day. Their eyes get blacker, their performance drops day by day. They are a puppet on your string. Wonderful!

The irony in this tactic is that as you move them up higher on the list, their daily demise gives you the control you desire. They seem less of a threat again, so they move slowly back down the list.

If you trust your Assistant, they will appreciate this little tool too, but be careful who you share this information with. I usually kept my top fifteen list in my head. Within minutes of someone taking over the Number Two spot, I could delight in their death and feel better instantly.

The Death Wish List technically starts at Number One (being the closest to death). However, the Director of Sales will almost always occupy this spot. Therefore it is completely counter-productive to put someone else in this spot, even temporarily. You don't want to focus all of your anger on one person. Share it around. The Number Two spot will change frequently, which means you can stay more motivated.

I checked the schedule. When is that bastard in next? Two days off: typical. This is the First Law of Food and Beverage Dynamics: the person you most need to strangle will be off for at least two days; without fail.

Depending on your outlook, this can be good or bad. In scenario one, you enjoy two glorious days of daydreaming about how, where and when you are going to kill the offender. Like a game of Clue: Santa, in the back office, impaled by an umbrella. The only downside to this theme is that you may calm down after forty eight hours, and not be as brutal as they deserve for embarrassing the poor F&B Manager and costing the hotel two breakfasts.

In scenario two, the poor F&B Manager has two days to build up stress about the situation. The ensuing anxiety causes a high level of frustration about not being able to do anything about it immediately, which can lead some F&B Managers to partake in an occasional drink after work; purely for medicinal reasons, of course.

You may have surmised by now that Santa had done this on a few occasions. I could not honestly guess how many times this actually occurred, but I am certain I could not have counted the number on his yellow fingers.

One busy night, I had to stay a little later than usual to finish some paperwork. There were two arrivals left when I called my taxi just after midnight. As I waited, the two arrived just seconds apart. Strangers when they arrived; you would have thought they were long lost sisters by the time they were checked in. I watched in wonder, cringing as the action unfolded in slow motion.

'Every guest must be checked in within five minutes' the training manual stated. Unfortunately I hadn't started the timer at arrival, however it would be fair to say that it was well over the ten minute mark before Santa had the correct spelling for Lady One's last name. 'Smith' was obviously not a very common name under the rock where he had somehow managed to crawl out from under.

Finally, her ordeal over, Lady One was checked in. She bid her friend a good night and disappeared into the elevator. Lady Two inched tentatively closer to the desk. After another fifteen minute fiasco, she eventually followed Lady One's footsteps into the elevator. I breathed a sigh of relief.

My taxi pulled up just as Lady Two reappeared down the steps. I could tell she was thoroughly displeased with something. "I just opened my door and guess who was undressing in the room when I walked in?"

Incredible! Probably a total of thirty minutes to check them in and with only two rooms to choose from, he put them both in the same room. To explain how hard this is to do; the two rooms stated 'VC' (vacant and clean) on the screen. Every other room number had 'O' (occupied) beside it. When he typed in the name, the room numbers would have come up in big letters. Then you have to type the four-digit room number to 'cut' the key. It is not the most complicated of systems, even by Night Standards (if you'll pardon the oxymoron).

In order to 'speed up the process,' he had not checked her in on the computer, so both rooms were still 'vacant' in the system.

How he had not realized: 'Hey, I think I may have typed those four digits in the last fifteen minutes,' is a good indication of how long his memory span is. It had occurred to me that his memory could not match a goldfish in a three liter bowl.

But she was holding back: not good. That means she's saving it up for someone else in the morning. She knew she was wasting her time telling Clown One anything as he was totally incompetent: well spotted! 'If only she worked in HR,' I thought.

I slunk into my taxi. One glass of wine put me to sleep. Santa had certainly jumped into the number two spot on the Death Wish List and I dreamed sweetly of him dangling from his belt at the gates of Edinburgh Castle.

The adrenaline was going as soon as I hit the shower. I was totally focused on the Service Recovery. Forget Santa; I would deal with him when this was resolved.

I jumped into my taxi as fresh as a daisy in the morning. The anticipation of Service Recovery always made me alert. I never needed an alarm clock on those nights. At least I knew who the complimentary breakfasts were going to this morning. I could surprise them when they came down to the restaurant; thereby putting them on the back foot and gaining the upper hand. Knowledge is indeed power. Jim had neither.

On the positive side though, Santa didn't want power. I knew there was never any ulterior motive to any of his cock-ups. He couldn't spell his name, never mind 'politics.' But I still had to be prepared every morning for the complaints from his inevitable 'opportunities for training' as HR put it.

Fiona, our Head Housekeeper, arrived in her taxi, right in front of me. Chatting casually as we walked in, we opened the door to Reception. I walked past Santa to the back office while Fiona went to the computer beside him. "How's the house count looking today Fi?" I called out.

"Not bad, mostly single occupancy," she gave back.

The Duty Manager keys were lying on the safe in the back office. I opened the safe and got the hotel float out to count. "Alright Jim, ready to count the cash?" No answer. I waited. I finally poked my head out the door when there was still no answer a few seconds later. "Jim. Ready?"

Fiona was bent over double: face red as a beet, tears streaming down her face. I panicked. She's choking! "Fi, are you okay?" She pointed at Santa and finally let it all out.

And when she did, I'm not sure who got the biggest fright: me, for realizing what had happened; or Santa at being so rudely woken up.

Now Santa worked nights five nights a week. It's not like his body had to adjust to it every few days. The fact that someone could have walked in banging a drum, opened the safe and disappeared with all the hotel cash, keys and computers without him even losing any beauty sleep was certainly impressive.

As a Manager, constant cock-ups are frustrating and most take a little while for the ink to dry on the Written Warning before you can see the funny side of things. Not this one. Fiona and I went for a coffee. We were in tears, laughing all day long. Everyone in the company was enjoying Sleeping Beauty's latest and perhaps greatest within an hour.

We were about an hour into breakfast service when Lady One arrived at the dining room. I had reserved the two best tables for them, next to each other.

"Are you the…" was all she got out.

"Ms. Smith. My name is Mike. I am the Food and Beverage Manager at the hotel. I believe we had a problem with your arrival at the hotel last night."

"Oh! Yes." She was on the back foot already. I moved in.

"I am so sorry. I have already begun an investigation. Please accept my apologies."

"Yes, it was just such an inconvenience after a long day."

"Quite. I understand. I really do feel badly about this. I'd like to buy your breakfast for you this morning if I may?"

"Oh really, that's not necessary. It wasn't your fault."

'Better believe it! I didn't hire him,' I grinned.

Lady two came down moments later. I led her to the table opposite Ms Smith. "I believe you two are acquainted?" Slightly embarrassed, but seeing the lighter side of things now, they laughed, shook hands and sat together.

I walked them out after breakfast and felt the warm smug glow of success envelope me like a puff of cigar smoke. Time to celebrate.

I carried my latte confidently up the stairs at the side of Reception to my shared office immediately above it. Better check on the previous day's business results. I took a sip as I opened the door. Like a shower on a sunny day, the coffee sprayed out in a fine mist from my mouth, narrowly missing our IT Manager's feet, as the door closed behind me.

"Neil, what's going on?" It was early. Way too early for the IT guy to be up and about anyway. We shared two IT guys between our three closely situated hotels. Being the smallest of the three hotels, we didn't see much of them. My body, sensing the oncoming trauma, rejected the coffee instantly.

As he turned to answer me, I could see the Accounts computer over his shoulder. Naked bodies, horses, lots of naked bodies; yikes: porn! It wasn't your run of the mill ads that kept popping up either. This was hard core.

At my right side, leaning back in a chair was the Group Financial Controller, Dianne Monk. As far as Dianne was concerned, it was an accounting firm we all worked for, not a hotel. Our hotel Controller was on holiday, so nobody else would use her computer, or so we had thought (I had actually thought the computer was turned off all that time). So Dianne would arrive at 7:00am sharp each morning to collect the Accounts paperwork and take it to Head Office.

According to Neil, Dianne must have walked in, bumped the mouse or keyboard, thereby activating the screen. She phoned Neil immediately and screamed at him to 'get down here, it's an emergency.'

Strangely enough, for someone so traumatized, she never left the scene of the crime. Neil let me in on another little secret later too. It took him over twenty minutes to get to the crime scene. The screen saver would have blackened the screen show in ten minutes. However, when he walked in the 'show' was still on the screen!

Dianne was an old battle axe. Nearing retirement, she was cutting and nasty. She also liked a few drinks and was therefore usually in a bad mood in the morning. I liked to avoid her wherever possible, but if I had to hear from her, I tried to ensure it was after lunch. She tended to soften up a bit as the day wore on and she got closer to her next tipple.

She looked like she could use one now. "Oh God Mike. What a shock. It just popped up right in front of my face. How long has this been going on?"

I shrugged and looked at Neil. Neil shrugged back. "I can't tell. SD wouldn't pay for the software that could track this. We asked for it a year ago." That was typical of Steven Duncan, the Managing Director.

Anyone in the last eight days could have been on these sites. This could be hard to trace.

We did not have a Human Resources representative at our hotel. Again, two were shared for the three hotels, but stationed at the other two. "We're there in spirit," was what I got occasionally in an e-mail from HR: very reassuring!

I often wondered if we had been quarantined. We certainly weren't that morning though. Not one, but two ladies claiming to be our HR reps arrived shortly after the crack of 10:00am. After I'd verified their ID, they said they wanted to get statements from everyone.

The investigation that ensued was of the Keystone Cops variety. Nobody of course, had seen the computer, knew anything about it or had a clue who could have committed such a heinous crime. Privately of course, everyone suspected the Nocturnal Mafia. Who else had enough time to do it, and enough privacy to ensure they wouldn't be disturbed in that room? Certainly nobody working from 6:00am to 10:30pm.

A lot of fingers pointed to Santa, as he had been working most of these nights, but I concluded it was more likely a Night Porter. It just didn't appear to me that Santa could muster enough effort to take the elevator up one level to the office.

HR's thorough investigation continued for most of the day. Some were brave enough to suggest it could only have been a member of the Nocturnal Mafia. However, as we have already learned about the Mafia: solidarity reigns supreme. With no clear evidence, the case was thrown out within a few days.

It took a little longer to clean up the computer. Steven never did buy the software required that could catch someone if it were to happen again. At the Executive Meeting he offered the reason: "everyone will have been warned off after this episode."

Quick, darting glances were exchanged around the table, but nobody asked just how he arrived at this conclusion. Possibly everyone knew the answer. He wasn't just tight with money; he was the reason that Scots had a bad name. And he loved that everyone knew it!

The staff of course, in their typical Scottish nature, decided it must have been a ghost. "Randy the ghost' he was nicknamed. Within a few days, paper ghosts were hung up, flying around the office. Randy got the blame for a lot of things thereafter; missing pens and staplers mainly. But SD was right. Maybe 'Randy' had learned a lesson. It never happened again.

That's the way it goes with the Nocturnal Mafia: win some, lose some.

Chapter two - Accounting Hell

I slipped up the narrow spiral staircase in Reservations to the deathly quiet above. Quietly, I tiptoed down the corridor and peered around the corner. Nobody there. I glanced at my watch: 2:01pm. Game on.

Tapping softly on the glass window, I watched through the glass partition. I could see the hairs stand up on the back of his neck. The neck turned a deep red color, almost but not quite purple. Still no movement. I waited. Maybe he didn't hear me in there. I tapped again, a little louder. That did it!

The shoulders sank quickly then heaved up. Still facing away from me, but staring at the blank wall in front of him, he slowly removed his glasses. Then turning sharply like a shark on his prey, he got it out through clenched teeth: "You bloody people in this hotel."

I said nothing as I slipped the cash and list of required change under the partition. The tension was electric. You'd have thought I was asking him for $100,000 in unmarked bills rather than change for the bar!

That was the chore some poor bugger from each department was tasked with at 2:00pm each day. Everyone dreaded being asked to get change. Well, almost everyone.

Cardio didn't bother me. I was more intrigued by his reaction. How could anyone become so incredibly agitated when they knew it was coming? After all, he was the one who insisted that change only be issued between 2:00 and 2:30pm.

I really expected Cardio to just keel over clutching his chest one day when I tapped on the window; but it was the only thing that would annoy him enough to turn around and give you the change. He would completely ignore any of my pleas. I am sure I could have stood there for thirty-one minutes yelling and pleading for change; and he would have walked over at 2:31 to say: "Too late; now piss off."

I never did get Cardio's real name. It wasn't likely to come up in anyone's interactions either, so everyone just knew him as Cardio. Then one day he just wasn't there. I didn't ask why; I doubt anyone did. I just wondered what the other managers would do with the extra forty minutes in their day. It took them ten minutes to find someone around 2:00pm to assign Hercules' task to; twenty minutes for the doomed employee to get the change; and ten minutes of counseling to calm them down afterwards.

Issuing change may be a relatively minor use for an accountant; however, the smart F&B Manager is not fooled by this. Even the most menial of Accountants can pose real problems for the dedicated F&B Manager. It is therefore important to learn their idiosyncrasies and find out exactly what their 'special needs' are.

Sheri took over within a few weeks of Cardio's disappearance. She definitely had special needs, but I was not going to fulfill them.

About four weeks after she started, blinds were put up on the glass window when I went for change. "New security measure," she told me. Why not? It is where most of the cash is kept.

Dave, our Financial Controller, had moved to Edinburgh with his wife and six month old daughter about eight months prior to Sheri. He had changed a lot of our Financial Reports in those eight months. As a new manager, I was constantly knocking on his open door, prying for information. During Cardio's time, Dave was all access; but changes were afoot.

I would go over twice a day; no small task for a start. To reach Accounts, you had to go downstairs and enter Reservations, behind Reception. From there, a narrow spiral staircase led you back upstairs. Turn right and you looked down a long, empty and quiet corridor. Pretty secure…and very isolated.

I passed the glass 'change' window (shutters down) to knock on the always-locked Accounts door. Ron opened the door to let me in; it never failed. Nobody ever asked: 'Who is it?' or 'Are you going to steal all our money?' There was no peep hole to see who it was either. They just opened the door every time.

Dave's door: locked again. I turned to Ron: "Where is he?"

He grinned and pointed with his pencil to Sheri's door.

"They're always in meetings these days!" I remarked. A snigger came from the partition behind Ron. That would be Ian Cross, IT Guy. Ron banged his palm on his desk, trying to keep the laughter in. "Can you ask him to call me? We were supposed to meet at three o'clock."

A light went on somewhere above me as I walked out. 'Surely not,' I thought. Sheri was game alright, but her son worked in the restaurant; and Dave was a new father. I didn't want to believe it, but it turned out to be true. It was only later I discovered Sheri was married as well! That thought had never even occurred to me.

Two months later: Sheri was gone (inappropriate conduct); her son had left the restaurant (embarrassing conduct – third party); and Dave remained. Money talks.

Every morning and afternoon, Sheri and Dave could be spotted (if you had a strong stomach) in each other's throats at the coffee shop across the street.

I was sorry to see Sheri go. I guessed I wasn't the only one either. Since Sheri had been with Accounts I had noticed that more and more managers had been going to get the change themselves. I always got the change quickly, and she was very flirty, so it was an ego stroke too.

Nobody in Accounts seemed terribly upset by the whole affair. Normally, there is a rash of brown–nosing with the boss when a position becomes vacant. Back-stabbing is even more common than usual at times like this; but not in Accounts.

Accounting Teams are unique in that they are not usually out to climb the corporate ladder. The reason for this is, as far as they are concerned, they are all department heads already. Accounts Receiving; Accounts Payable (I liked to think of these as Complaints Receiving and Complaints Payable); Change Dispenser, etc. Everyone is in charge of something.

The problem for the clever F&B Manager here is that you have to be careful with favors. You can't afford to trade an Accounts request for future favors (say when the Accounts Receiving guy becomes the Controller). So you can only trade small requests for short-term favors or information. This can be costly, as you are now trying to buy an entire department (or many small departments in their eyes) rather than one manager.

The sharp F&B Manager must monitor the reports and decide what information they need and who can fix the numbers in their favor. Then they must approach that accountant and find out, without making it look like entrapment, what they might like in exchange for favors of an accounting nature. It may be as simple as chocolate. Chocolate is a good bribe, especially if you have access to the Chef's stash. It may be wine, or champagne. Champagne is obviously expensive. If anyone hints they would prefer something along those lines, steer clear. They are obviously a professional inside trader. Get your favors and info from the chocolate lover.

Ron certainly didn't have any delusions of grandeur; just delusions. I remember waiting for Dave outside Sheri's office one day. My eyes caught Ron's wall: postcards...hundreds of postcards from every corner of the world. "Who sends you all these?" I asked.

"I do. I send them back here when I'm away on holiday."

I thought quietly for a moment. Although I hadn't worked in Accounts, the math seemed pretty straight forward here. Ron was either: a) a millionaire who holidayed nine months of the year and worked in a hotel as a tax dodge; b) a millionaire illegal immigrant from India; or c) full of shit.

My spidey senses told me 'C.' The sharp instincts of the F&B Manager are rarely wrong. This was confirmed with another snigger from Mr. Cross.

I saw one from Victoria, Canada. I was pretty sure Ron had no idea I grew up not too far from there. "What was Victoria like?"

"Cold. Big city with great night life. Lots of hot chicks." He intimated with his hands that even this loser could pick up there. I knew however, that Victoria was not a society of deaf and blind females.

"What time of year were you there?"

"June. It was a few years ago now though. There were whales everywhere!"

"Oh really? Did you go on a boat to see them?"

"No. They swim right past the shore."

Just as I thought…C - full of shit. According to Ian, Ron booked two holidays to exotic destinations every week, and then cancelled them when the deposit was due.

Sheri's door opened suddenly behind me. She came dancing out and twirled away out of the office. "Ready?" Dave nodded to me and walked into his office.

"Be gentle with me," I whispered to Ron. Mistake.

Ron banged his desk with his fist. "Be gentle with me!" he parroted. Idiot! I made a mental note to myself: be very careful what I say to moron in Accounts.

I closed the door behind me as I sat opposite Dave, trying to make light of it. "What's his problem?"

"Alphabetically or chronologically?" was the dry, cold reply. Not a hint of humor in his tone. But that was probably as close to a smile or a laugh anyone outside of a 'shutters-down' meeting ever got from Dave.

He was spot on with Ron too. This nutter extraordinaire kept most of the entire hotel entertained for almost two years. And entertainment was what Ron liked.

Ron was always so chipper and cheerful around lunch time, it was ridiculous; he was almost giddy. If you caught a glimpse of him at 9:00am and then 11:00am, you would have thought he was dropping some serious amounts of ecstasy in between.

Helping out our restaurant over lunches one busy week, I noticed Ron returning to the hotel from the far right corner of the plaza that the restaurant overlooked. This happened every afternoon at exactly 12:55pm. I brought it up with Drew, our Purchasing Controller, and Ian Cross over a beer after work one day. Drew nearly choked on his pint.

It turned out Ron visited the Fantasy Bar (a very exclusive strip club) on his lunch hour every single day. Table dances, private dances, the lot! I was gobsmacked. An hour for lunch!

Ron didn't just like to be entertained either. He was also quite an entertainer himself and all too frequently enjoyed a drink with the boys. Sadly, 'a' drink was where he should have stopped, and never did. Ron didn't normally attend many leaving parties...but he wasn't normally invited, to be fair.

In large hotels, there is a leaving party almost every weekend. Sheri's came on a payday, so there was a large attendance.

Despite our efforts, Ron spotted us at a table at the back and graced us, pint in hand, with his company. At least we had a good seat for the cabaret. By the time Drew returned with our first, Ron had already quaffed his.

It only took three beers for the entertainer to kick off the festivities, warming us up with stories of his recent wife swapping escapades. It certainly got the crowd going. The thought of him as married seemed ridiculous and had never crossed my mind. Someone who obviously couldn't hear Ron's tales of intrigue suggested to him that he should probably leave.

Strangely, although strange had new connotations around Ron, he agreed. He reached below the table for his umbrella and stood up, and then up, and then up again. Standing on the table, he opened his umbrella. Only a couple of drinks were lost as Ron's crowd backed a few feet away to get a better view of the stage. The crowd cheering him on, Ron delighted his fans with a rousing rendition of 'singing in the rain.' I would have liked to see Freddy Astaire try his little show on a bar table. It couldn't have been easy.

Sadly, it was over as quickly as it had begun. Two bouncers waded in through the tsunami of fans. The crowd reached a fever pitch of applause as he was surfed above them and gently thrown, broken umbrella not far behind, out on the wet sidewalk. When he managed to pick himself up, Ron peered in through the window at his adoring throng of fans to take his last roar of applause, and wish the bouncers a pleasant evening with his two fingers. Inspirational stuff!

On Monday morning I aimed straight for Accounts at 8:45am. I always looked forward to reminding the guilty party of their incident, lest their memory suffer from blackouts. Played expertly, the price of favors can be reduced drastically at these times. They will not barter because they do not want to be reminded of their stupidity and are more worried about their 'indiscretion' being spread around the hotel. F&B Managers should not feel guilty about this. As long as you don't threaten to spread it, it isn't blackmail. It should however, be implied.

My tactic was wasted on Ron of course: he enjoyed the notoriety. This visit was purely for personal entertainment. Like so many others, I didn't know what he did in the hotel anyway, so I wasn't about to get anything out of him.

He was just hanging up the phone when Ian opened the office door and let me in. "That's me just booked for two weeks in Zanzibar," Ron smiled.

"Hey Ron, how was your weekend?" I grinned.

"Great!" he laughed.

"Someone asked me to give these to you after you left early on Friday night." I threw him a pair of leopard-skin ladies briefs, picked up from the Lost and Found that morning.

He picked them up off his chest and held them up high so everyone could see them. A sick grin slowly crept from one ear to the other. "Great. I like 'em big."

Mr. Cross and the rest of the Accounts Team were enjoying this. Raucous laughter filled the room. Ron was enjoying it too. Holding his prize aloft again, he gave them a good sniff. "No, I don't think I know her."

"So which table are you dancing on tonight Ron?"

"I'm having dinner in the Grill Room tonight actually," he smiled. "It's our anniversary."

Silence. "The Stacker" as Dave was known when he wasn't present, had slithered under the door. 9:00am on the nose. He didn't look happy. He didn't normally look happy, but today he wouldn't be having any stress relief in the cash office. Laughter turned to muffled grunts; grunts turned to coughs; smiles turned to frowns. Accounting is all business when the boss is around. I made my excuses and left.

The Grill Room. This was our fine dining restaurant in the hotel. It was one of only two restaurants in Edinburgh with 3 AA Rosettes. Staff were allowed, with the Restaurant Manager's approval, to dine in The Grill Room. However, even with the fifty percent discount that staff received, the prices were a good deterrent to this perk being abused.

Ron and his alleged wife would definitely be fish out of water in this arena. Quite a few of us eagerly anticipated this little soiree. Finally we would get to see who could have married this clown.

"They're here," Patrick whispered through the swinging doors into the kitchen. Patrick had been the Supervisor in the Grill for as long as I could remember. He was quite young, although he looked older than he was, French and very professional.

I walked through the Grill Room. They sat at a table near the entrance (or exit, depending on your outlook) against the beautifully cut glass bay windows. I stopped by, expecting an introduction to Ron's undoubtedly better half. As it was not forthcoming, I wandered past, straining my eyes at her. It was not the usual attire for this restaurant. 'A good match for Ron,' I thought.

She was in a tight, red leather one-piece suit. I'm not sure how the black high heeled shoes fit in the look, but with Ron on her arm, it would probably go unnoticed. I had to admit, she was better looking than I had imagined; although like Ron, there was something a bit odd about her.

I went back to the kitchen where Patrick was entertaining the chefs with details of her outfit. "Patrick, the Gimp is ready to order," I called.

Patrick returned to the service area a few minutes later. "Moet," he laughed. "How passé." Patrick was also gay. He was only ever critical of two things in his restaurant: women's fashion, and wines. He would never deny he was a wine snob. I offered to take it out, since Patrick 'didn't do Moet.'

A three course meal in the Grill Room was an event. Typically it would take about three hours. You were always kept busy with the servers bringing a small 'amuse' here and there. It was a very relaxing and romantic setting. After a few glasses of Patrick's finest, the mood, or the Moet, was having a devastating effect on this couple.

The hands were wandering alright. Standing a few tables away, I could see the groping that was going on under the table. Ron's hands cast an easily identifiable shadow over her garb, fluorescent in the candlelight. I shot a glance at Patrick. He was definitely worried, and with good reason; they hadn't even got to their main courses yet.

You could sense that other diners were keeping at least one eye on the enthusiastic duo as well. Whether or not they were enjoying it was quite another matter. Patrick went to spend some quality time at the table in the hopes of cooling them down to sauna temperature. No success. After a few minutes of being ignored and having to watch it close up, Patrick was sent back for another bottle of his favorite champagne.

"Merde! Imbecile!" Patrick had a fabulous tendency to mumble and swear in French when he was angry.

The champers went out, followed closely by the main courses. The kitchen were under orders now to rapid fire this meal out, at risk of court martial. Although it would definitely go unnoticed, food quality was taking a back seat at this table. I felt sure a back seat was where this date was going to end too. Ron ate with one hand. Where the other was I could only guess.

Clearing his plate, Ron wolfed down another glass of bubbly and cut a not-quite-straight line to the bathroom. Here was my opportunity.

I walked over to introduce myself. "Good evening. I trust you're enjoying your meal with us tonight?"

"Yes," she giggled, reaching for her glass.

"You must be excited about your trip to Zanzibar?"

A confused look. Maybe it was a surprise. Time was of the essence; Ron would be back any second now. I looked nervously at the entrance. "How many years are you celebrating tonight?"

"What do you mean?"

"Well, how many years have you two been together?"

"Years! I've seen Ron at the club a few times. That's about it."

Aha! I knew it! Ron's pace increased as he approached the table, no doubt sensing my line of questioning. The champagne obviously winning the battle for self-control, Ron fell into his seat and leaned over to start kissing her neck and chest, ignoring me brilliantly.

Thoroughly blushing, I turned and walked into the kitchen to escape the heat. "Holy shit! He's brought a prostitute into the hotel!" I whispered to Patrick.

"Of fucking course," he gave back. "Who did you think could wear an outfit like that in here?"

I had to admit, looking at it now; it seemed obvious.

We returned together into the restaurant and stared in horror as Ron was nearly straddling her on the sofa seat. They were kissing wildly. Patrick went straight for them. "Ron. Ron." Nothing. "Excuse me. Ron!"

Ron turned around; a nice lipstick smear on his cheek. One eye tried to home in on Patrick, the other was so far askew that I couldn't hazard a guess as to where its gaze rested.

Patrick spoke slowly and clearly now: "Ron, you must leave at once." Fortunately, I could see Ron understood. Unfortunately, he wasn't having any of it.

"We haven't had dessert yet."

"Mon Dieu, No. And you are not going to get any either. You must feeneesh your Moet and leave tout de suit."

A bit of a compromise there; and not a good one. Ron paid no attention. He turned back to his business while Patrick went around the tables to offer his sincerest apologies for this most inappropriate behavior.

This was obviously a very uncomfortable situation for almost everyone. Patrick couldn't remove him without causing a bigger scene and risking Ron letting everyone know he was actually a member of staff.

As it turned out, the other tables ate rather quickly and left before Ron and 'Candy' (as the chefs had dubbed her) could drink up and leave. The last table walked out, straining their heads impossibly away from the disgraceful couple near the exit. Patrick banged the bill down on Ron's hand, which was momentarily making a surprise appearance above the table: "I suppose you'll be paying for this as well?"

"You must leave at once," Patrick seethed as he whisked the nearly-done bottle of Moet and two glasses off the table.

Eventually, Ron paid up and staggered out, one hand on Candy's ass as they gracefully, and thankfully, disappeared to God knows where.

I breathed a sigh of relief as Patrick called out to no one in particular: "Merde! Fucking arsehole. He didn't even tip!"

Ron's notoriety around the hotel was picking up as fast as his popularity was increasing each day: exponentially. This latest little escapade had bought him a special invite to discuss etiquette with Jane in Human resources.

Poor Ron was barred from using any of the staff perks in the hotel. No discounts on rooms or spa treatments; and absolutely banned from the use of any restaurants, with or without the discount. Some accountants just didn't understand where the line was laid until they had crossed it. Sharon was cut from a similar cloth.

"Oy, where the fuckin 'ell are you from?"

"Uh, well I'm from here originally, but I grew up in Canada and moved back here a few years ago." I'd been asked this question, sans vulgarity, so many times that I was able to reel of my well-versed, standard reply. This time I'd been caught off guard though. The F-bombs were not very lady-like…although it soon became ridiculously apparent how inappropriate this term would be when relating to Sharon. At the first point of introduction too! She was as subtle as a brick in the face.

Sharon was from Kenworth. I have never been there, but the way she threw it around gave me the distinct impression that 'fuck' was the first spoken word of half the Kenworth population…the female half. I'm sure her grandmother would have been proud.

"Oh, fuckin right. Nice to meet you."

I smiled. "Nice meeting you too." Sharing an office with Sharon Fucking Evans was going to be entertaining if nothing else.

The entertainment value of Sharon was a benefit that Human Resources failed to mention when interviewing me for the position. It should have been brought up right after the fifty percent discount on food and beverage: 'You'll be sharing an office with Sharon. She has a master's degree in vulgarity. Sharon will keep you entertained throughout your stay; whether you are eavesdropping on her phone calls to clients and friends, or listening to her parlaying stories of her weekend debauchery to you directly. We also supply ear defenders should it become too much. This benefit is also tax-free!'

Sharon's shtick never varied. The intensity of the limited pool of vocabulary she could draw from however; was ear-numbing.

Every morning I would walk into the same complaint, yet I marveled at the variety of ways she could get her point across, and with such venom! For example: a pet peeve of hers was that the restaurant servers could not seem to remember to sign their name and write the date on their cash pay-in sheet after each shift. The fact that all their order chits (stating the date and the server's name) were attached to it seemed to make it all the more sinister to her.

The Accountants view: These morons obviously have no desire to continue working for this Accounting Firm. They make these mistakes on purpose to piss me off. I'll show them who's who in this Firm.

The Server's view: I'm two minutes from finishing my shift and getting to the pub to meet my mates. It's not balancing…stuff it, Accounts will fix it.

The Manager's View: If this is my Accountants biggest issue with Food and Beverage, great! I will see HR about that raise immediately. Do not fix the issue as Accounts may find something of relevance to focus on in its place. I must avoid a meeting between the staff and Sharon at all costs, to maintain the status quo. Try to keep a straight face.

I decided not to tell Sharon that they seem to have a problem writing down orders and bills correctly as well. This may have had the effect of cancelling my entertainment package benefit.

"Good morning Sharon. How are you?"

"Fucking idiots! That Fucking Caroline is fucking useless down there." By 'down there' I assumed the restaurant. But to Sharon it didn't matter where they worked. If they weren't part of the Accounting Team, they were only extended employees of The Firm; exiled lepers.

"It's a training issue. I'll speak to her about it." This was a reflex response from years of not being able to get rid of some staff that would have been out of their depth in a parking lot puddle. Every time I would run smiling to HR thinking I finally had enough to get rid of the bastard that was giving me nightmares. Every time I came out suicidal after HR's 'they need more training' response. My sharp instincts took over now and turned the tables. Here I was using the phrase I had dreaded from HR, for my own benefit.

"Training my fucking arse. She's been here for two fucking years."

She was right of course but I had played my hand and had to either up the ante or fold. The F&B Manager never folds. "What do you suggest then?"

I knew damn well what she would suggest. To coin a phrase she had uttered many times: sweet fuck all. The only action Sharon ever took was to write nasty and inappropriate comments on her Accounts Report that was sent to every manager in the Hotel Group each day. This was her idea of training. The manager is then supposed to take her comments, always capitalized, bold of type and font 16 (just so it embarrasses the person enough to make sure it sinks in their thick little skulls), and use them as a training tool.

Obviously her action always had the exact opposite reaction than the one she wanted. When they saw the report, I usually got something along the lines of: 'What a bitch! Why doesn't she come down and show us how she wants it done?' I had asked Sharon this many times myself, only to get a disgusted look accompanied by a rousing rendition of: 'That's not my fuckin' job.'

Unfortunately, this time I was disappointed…very! "Dianne Monk is coming to speak to them."

I could hear my heart rate increasing as I vainly tried to muster a smile. I hadn't met Dianne yet, but I had heard plenty of rumors going about the hotel. 'Hard as nails. Hard drinker. Hard on the eyes, and especially hard on the ears.' These were just a few of the comments I had heard, so I did not want to get off to a bad start with her. "When is she coming?"

The door opened. I inhaled sharply as she took two steps past me, placed her handbag inadvertently on my desk, swung around sharply and leaned back against my desk. She quickly glared me up and down.

"Mike this is Dianne," Sharon smirked.

"Hi Dianne. I've heard a lot about you." I wanted to continue but was quickly cut off.

"Mike what the fuck is going on down here? I mean, there's something wrong on every fucking cash pay-in from what I can see on Sharon's report." She kept her arms folded. No doubt she had never shaken a hand until she could be sure it didn't hold a knife.

I wished I had one now. This wasn't going well. I didn't know what to say. "Are you from Kenworth by any chance?"

"No. Why?"

"No reason." Shit! "Anyway, I was just saying to Sharon, that I would like to arrange a training session with the restaurant staff and Sharon so we can document the training and that way, we can punish the bastards if they keep getting it wrong."

I could see in an instant that she wasn't down here to arrange a training session. She wanted blood; no doubt anybody's would do. The idea of being able to 'punish' anyone trying to bring down The Firm by neglecting to put the date on a pay-in sheet would appeal to this bloodthirsty tyrant.

"Okay. This better be sorted out by next Monday. Mike, I can't run fucking Accounts like this."

There was no way around it now. My benefits were on the line, but Dianne didn't look like one to piss about. Anyway, I was sure the training would be a good laugh in itself.

In the end, the training session was superbly conducted. Sharon's decision to speak to her audience as if they were three year old toddlers rather than the twenty-something alcoholics that they were, was a magical touch that created a brilliant environment for learning.

The toddlers sat quietly and impatiently as Sharon loosely threw around terms such as: "Does any of you lot not know how to write your name?" and, "…is that too much to fucking ask?"

Sadly for Sharon, being such a young audience, she did not receive the standing ovation her well planned session deserved.

The next morning I held my breath as I walked in. "Good morning Sharon."

Not a peep. Her back faced me soundlessly. Maybe she's on the phone. I peered over her shoulder. Nope. "Good morning."

She turned to face me; mascara sprinting from her eyes as she screamed at me: "Fucking bastards. Fucking bastards!" She was too distressed to get any more out. Instead, she held the sheets up for my inspection. Every toddler had failed to sign their name and the date on their pay-in sheet. A protest.

I stormed out of the office and made it all the way to the far stairs and into the fire escape stairs before I let it all out. Fiona, smoking as usual at the bottom of the fire stairs, came racing up to find out what all the laughter was about.

Sharon had needed pulling down a few pegs. This had been made difficult because of the Dianne Monk factor. However, I was now confident that this had done the job. Sharon needed to see that: a) it wasn't an accounting firm she was working for; and b) she was part of a much larger team.

This was what I had been working towards. Now it was crunch time. I had to make her feel like she was part of the team and turn her attitude around before The Monk could tighten her grip on this wreck. I couldn't afford to leave her alone for long lest she make a call for advice to her superior. Not so coincidentally, Dianne's extension number at head office was 666.

I returned to the office with a latte and a donut from the kitchen. The mascara slowed to a drip when she caught sight of the donut. I knew I was in with a good shot now. I threw the words at her feverishly while she inhaled the sugary treat: 'respect, teamwork.'

At lunch time I dragged her down to the staff room. An awkward hush fell over the room as she walked in there for the first time. I'd made sure everyone knew the script: Chef shared his politically incorrect jokes. They only got a smirk, but I knew she loved them. The server in the restaurant brought her a latte. This cost me a $3 tip. The Housekeepers she normally ignored all commented how nice it was to see her 'down here.' I was calling in every favor I was due.

In the end though, it worked. The toddlers suddenly regained their memory when it came to putting a name and a date on their pay-in sheets. The Daily Accounts Report went out without capitalized sentences condemning the children (and their manager) to the fate of The Monk. Any time there was an issue, Sharon would storm 'down there' to speak to 'the person' and not the 'fucking moron' involved. It began to feel like a real team.

And best of all, I kept my entertainment benefits. Except now, instead of abusing the staff, Sharon took it all out on the clients that owed us money.

As she was the only one in Accounts in the hotel, Sharon was 'complaints payable' and 'complaints receiving.' It didn't take a genius to figure out which one she excelled at, and which one was going to need a lot more coaching on.

But now that I had her trust, it was relatively easy to get her from phrases such as: 'Oy, that's four fuckin' weeks overdue. I'm going to pull out any reservations for your company immediately;' to 'I will have to escalate our request for payment of this outstanding amount to my Group Financial Controller and your superior. May I please have their contact details and your full name?'

Sharon then picked up the phone, dialed 666 and passed it on to the pit bull at Head Office. I could imagine the fear Dianne would put into anyone owing her money. God help them!

Strangely, Dianne began coming around more often when things were going well than when Sharon was filling her Daily Report with unsuitable comments. I could feel her cold eyes boring a hole in my back when she was around.

I would walk into the office to find Sharon talking to her while Dianne perused my desk, browsing my notes and inventory details. I clued in quickly. She was trying to woo Sharon back to The Firm. Something had to be done.

"Dianne, I have a problem I was hoping you could help me with." Her lips clenched tightly. Only her finely trimmed moustache differentiated her mouth from a sphincter. I continued: "We had a beverage delivery three weeks ago. I received a bottle of champagne that we weren't invoiced for. It's not one we have on our list so I can't sell it. What should I do with it?"

Her eyes narrowed through the thick lenses. When she'd gathered enough saliva to relax her sphincter muscle, she was able to respond. "What kind?"

"Bollinger."

"Well I guess you could give it to someone." A moment of silence that must have seemed an eternity to her elapsed before she hastily added: "Or I suppose you could just take it yourself, I mean…if you drink champagne?"

"Well, I don't really drink the stuff." Of course, this was a lie. Every F&B Manager drinks champagne, but I hoped she would oversee this with her thoughts on the prize. "I don't want to look like I'm playing favorites with the staff, so would you take it?"

It was a good thing she was well past her mascara years. I sensed she was very close to tears. It may have cost me a bottle of Bolly, but I had The Monk in my back pocket now. As the Group Financial Controller, there was no way around her.

This tactic is called 'over and upping.' Quite simply, the Hotel Accountant (Sharon) now knew I was well in with her boss, so she had to watch her step around me now. How sweet it is when the tables are turned by the F&B Manager; slowly, carefully and with malice aforethought.

If there is a downside to this tactic, it's that there can be no bragging about it. Not around the workplace anyway.

Any manager found discussing the success of this type of venture (or more likely, when a colleague grasses you up!) can expect a visit from their over-bubbly HR person. Expect not the proverbial pat on the back you deserve. HR will misconstrue this metamorphosis in staff morale as bribery and manipulation.

It is therefore recommended that the champagne (or similar 'bribe,' for lack of a better term) is untraceable. If you work for a group of hotels, or have a good relationship with a nearby pub or restaurant, borrow it from them (as I did on this occasion) so that when your 'Dianne Monk' checks your invoices (and she will!), they find nothing. In a few weeks, you can add it to your weekly order and replace it. Brilliant!

At least Dianne's was a one-off. The first time I met Nina, I knew she was a long-term planner. Nina knew where her bread was buttered; or more accurately, where her chocolate was wrapped.

Every time I walked within nine feet of her desk I would hear her 8-track tape playing the tune: "Mike. Hello. Brother how are you?" it whispered in a Russian accent. "Listen, brother... (here it was always made to sound like an afterthought as a hand patted my knee) Do you have something for me?"

At this point Nina would lower her nose, allowing her glasses to slide forward. Two large puppy-dog eyes peered out at me above the rim of the glasses. Her bottom lip quivered slightly until it formed a pout. She also had a rather large chest, which nobody could miss with the low cut shirts she wore. Nina was in her early fifties, and had probably been perfecting this little game of hers effectively for thirty years. I recognized at once I was dealing with a professional inside trader.

Nina's tactic was to hit small, but often. If she had been a champagne lover I would have resigned on the spot. No F&B Manager can afford to give out 'gifts' at every visit. But Nina was a chocolate addict. I don't even think she ate it all; but she had to have it. I learned to carry a small supply in my coat pocket at all times. You never know when you are going to bump into someone.

My chocolate supply chain was simple. They don't call it Human 'Resources' for nothing. HR always keeps a jar of candy near their office entrance, designed to entice unsuspecting staff near their office. Once the hand has reached into the candy jar, and the HR Manager is confident they are preoccupied with the candy, he begins his solicitation for information.

Offering candies to children in exchange for favors outside the hotel may land you eight years hard time. In a hotel however, the HR Manager will without doubt receive a large pat on the back (and possibly a 'well done') from the General Manager for any juicy info the staff member divulges while on a chocolate high.

Every day I would make an excuse to stop by Isaac's office and dip my hand in the jar, commenting on the quality of the candy so I had something different for my chocolate wolf. "Isaac you had these same chocolates last week. You need to change them up a bit. I haven't seen many staff around here lately. Try the mini smarties."

He took the hint. I would walk past, ask a question, grab a handful and store them in my desk drawer until I needed to top up my pocket supply.

Occasionally I would pass Nina's desk when she wasn't there. I would leave a little Hershey's chocolate kiss on her desk with a post-it note that stated: 'Enjoy! Mike.'

This was a big hit with The Wolf. Finally a manager who could fulfill her needs! My goal had been achieved. Now I had to be careful not to over-achieve. I didn't want another 'Stacker-Gate' on my hands. I wanted her close, for information; but at a distance, to avoid a nuisance.

It wasn't easy. My problem started with the classic Achilles Heel of all F&B Managers: remembering names. All F&B Managers suffer from this ailment, in varying degrees, because their minds are constantly working on so many different levels. Names, like the people, therefore become unimportant. They are either obstacles in your way to achieving, or the grunt that you use to achieve your goals.

Rather than constantly calling people the wrong name, I began using a non-confrontational approach. I called everyone 'brother' or 'sister.' Most loved it; mistaking it for a term of endearment.

My assistant at The Plaza, The Dick, had to learn this valuable lesson the hard way. He foolishly tried to recall individual names at peak times. This had the obvious result in confusing the staff when he stuttered (searching for a name), and used the wrong one. On one occasion he addressed two girls at the bar as 'Dick'…his own name! Not even in the ball park!

This is a rather obvious de-motivator for staff, as you are showing them that you don't care enough about them to learn their names. Occasionally I held out hope for The Dick; like when he started calling some staff 'sweetie;' however, all too often he used it for male staff, and he soon reverted back to trying to use their real names. You can lead a horse to water!

Nina soon became enamored with the 'sister' moniker. She called me 'brother' at every public opportunity; sometimes shouting it at me from across a crowded lobby. I made sure I never addressed anyone else as 'sister' in her presence, lest she thought I was cheating on her. Fortunately all her co-workers in Accounting Hell were 'brothers.'

Nina was also obsessive compulsive. When I started at The Plaza, my first assistant had been left to run the department by himself for three months. He had made the fatal error of neglecting the purchasing and invoicing procedure, which had driven Nina even crazier than usual.

I tried to instill in Aaron the importance of making Accounts feel important, but he wasn't having any of it.

In my first week Nina was down to the F&B Office at least three times each day, chasing me for Purchase Orders and delivery notes from the last three months that either didn't exist or had long since been discarded.

She drilled me on her procedure:

STEP ONE: when receiving a delivery, sign and date the packing slip (or delivery note).

STEP TWO: staple the delivery note behind the Purchase Order. Here was the tricky bit: they had to be stapled at a forty-five degree angle at the top left hand corner. "Otherwise Mike, (here she flipped the top page over as an example, and threw a hand up in despair) look, you see? They just don't look right. This is not professional Mike."

I couldn't help laughing. "Nina I totally agree. I can't believe how sloppy some people can be!"

"Mike. Thank you. Listen, I know you are going to fix this for me. It's important. You know. I can see you know this."

I knew alright: 'beware lunatic in Accounts' registered thoroughly. A pleasant lunatic though; she wasn't nasty like The Monk.

STEP THREE: when you receive the invoice, it must be paper clipped (any angle; not stapled) to the top of the delivery note and purchase order. These are then passed on to Accounts for payment and filing.

Aaron had been placing orders without purchase orders, so the delivery notes were crucial to her. The few of these that he had kept had been thrown in a large pile with invoices and other unimportant paperwork. To Aaron, all paperwork was unimportant.

The only way Accounts knew when to pay someone was when they called Nina to complain that it was overdue. This did not sit well with Nina. It put her straight on the defensive. Accountants in general can be quite pedantic, but when they are made to look incompetent, they become aggressive. Nina was a Siberian Tiger by the time of my second week.

The sensitive F&B Manager notes that when someone makes such a fuss over something as ridiculous as the angle of a staple, there is a bigger issue at stake. Nina needed attention.

I typed up the 'purchasing / invoicing procedure' and ran over it with Aaron for a laugh. When he reached the 'staple the delivery note behind the purchase order at a forty-five degree angle' bit, he grimaced and poignantly added: "Yeah, if you're a fucking freak!"

I decided to look after the purchasing myself from this point on. Hurricane Nina flew into the office and assumed the space Aaron had vacated only seconds earlier. Before she could get out her first pout, I rammed the full-page written procedure in her face and pleaded: "Nina, could you please read this over for accuracy?"

She read…slowly. I watched carefully as she read a few lines, rolled her eyes to the ceiling and let out a series of "uh-huh's" as she flicked the page with the back of her left hand every moment or two. Success!

I moved in for the kill. "Nina, I'm really sorry about all these issues with missing invoices and purchase orders. I turned my back on her briefly so she could watch me taping the written procedure to a sparkling new two-tiered filing folder. I explained it to her as the tears welled up in her eyes: "The first tier is for P.O.'s. They are dated when the order is placed. The second tier is for the delivery notes and P.O.'s that are attached, but awaiting the invoice. When the invoice arrives, it is attached and sent up to Accounts on the same day." This part actually made no sense at all to me.

When an invoice is sent to the hotel, it is always sent straight to Accounts. Accounts then have to send it down to the correct department, and then wait for that department to attach it to the delivery note and P.O., and then back it went to Accounts. Getting these three items attached and back to Accounts quickly is vitally important to the conscientious F&B Manager.

The F&B Manager eagerly anticipates the food cost and beverage cost at the end of each month; as if their bonus was on the line. However, if invoices are missing, these 'markers' can't be accurate. You will look utterly brilliant one month with a food cost of 20%. However, you will be looking for work in the staff cafeteria the next month when it comes in at 40%. Consistency is king here.

I tried to speak to Kent about this. "Why don't we just send you the delivery note and P.O. when the order arrives? This way, you will at least know if there are outstanding invoices each month. It also speeds up the process; we have two extra steps in the current process."

Happy with what seemed to me an irrefutable point, Kent countered by blowing his cheeks out like a puffer fish. This was his reaction to any question at all though.

For this reason, I would always give him some warning about when I wanted to buy an expensive item. Accountants just move the money around on the Financial Statement each month, so when you need something, don't be aggressive. Give them an estimate on the cost (always estimate lower than the actual cost obviously!) and the time frame you are looking at. They will find the money.

Also drop little hints that it's a much needed item: 'the General Manager and I were talking about a new toaster,' or 'we had several complaints recently that the toast is burned. A new toaster would be great.' These 'pressure points' cause The Controller stress, and the best way for an Accountant to beat that stress is to buckle under the pressure.

I waited patiently, looking up expectantly for an oxygen mask to drop as I felt the carbon dioxide level in the room peak sharply.

I had a lot of respect for Kent. He was Nina's boss and anyone who could put up with her on a daily basis deserved my unending respect. But the one down side to Kent was that he did not like change. Most of the reason for this was because he couldn't figure out how to make the changes he should have…like the Daily Revenue Report, for example.

Every hotel issues a Daily Revenue Report of some sort at their daily 9:00am meeting. The Daily Revenue Report is the bane of every F&B Manager's existence. This stat sheet is supposed to help the F&B Manager. In reality, the report is a tool to demoralize and humiliate the F&B Manager.

The GM will read the report and tell everyone who is pretending to listen how overstaffed F&B is throughout the month. My defense to this plot prior to this particular hotel was to avoid the meeting altogether…due to a 'busy spell' in the restaurant, if questioned. It seemed ridiculous to me: a hotel has only so many rooms. Therefore the Rooms Division knows pretty accurately how many rooms will be used each day. So they know very accurately how many staff they need each day. In F&B however, you have no idea how many guests will call for room service, or come into the restaurant, or come from outside the hotel itself…never mind what time they will show up or call down.

In Accounting Hell, however, I used to laugh at the stats before the GM could make a mockery of me. This was easy when Kent and Nina were compiling the report because none of the stats were correct. At first glance I could see that they were wrong.

I remember walking into the GM's office one busy morning. She eyed me coldly as she glanced from the report to me and back again, several times. I smiled bravely and swallowed hard as I risked a wink, knowing that would piss her off and make her bite all the harder at the cherry.

"Okay let's go with the Revenue Report. F&B." This was a clear breach of etiquette as she always started with the Rooms Division. This was going to be all the sweeter after going for my throat like this. I calmly read out the stats. I had to admit; they did make for grim reading.

The echo was still reverberating in the packed room as she eclipsed it: "Overstaffed twelve and a half percent to budget!" Kent's reports weren't sophisticated enough to contain percentages. She had obviously done a little homework.

Like a wolf stumbling on a pork chop, I thought: it just can't be this easy and this good. "I couldn't agree with you more. This would be absolutely disgraceful (I delayed slightly here so I could count how many mouths were wide open), if the stats were accurate."

My gaze quickly flashed across the room and rested on Kent. All eyes fell upon The Puffer as I continued: "However the revenue is wrong, the payroll is wrong, and there is clearly an issue with last year's revenue figures too." I rested my case.

The tension in the air was enough to pop The Puffer, but he exhaled just in time. "Uh, yeah." He was trying to buy time. "I think there is a problem with the links. I'll look at it."

There was a problem with the links alright. The hotel had been open for eight years at this point. All of the Accounts Team had been employed here since pre-opening. They had built so many spreadsheets (and not labeled or e-filed them properly) that when something needed to be changed, it was the proverbial needle and haystack job. They had no idea which spreadsheet was linked to another, and had nobody to blame but each other.

There was a problem with every spreadsheet we had: ridiculous, obviously. To demonstrate what the impact of this can be for the meticulous F&B Manager: take the 'covers' issue as one example. 'Covers' are the number of guests you serve in an outlet.

We had started the annual budget process only weeks after I started in Accounting Hell. After weeks of studying the history of 'revenues,' 'covers' and 'average checks' from the last two years; the numbers just didn't make any sense to me. There were huge swings in covers and average checks, but not revenue. Apart from being very odd, how was I going to gauge which one we should try to increase?

Stumped for the first time since doing budgets, I brought it up at my first budget meeting with The Puffer and Nicole, the GM. "How is this possible? Where are you getting the cover counts from?"

They stared at each other until The Puffer finally exhaled. "Well, they're the budgeted numbers from last year."

"But surely you update this with the 'actual' numbers at the end of each month right?" I tried in vain to give him the answer I so desired to hear.

"Uh, no. We don't track covers."

"Who does?" My heart sank even before he could puff up again. "You're telling me that for the last seven years, you've been doing a budget with average checks and covers, but nobody has tracked the actual covers?" It was as close to tears as I've ever come at work.

If you've never been involved in the budget process, it can be simple: track your covers and average check. Multiply these to give you the revenue. As a business, you will want to increase your revenue. In order to do this you will set monthly goals for increased covers and / or average check. This is how most places put a budget together.

The clever F&B Manager tracks his covers and average checks, knowing accounts may not, so he can see where his opportunities lie. But what can you do when you have to guess at the previous seven year history?

In Accounting Hell, you will find the easy budget made difficult: just plan to increase your revenue every year by five percent. Then calculate how many covers you should be doing to give you (what appears to be) a consistent average check.

F&B Managers will have already noted: this appears to be fairly easy until roughly the end of the first fiscal month, when everyone realizes the annual budget is so cocked up already that drastic cuts have to be made in staffing. This will affect F&B first, so the moment the ink has dried on the approved budget, the F&B Manager should book their holidays for the first two weeks of January.

By February 1st you will have to explain to your boss, or the owners at the kangaroo court known as the strata council meeting (for all franchised hotels), why the revenue isn't coming in as predicted. If you have walked into this scenario as newly hired in January, do not despair in missing out on the holiday window of opportunity. You will soon have another eleven months to do whatever you like.

Within three weeks of starting in Hell I had realized the depth of my Accounting woes and started tracking the covers and average checks on my own little spreadsheet. I produced and issued the much-anticipated Food and Beverage Report on a monthly basis to ensure we were all working off the same (and accurate) numbers. Coincidentally, it was around this time that I decided I would scrutinize my pay slips with a fine-toothed comb. The glorious F&B Report involved countless hours of breaking down information that is normally calculated by people like The Monk. How I missed her now!

The Puffer and his merry band of missing links however, were out of their depth here. To be honest, they would have been out of their depth in a parking lot puddle, so perhaps they were over-achievers when you looked at it that way.

F&B Managers beware: I became an instant hero with the F&B report. I floated into every financial meeting to enlighten and delight my fan club with real stats and percentages that Accounts could only have dreamt of linking to one single page. I would fantasize about hearing chants of 'long live the King' as I left the Daily Revenue Report meetings.

Unfortunately, there was a price to pay. I was nearly sucked into the dark world of accountancy and statistics, and could have ended up in their office had my razor-like instincts not carried me back to the glorious early-morning wake up calls from staff too hungover to get up at 5:00am.

I knew something was wrong. I was spending up to an hour trying to correct the Accounts-issued Daily Revenue Report (I wondered why they bothered at all), for a meeting that lasted less than five minutes.

My original aim had been to shame the bastards in Hell into getting the statistics and reports accurate; but they had turned the tables on me. With the F&B Manager's almost-embarrassing attention to detail, they had obviously decided to ignore this, possibly through fear of not being able to reach the high standard that had been set. Now I was stuck doing countless hours of stats: a victim of my own success.

It also occurred to me that if they couldn't get the simplest stats right, just how accurate were my food and beverage costs were going to be?

The first day of each month is dreaded by every F&B Manager for one reason: inventory. It is a boring, tedious and back-breaking process. Hours are spent lying down in your suit, on your stomach, trying to shine a flashlight to the back of every conceivable little cupboard where bottles can be stored; counting hundreds of rows of bottle tops. Most vagrants wouldn't go through this in the hope of finding one more bottle.

It is usually an early start on inventory day too. Sometimes 5:00am, so that nothing is issued or sold before they are counted. So it was with a heavy heart, and even heavier eye lids, that I drove in for my first inventory day in Accounting Hell. In Hell however, nothing was as it should have been.

Todd counted the food with Chef first, so I strolled in happily at the crack of 8:00am. When he did arrive upstairs, he handed me the sheets to record the count and got down on all fours to count the first cupboard. I had to check the date to make sure it wasn't April 1st. I was doing the recording! I could feel my heart beat begin to race. The Accounts rep always records the count for two good reasons: 1) I could write down any number and he would never remember it later, and 2) my hearing could be suspect. I could record 'fifteen,' when he actually called out 'one.'

I smiled inwardly and kept very quiet. The bar itself was quite small, so it did not take long to count all the beverage in the outlets. Now it was time for the storage areas.

"Okay, see you tomorrow," Todd said as he walked away. I had to chase after him.

"Todd, what about the storage areas?"

"No, no," he waved me away. "You guys count that yourselves."

I thought he had to be kidding. This was like putting the cat in charge of the canary. Apart from The Dick and I, nobody had any idea how much beverage was stored in the cellar.

I knew approximately how much beverage revenue we had taken, from my 'sister's' much maligned Revenue Report. I knew from the invoice copies I kept how much I'd spent. So I could have acquired any beverage cost I'd wanted, to the hundredth of a percent, every month. How the Manager before me had achieved such poor results was beyond me; but it was more credit to me when it was quickly turned around. This was quickly becoming Accounting Heaven!

But why would Todd bother to count any of the beverage with me when he let me count the rest on my own? I smelled a rat. Perhaps it was a trick to test my honesty. This of course, was ridiculous: testing the integrity of a Food and Beverage Manager! I marched into the GM to ask why such an amateur practice was being carried out each month.

The blush disappeared from her face faster than you could say 'fake tan.' She reached for the phone and The Puffer appeared within seconds, cheeks a-puff, to explain. Obviously this had not been a trap. Any Restaurant Manager posing as a F&B Manager would have kicked himself at this point; noting that he could have opened up his own beer and wine store with the takings that had, just minutes ago, been available to him.

When The Puffer was again at a loss for oxygen, I tallied the final score in my head: F&B Manager 5, Accounts 0.

Chapter three - The Nam: How to Open a Hotel

I had always been told that it was important to have 'opening experience' on your resumé if you wanted to get to the top of the hotel world. I didn't understand this. After all, it was still a hotel you were working in. How could it be so different from putting procedures into place in an existing hotel?

Looking back now of course, this was a very naïve outlook. I was doing cartwheels when I got the phone call from Jackie offering me the Assistant Conference and Banqueting Manager position. After eight years at The Park, I decided I needed more Banqueting experience if I was going to be a F&B Manager. I was not only going to get that, but opening experience as well. This hotel was paying top dollar too, and made sure everyone around town knew it. Unfortunately, as the saying goes…if something seems too good to be true…

My tour of duty lasted just a few days shy of a year in 'The Nam' as it was known to those of us in the pre-opening positions. I learned quickly why HR looks for opening experience: if you can survive this, you can survive anything. Graeme, the Head Chef, had moved back to Scotland for this position after several years as Head Chef at The Kempinski, in Moscow's Red Square. He assured me several months into this debacle that it was easily the worst opening he'd ever experienced. Even so, I would have to think long and hard before taking another crack at a pre-opening.

The Nam is the model for how a hotel shouldn't be opened. If you are pretentious, rich and wondering how to throw your millions away, here are five sure-fire steps to guarantee your hotel will be a disaster:

Step One: Find a group of owners that know absolutely nothing about hotels. Ensure they are involved in every decision.

This is crucial in getting off to a superb start in losing millions. In a perfect world, you find an art aficionado in the middle of England. He meets two other gentlemen at a champagne charity auction, who also have more money than sense, and are desperate to prove it. They agree to buy a small hotel in Leeds. Unfortunately, as the hotel is already built and quite established, it makes money.

Undeterred, they find a bank gullible enough to lend them enough money to buy an iconic building in the heart of Scotland's beautiful Capital. Built in 1904, the building is all marble, paneled wood and stained glass windows, with stunning views throughout the 31 stories. The building is impressive.

The owners: less so. They were far too important to be introduced to, or be seen talking to the likes of anyone below General Manager rank. Only one in fact, seemed to take any interest in the hotel at all. Crawly by name; decidedly creepy by nature. He could be seen wandering around the hotel from time to time like a hard-hatted ghost.

Sightings of him were always eerily similar: staring at boarded up walls in empty corridors. His pose was the same as well. Two fingers of the left hand tapped the lips, the remaining digits stroking the pointy chin. Right hand supporting the left elbow that dangled like a spare part a few inches in front of the body. Had the elbows not been bent and locked in this impossible position, the ridiculous tweed sports coat would have slunk, silently from the gaunt frame. The left foot shot straight out in front of him, heel on the ground, toes pointing up. The heel rolled left to right, almost non-stop, as if they were directing the toes to where his gaze should follow.

Benjamin Stix gave the impression he was a David Hasselhoff impersonator in his spare time. His main involvement was picking the art work that would adorn the bathrooms in each room, and stenciling his name on everything and anything that would go into a frame. He was most often seen in the restaurant, always arriving late for dinner. It wasn't hard to spot him. He was the only patron all day for several months. He endeared himself to the staff in this way, by adding an extra three hours onto our twelve hour shifts.

The dining room was bare and soulless. No music system was hooked up yet; the floor was hardwood and there was precious little furniture dotted around the room. You were scared to breathe, never mind walk across the floor, listening to the tapping of your shoes echoing around the room. And there he would sit, alone (unless the ghost of Crawly was sitting across from him), for hours. The complete silence shattered only by the hourly: "How much fucking longer is he going to be?" that crept through from the kitchen door. Graeme hailed from Glasgow.

Step Two: Pick a site that is impossible to secure.

It must have taken the Dynamic Duo years to find the most insecure building in the UK; and The Nam was certainly that.

The main entrance to the eventual Reception / Arrival area was on Level Five. This was at the North end of a bridge that spanned a train station below. The bridge was appropriately enough, a favorite spot for suicide jumpers. There was also a smaller entrance just before the main entrance that for some reason opened into a no-man's land area between Reception and the Brasserie. Anyone entering here could not be seen by staff working in these areas though. Once inside this door, every area in the hotel was accessible; but right at this entrance was a staircase leading directly to the bedroom floors...very handy for thieves.

When the Hotel's brasserie eventually opened, several months after the hotel, its entrance was around the corner from the hotel entrance on the bridge. The hotel however, could be accessed from two doors inside the brasserie; and on two different levels.

On Ground Level, beside the train station, there were four known entrances. The first led to an underground storage area that was to be used as a goods receiving / storage area. All food and beverage would be kept here for departments to 'requisition' up to their individual outlets. This area was found to be not exactly secure however, when a couple of derelicts were discovered, in quite an inebriated state, gorging themselves on wine and food one morning. It turned out that there was a small cavernous tunnel full of rubble at the back of this dungeon that, if followed, led to a series of other tunnels; one of which came out at the train station tracks. One would truly have to be desperate to enter these tunnels. However, this area we were using for storage had been probably been unused for so long, that it could have been a refuge for a number of derelicts.

The second Ground Level entrance was a winding staircase that led to the Level Five main entrance. The third was the little-used 'official' staff entrance. Entrance four went to the Health Club. This entrance split in two directions immediately inside the door: a set of stairs on the left led directly to the Health Club; the elevator to the right led to the Level Three meeting room area, the movie theatre and the staff cafeteria.

On Level Four one could find another set of meeting rooms. One of these rooms had an outdoor patio. Although the patio belonged to the hotel, the building that enclosed the area was a youth hostel that had dozens of windows, including its very noisy kitchen, overlooking this area.

An alley ran down the west side of the building. This was an especially fantastic place to hang out if you were homeless, or begging terrified tourists for change. Three of the hotel's fire exits emptied out onto this boulevard of beggars.

These were all the main routes intended for entering and exiting the hotel. Other routes were used however.

The Royal Scots Guards, just a few blocks away at Edinburgh Castle, may have stood a reasonable chance of protecting this many ways in and out. The security squad of two that were employed to guard them at night, did not.

Step Three: Find a completely incompetent group of Managers. Give them precious little direction and drip feed information to them.

Of course, to get this project off on the right foot, the owners had to find the worst HR Manager in the UK. This was one of their very few successes.

Chelsea was also from Glasgow. To be fair, I did not envy her job. I knew a thing or two about behavioral interviewing; and hiring an entire crew of managers was never going to be easy.

One of the real difficulties in grouping so many managers together at once is that you don't know how they are going to get along together. In an already-operational hotel, you may have to replace one or two managers at once. In these cases, you know what type of manager you are looking for because you know the dynamics of the current team, and what type of personality you want to fit in with them. At a pre-opening, you don't really know any of the personalities yet, so you can't tell how, or if, they will work together. You are also in an environment where everyone is trying to prove themselves. There is a lot of jealousy and a lot of ego.

It was not Mission Impossible either however. How she could have hired so many poor managers seemed to defy the odds. I'm sure I could have picked a better suited crew from the Boulevard of Beggars. Chelsea was not a very good interviewer. I wasn't about to condemn her for hiring me, but I was amazed at how quickly I was hired…even with my glowing references and wonderful resumé.

I'm not sure who hired Chelsea, but the fingers pointed at one of the Richard's: either Cameron, Director of Operations; or McNeil, General Manager. McNeil was a puppet, and everyone knew it. You could almost see the strings propping him up from the back when Cameron was around.

Cameron had an ego like no one else I have ever met, or wish to. I'm sure he did not have to work hard at perfecting his condescending nature. Sporting a starched white shirt with the cuffs rolled up and the top two buttons undone, Cameron would always stroll casually into a room. At the precise moment the door banged closed behind him he would stop, hand on hip, and sling his coat over his shoulder so that all the heads that turned would see the magnificent sight that had entered their presence: the epitome of relaxed, casual arrogance.

I have to admit, the timing of this was a wonder to me. He must have practiced it thousands of times to make it look so nonchalant. It wasn't hard to imagine him doing so at home in front of a mirror.

McNeil could not have been more different; he was a really nice guy. Whenever there was bad news to deliver, R Cameron was usually seen leaving the office only moments before R McNeil had to carry it out. McNeil would squirm uncomfortably in his chair trying to find a way to get bad news over to people. Everyone felt sorry for him, having to play the bad cop all the time.

The main antagonists in the Food and Beverage Team were Timmy Buchanan, Conference and Banqueting Manager; and Blair, Fine Dining Restaurant Manager. They were both about 6'3", and that was where the similarities ended. Blair was a free spirit.

He had good looks, style, a touch of class…and very sticky fingers. He had a mid to fair sized ego, but he was a good guy. More importantly, he was 'one of the guys.'

Timmy on the other hand had no endearing qualities whatsoever. He was extremely arrogant and void of any of style or class. He loved his title and made sure to use it at every opportunity. Timmy could be talking to us normally one minute, and when someone walked past, his voice dropped ten pitches until it sounded like Barry White introducing himself as: 'Tim Buchanan, Conference and Banqueting Manager.'

The deeper the voice: the more important the person, according to Timmy. Only the extremely large chips on both shoulders gave him any balance at all.

Timmy also had no work ethic. He was always last to arrive and first to leave. He would actually call twenty minutes after he'd left the hotel to say: "Sorry, I just realized the time and had to run for the last train." All ego, no substance; Timmy was definitely not 'one of the guys.'

Adam Keatinge was Blair's Assistant Fine Dining Manager. Until recently, Adam had been a sommelier at the Gleneagles Hotel. He was a slightly shorter, younger version of Blair, without the sticky fingers. I took an instant liking to Blair and Adam. Unfortunately, Timmy was my superior, in title anyway…at least for now.

Luca was the Bar Manager. He was very quiet and liked Formula One racing, particularly Ferrari, and did not have the greatest grasp of English.

Lucy was the Director of Sales. The only Director of Sales I have ever had a great respect for; perhaps because she had Timmy on a very short leash and wasn't afraid to give it a good, hard tug. Timmy referred to her as Lucyfer, although never in her presence. Amanda played the part of Lucy's flighty, flirty, very girly assistant.

Andrew 'Shakey' Blakey tried to keep the IT department together. This must have been hard when computers were being stolen from every floor and even seen being passed down the scaffolding by the 'workies.'

Chandler and Fiona ran Housekeeping. God help them. I have never seen anyone sweat like Chandler. It is no exaggeration to say he say he lost at least forty pounds in the first five months of opening.

There were of course, many other bad actors in this soap opera; however these were the main protagonists.

Step Four: open on the initially agreed date…at all costs.

'Thank God. He's finally come to his senses.' That was the thought going through everyone's mind when Richard Cameron called a Manager's Meeting the day before the hotel was to open. We all knew the hotel was in no shape to let the public in. As far as most of us could see, we could not count off one area in the hotel as 'completed,' or 'ready for service.' We removed our hard hats and took our seats in the drawing room as we waited for the big announcement.

Mr. Cameron strutted in, cuffs rolled up, and got straight down to business. "If anyone in this room thinks we are not going to open this hotel tomorrow, they can leave right now."

I waited for the punch line, but it never came. Even when it was opened, the drawing room had never heard silence like this. I don't think anyone heard much more after that, but he did continue with a short speech. I recall something about him having had more people in his kitchen for a party.

As far as motivating speeches went, it was right up there with my dentist telling me I needed a root canal.

Step Five: Ensure controls of any kind are not in place.

There are effectively three areas of security that are crucial to every hotel and surely most businesses:

1. Financial. Money and products going in and out of each department obviously have to be controlled. Department Heads should be working with a budget for revenue and expenses, including payroll. All purchases are usually approved by the Financial Controller before anything can be ordered. A daily revenue report (DRR) is usually issued by the Controller as a tool for Managers; to help them control their payroll compared to their revenue.

Not in The Nam. There were no rules here. In all the time I was there, I never saw a budget, DRR or purchasing procedure in place. Everything seemed to be done with a handshake and a wink. Receipts for everything under the sun, including Timmy's home grocery bills, were being handed in left and right.

2. Staffing. This is the largest operating cost that every hotel incurs. A lot of hours are spent in the hiring and training of staff to get them familiar with the hotel and up to speed with the service standards. Therefore, hotels try to streamline processes and reduce turnover to get the most out of people for their money. Every hotel that is, except The Nam.

In The Nam, they made sure everyone knew that they 'want the best staff available and money is no object.' At least, that's what I was told at the beginning of my interview. Chelsea asked me what I was currently earning ten minutes after this bit of bravado. I quickly added £5,000 to it, and to be fair, they did beat it! How they knew they were hiring 'the best' I did not know. They obviously didn't waste a lot of their valuable time doing reference checks. If they had, they may have thought twice about hiring Timmy after his dishonorable discharge from his last hotel for harassment of a sexual nature.

3. Security of the building and contents. Theft from hotels is unfortunately very common. It is hard enough trying to stop guests from packing your cutlery and salt shakers in their luggage, and even harder to catch staff from kitting out their rented flats with everything from towels and soap to plates and staplers.

One F&B Manager I worked with told me that he estimated forty percent of the restaurant cutlery was stolen by staff in every hotel he had worked in. I never asked how he came to that conclusion, but after my many years of ordering cutlery, I would guess it to be at least in the thirty percent range. Teaspoons are definitely a hot commodity for transient staff, and the smart F&B Manager will ration these to departments at all times.

The idea being, the less there are in operation, the less likely staff will be to steal them and leave themselves scrounging for them at work. Nobody in The Nam was bothered with small-time stuff like this however. Bathrobes, TV's, DVD players and other large items were there for the thieving; and Blair smelled opportunity like a starving rat on a plate of cheddar.

Access to some areas should be limited and access keys for all areas should be signed for. This is basic in hotels. In the Nam however, nobody knew who had a key for anything. In fact, in a fit of panic with a delivery one pre-opening day, The Puppet gave me his master key to the entire hotel, and completely forgot about it. What this would have been worth on Blair's black market I shudder to think now. I'm sure I could have retired.

The normal security procedure when a key goes missing is to cancel the key that was lost. This is done by re-cutting the series of keys, or changing the locks. Not in The Nam. The Puppet just took another master key and disregarded 'my precious.' Every time something disappeared in The Nam, gossip spread quickly as to who was seen in the area and whether they could have a master key. I'm sure controls were meant to be in place; however, they were catastrophically compromised due to the cumulative effects of steps one to four.

Ninety Days Before Opening

I arrived in the freezing cold at 7am for my first day, signing in at the building site office. I picked up my hard hat and made my way to the staircase the foreman pointed towards. He whistled me back: "You'll need this." He spat on the dirt as he disinterestedly handed me a flashlight.

Eight years in the last hotel and every day of it in a suit and tie. Wearing jeans, several layers of t-shirts and boots felt like a great change now.

Another hard hat greeted me at the top of the stairs. "Mike? Blair. This way." I followed him through the maze of scaffolding, sticking close in the dark. We came to a bedroom; at least, I guessed it was a bedroom. My flashlight scanned the room. One bed, five chairs, one phone and one garbage bin…overflowing with coffee cups.

"This is our office," he smiled proudly.

"Oh. I thought I was working with Timmy?"

"Yeah. He seems to be running late. Coffee?" We re-traced our steps, turned into the General Manager's office area, made our coffee and headed back to the office. My flashlight searched the wall for the light switch.

"Sorry, no electricity hooked up in here yet, or heating."

"Okay, what should I be doing?"

"Not much we can do until we get daylight." In mid winter, that was at least two hours away.

He beat me to the question: "Who told you to come in so early?"

"HR. I guess Timmy told her what time I should be here."

Adam and Luca arrived at 9:00am and brought more coffee. Timmy finally arrived shortly after 9:30am. "Sorry guys. Bloody trains are running late again." I caught the disgusted glance Blair shot at him.

Blair and Adam worked on one side of the bed, our desk, while Timmy and I sat opposite and Luca leaned over the bottom of the bed. Adam and Blair spent most of their day jumping between their laptop, several brochures and catalogues, and the communal phone. Adam was furiously writing down codes, prices, sizes and availability of everything in the catalogues. Luca, at the bottom of the bed, worked out of his briefcase. I couldn't see what he was doing, but there were a few Formula One magazines in there.

Although there was nothing of note to talk about, Timmy managed to spend the first ninety minutes talking about his weekend. At 11:00am Jackie, the GM's assistant, came in and dropped off a lunch order sheet. After writing his own order down first, Timmy volunteered himself 'and my assistant' to collect it.

We left immediately to pick it up, although it hadn't even been ordered yet. We returned to the hotel with lunch, after doing some personal shopping for Timmy's fiancée, at 12:30pm. Stuffing down the last of his burger, Timmy scrunched up the wrapper, threw an air shot at the garbage bin, leaned over and stared into my eyes. "Everything here has got to be regimental man. Regimental!" He was already half-right: it was mental!

"I've got all my banqueting manuals from my last place," Timmy sniggered towards Adam and Blair. "All we have to do is copy all the standards over from those. Easy peasy." He sat back in his chair, content with himself. I wasn't so sure about this. I had written several training manuals in my time, and I knew one thing for certain: what works for one department may not work in another. You can't copy an entire training, or standard operating procedures (SOP), manual. I also recalled the briefing I had at my interview. It had been stressed that this hotel was to be 'different. We are not going to be like a Sheraton or a Hilton.'

"Why did you leave your last hotel?" I asked Timmy casually.

He shot me an inquisitive glance and drew a deep breath. "Why? What have you heard?"

"Nothing! I just wondered why you left. You were there a while right?"

The door opened at this point, breaking Timmy's concentration. The first one to step into the overcrowded bedroom introduced himself as Peter, our Food and Beverage Manager. He shook my hand and made room in the doorway. Nobody quite heard Peter's introduction of our new breakfast restaurant supervisor as Wilma stepped forward into the room.

She had an unusual look for sure. She was about five foot two, with a large afro that took her to five foot ten, and huge spots of rouge on her Dizzy Gillespie-like cheeks. She wore a thick wool jacket and her two hands met in front of her stomach, clutching a bag, presumably containing her worldly possessions. Was this what they meant by wanting to be different? It was obvious some of us were in the wrong place already. Exactly who, I wasn't sure.

Wilma croaked out an: "Allo everybotty" in an extremely high-pitched Jamaican accent that cracked at every syllable.

Peter left to find her a chair for the small side table that he placed in the corner of the room. Handing her a catalogue, he gave her the instructions that she would take to heart, breaking ours: "See if you can find some hessian sacks for the breakfast cereal display."

She carefully placed her worldly possessions under her desk and picked up the catalogue. "Okay guys, give her a hand if she needs anything, alright?" We all nodded, speechless. With that, he grinned, turned and left.

It was closing in on 2:00pm on my first day when Timmy stood up and put his coat on. "Well, big day tomorrow. Let's get away now so we can get an early start. Be here at 9:00am." And with that, he was gone.

Fourteen Days Before Opening

"Hessseee-yan sacks. Do you ave any hesseee-yan sacks? I'm looking for hesseee-yan sacks!" I wish I had a dollar for every time we heard that phrase over the last eight weeks. Wilma was relentless. She went through every catalogue we had very quickly, with no success. Every morning another dozen appeared on her desk, and she would call them all; again with no luck. She brought in the yellow pages six days later, when she finally realized someone was only shuffling around the same catalogues!

It was all fun and games at first. We would burst out laughing hysterically occasionally as the broken record went on and on in the corner: "hessseee-yan sacks." I wondered how long this could continue though; it was beyond the point of funny any more. Apart from the fact that the cracking, high-pitched tone was causing us sanity issues, she was being paid to sit in the office unsupervised and make phone calls for hessian sacks. What the hell was Peter thinking? She didn't report to any of us, so we didn't say anything.

"Where is Peter?" I asked.

"Thailand...got sacked last week. He got a huge payout too! Look." Blair swiveled his laptop around. There was Peter lying on a beautiful sandy beach, cocktail in hand: blue sky, blue water...definitely a million miles from the UK. "We had another guy before him. Can't remember his name, but he got paid off as well."

At the time I came on board, there were very few areas we could actually walk around and see due to the construction. Every few weeks we would get another 'artist's impression' of what each outlet would look like. I was surprised at how much the layouts changed each time we got a look. By this time, several staff had come and gone. Peter wasn't replaced, so we just continued planning for our own departments as we saw fit.

The Breakfast Room was clearly in trouble with Wilma holding the fort. However, it was a semi-finished room. There was a buffet table now, which could be filled with crushed ice each morning. Also newly-arrived at the entrance was the strangest service table I'd ever seen. It was fifteen feet long, so it was difficult to walk around, and it had no drawers. This meant everything was on display for guests: menus, checks, paperwork. It was only slightly above knee height too, so it would be fair to assume that ergonomics and usage were not at the forefront of its design.

Due to delays with deliveries, a lot of things around the hotel were being used as stop-gap. I hoped this service table was one of them, so I e-mailed Creepy Crawly to ask if this was just a temporary use for the table. I received an e-mail back within seconds: "It's Chilean Oak. £5,000. Look after your new service table."

I typed up a return message: "It's fucking useless." I don't know what stopped me from hitting the send button, but sanity (mine at least) prevailed.

The Point of Sale (POS) system (the till that orders are rung in on and sent to the kitchen) still hadn't arrived. As this needed to be programmed with every item and its price, this was a major concern.

Behind the Breakfast Room was the breakfast kitchen. Behind this was the bar: Room 399; so-named for the number of bottles of whisky that adorned the walls of the room. Each row of bottles was back lit by an orange light which gave the entire room a warm orange glow. Although very small, only twenty five seats, the room was taking shape nicely. Luca had also managed to bring in another bartender, Roberto, although his grasp of English was even worse than Luca's. While they were bantering away in Italian at the bottom of the bed, it was all hand signals and charades with the rest of us.

Blair's still-nameless fine dining restaurant was still nowhere near finished. No paint, no carpets, no doors. Blair was doing quite a trade in purchasing though. He'd just purchased two extremely top of the line cappuccino machines for the fine dining room and the Drawing Room.

Reps for wines and glassware were arriving with samples for him at an astonishing rate. Blair always led them out of the room when they arrived with his 'packages' so we couldn't overhear anything, but we could see lots of handshakes and smiles were exchanged. Blair certainly took a lot of samples away with him each night though, sharing nothing; sometimes in two or three trips!

Room Service was going to be run with the newly recruited Steve. Hired solely on Timmy's experience of him at his previous hotel, Steve was underachieving instantly. In fact within days, he was rivaling Wilma (and Timmy) for the coveted 'worst hire' at the hotel. This clearly embarrassed Timmy, who instantly decided to distance himself from Steve with comments such as: "Come on, I fucking got you here, you're making me look like an idiot."

It had been noted by many that Timmy could use a few management skills...notably when someone asked him a question. The most likely response to any question was: "Did I fucking tell you to do that?" Anyone trying to respond to this question would inevitably get the headshake with a touching: "Shut it. Did I fucking tell you to do that? No, so fuck off!"

Banqueting was not exactly overachieving either. My daily routine consisted of an afternoon stroll with Barry White looking for something 'different.' Glassware, centerpieces, you name it...Timmy had found none of it. We would come back to the hotel with the shopping completed and Timmy would rush off to find Mr. Cameron, who was putting a little pressure on Timmy for the 'banquet look.'

The pressure had increased daily over the last week after Timmy's first display did not go down well: "Timmy, this is all from your last fucking hotel. I told you I wanted to be different. Use some imagination for a change."

Timmy was deeply wounded. He would sniffle at me after each rebuke: "Why did they hire me if they wanted something different? I worked there for eight years. What did they expect?"

I bit my tongue and shrugged. This is good politics. Even if you know the answer, it's not always best to share it with your boss. Especially when everything I'd suggested to this point was given the: "Hey, who's fucking running this department?" from Barry White.

Luckily everyone who heard this knew the answer anyway: a complete asshole; so I didn't have to say it.

Returning from our latest shopping spree, Cameron had grabbed Timmy's latest offering, a water glass, from his trembling hand. He replaced it with his 'something different:' a ceramic cup that looked like it was partly crushed. Timmy, equally crushed, was dismissed with the wave of a hand. The effect was great. It cheered me up instantly, as well as Blair and Adam ten minutes later when they heard about it! Unfortunately, as much as I enjoyed the abusive treatment Timmy received, I knew it was perpetuating and justifying Timmy's behavior to others.

Richard Cameron and Timmy were birds of a feather actually, with Richard's fan club not growing in membership either. He had been throwing several pre-opening champagne parties for lots of his friends. These parties were thrown under the pretence of giving staff training for the real thing. Except there could be no training!

There was no Point of Sale system yet, and no manual inventory was being kept for any drinks being consumed. Chef Graeme had hardly any of the supplies he required either. Food actually had to be catered in for Richard's free-loading pals. Nobody would have really minded about this, except Richard was adamant that all of us stayed and served his guests until the party was over. Most of them ran until at least 3:00am.

With no happy ending in sight for any of these departments, my concern grew to the point where I wanted to know how the hell we were supposed to hit the ground running in fourteen days with all these problems. I went to see The Puppet.

Had my intention been to pull a few strings, I could not have dreamt of a more positive outcome. It seems The Puppet had bigger problems than the F&B department, but he was aware of some of the issues and definitely shared my concerns about Barry White and the overall direction of F&B. He looked over my resume that lay on his desk. "I see you have a lot of experience in all these areas. How would you like to run the food and beverage department?" As my mouth opened, he quickly added: "and be responsible for Health & Safety."

Bastard! The curse of the Health and Safety experience strikes again. Of course, with a Jurassic sized carrot like that dangling in front of me, who could refuse? Here was my chance to rid myself of Barry White as well as leap frog him in title. Surely there would be more money too!

"Well," said The Puppet, rubbing his chin: "Let's do a three month probation period and then we'll talk about a raise."

"Done."

"Now the problem is how we get this across to Timmy. Ask him to come and see me. And let's leave him alone in Banquets for now. So you're overseeing all the other outlets."

I flew out and down the stairs before he could change his mind. Timmy was on the phone to his fiancée again, writing down his shopping list. I mouthed it to him: "McNeil wants to see you." That brought a sharp end to the home shopping network.

I filled in Jeremy and Adam as Timmy plodded up the stairs. Their excitement brought about a series of wild high-fives and congratulations. Not everyone was happy though.

It was a very sullen Timmy that returned thirty minutes later. There would be no congratulations from him, surprising nobody. In fact for the remainder of his short day, even by his standards, Barry White seemed to be suffering from an overdue case of laryngitis…much to everyone else's delight.

Lucyfer even made an impromptu appearance in our dungeon-office to congratulate me. I have no doubt it was only to rub copious amounts of salt into Timmy's deep wound, and it worked. He left immediately, again without a 'goodbye' to anyone. Usually we were annoyed with him when he did this, however much he pissed us off when he was there. However this time there was a carnival atmosphere as the boys broke out in a rousing rendition of 'cheerio, cheerio, cheerio' usually heard at the local football matches when a player is sent off. We went out for a few beers that night, courtesy of the new Food and Beverage Services Manager.

Over the next few days, Timmy would still introduce me in his finest Barry White: "Good morning sir. Tim Buchanan, Conference and Banqueting Manager and this is my assistant Mike. Oh sorry, I don't have an assistant any more…what's your new title again?" It grew very old very quick. It was hard to believe he couldn't see that this was making him look an even bigger tit than before. When three days of this didn't get it out of his system, another tongue-lashing from McNeil did.

Opening Day

This was it! The day we had all been waiting for, albeit with the anticipation of a death in the family. I had worked until ten o'clock the night before to ensure nothing would go wrong. I had locked the door to the Highlands Meeting Room after setting it for its first meeting and left.

It was six thirty in the morning when I returned and made my way to the Breakfast Room. The first guests weren't checking in until around noon. The contractors had been working round the clock for the last fourteen days to try to get some of the rooms finished. When I'd left last night, there still wasn't one finished bedroom or meeting room.

'That's planning for you,' I grinned smugly to myself. Adam, Blair and I had worked relentlessly long hours over the last two weeks to get things organized. Shakey had managed to get our POS system wired in three days ago and the three of us took turns in four-hour shifts to program it. I felt confident we were in pretty good shape compared to other departments.

It was seven thirty when I started my walk around of the F&B areas. I unlocked the Highlands Room and inhaled a mouthful of fresh plasterboard dust as I entered. Tears welled up, and not all from the dust, as I tried to take in the scene confronting me. The contractors had obviously been in 'finishing' the room overnight.

The ceiling had been painted. The temporary plasterboard over some of the patio windows had been removed and real glass put in. They had even painted the plasterboard. It looked fantastic.

The thirty-five foot Chilean Oak boardroom table, aka Creepy's pride and joy, was finished too however…totally! The workers had not only failed to cover the table, which was too large and heavy to move, but they had walked all over it as if it had not been set for a meeting at all. Paint-splattered footprints paved the way from one end of the table to the other, as they kicked and broke the glasses that had been set on the table. The broken glass now a permanent feature in the table top, stamped in by heavy boots.

The carpet was a mess too. Apart from the paint all over it, there was a large pile of plasterboard in the corner of the room. Apparently this team had never heard of a splatter-cloth. As a meeting room, it was certainly 'different!' Even Cameron would have to admit that. However I did not want to be the one showing him or Creepy our new banquet look. That was for sure!

My mind raced as I tried to remain calm and prioritize quickly. Call Timmy? Pointless really, but as the person responsible for Banquets, he should know about it first. Where the hell was he anyway? The first meeting in the hotel was about to start in just over an hour and he was AWOL again!

"Timmy? Mike. Listen, the bloody workies have ruined the meeting room overnight for this morning's meeting."

"Shit. I was just about to call you. I missed my train. I'll be there in about an hour." As I expected: pointless.

Nothing else for it then: The Puppet. "Richard? Mike. Listen, I hate to tell you this, but we've got a problem down here in the Highlands. You better get down here now."

Richard's eyes and mouth widened. "Holy shit! What happened?"

"I left at ten last night and locked this door myself. The workies must have done it overnight."

"When does the meeting start?"

"An hour."

"What can we do? Where's Timmy?"

"Missed his train again. Get anyone upstairs in Admin and all of Housekeeping here with vacuums and dusters?"

Lucyfer was the first one down and within five minutes we must have had fifteen staff on the scene. The meeting attendees arrived just as we put the finishing touches to it and scraped as much glass from the boardroom table as we could. The Puppet gave them his sincerest apology and explained what had happened. "Please have a seat on the patio deck while we finish the room for you and we'll bring some coffee out."

I opened the patio doors to let some fresh air in as the guests walked out. Whistling the theme to The Great Escape, I walked back down the steps and into the room again. The frown on The Puppet's face put a sharp end to my tune. I turned around to see the group following me single-file back into the room. "I don't think we'll be sitting out there," one of them stated very matter of fact.

I went out to the deck for a look. Shit! Everywhere: shit. There were three pairs of filthy underwear dangling from the patio umbrellas. Some poor souls in the overlooking youth hostel had obviously missed the laundry or garbage bin when tossing away their soiled undergarments. A few broken beer bottles and some wet socks also lay about on the deck.

This one took a little more explaining from The Puppet; but with the promise of a completely free meeting, including breakfast and lunch, they seemed to understand that not everything can be accounted for, and that most of this had been out of our control.

Housekeeping cleaned up the patio while the rest of us adjourned to the meeting room next door for a debrief. It was quarter to nine; we were all breathing heavily and sweating profusely when my phone rang: "Hello. Oh, I see." I got no further.

Lucyfer charged at me from the far side of the room yelling: "Is that Timmy?" I nodded. She grabbed the phone from me. "Where the fucking hell are you? We've got the entire staff here trying to sort out your god damn mess…" She got no further.

The Puppet ripped the phone from her: "Timmy get the fuck in here now and straight to my office. How long are you going to be?" I didn't think he had it in him. I had found new respect for The Puppet. "His train will be here in ten minutes," he breathed out slowly, trying to collect his composure.

I nodded Richard over to the window as he returned my phone. Lucy followed. There was Timmy parking his car directly below us, across the street at the train station. "Fucking bastard!"

It was time for the daily nine o'clock meeting. Today it was held in Room 399 due to the number of attendees. I sat down next to The Puppet on the couch against the wall, with Adam on the other side of him. It was standing room only and everyone faced the three of us in the tight room. Luca kindly gave up his front row bar stool to Amanda who arrived fashionably late.

She was fairly forgetful at most times, and I wondered if she knew what time the nine o'clock meeting started. This time however, her watch wasn't the only thing she'd forgotten. An unshaven Timmy quietly slipped in late as well, largely unnoticed…temporarily at least.

Silence fell as The Puppet took a deep breath and thanked everyone for coming. He told us he was confident in our abilities as managers and was sure this hotel was going to be the best in the city. He thanked everyone again for their hard work to get us to opening day and told us to enjoy ourselves today.

You could almost hear a collective sigh around the room. It had been a long time coming, and I had to admit, it had all been a bit of a blur. Adam and I looked at each other behind The Puppet's back, smiled, and then peered back as the silence continued…and continued. We looked at each other again, and then looked at Richard. He stared down at his feet and then straight up at the ceiling. I looked straight ahead to see what he was trying so desperately to avoid. Amanda!

She was wearing a beautiful one-piece pink, wool dress that stopped half way between her hips and her knees. As she relaxed on her bar stool, she uncrossed her legs and revealed to her audience on the couch what else she had forgotten this morning: panties. It seems Timmy wasn't the only one who had not shaved this morning.

Poor Richard. He blushed and stuttered away for at least thirty seconds. Trying to avoid eye contact with everyone, he completely lost his train of thought. Adam and I had no such shame. We laughed uncontrollably on the couch after a good ten second glare. Amanda finally took our subtle hint and brought the curtains across on the show. "Okay have a good day everyone," Richard got out as Amanda bolted for the doorway, followed closely by The Puppet. As they filed out, everyone else stared at us as if we were mad: banging the sides of the couch, tears streaming down our cheeks.

We were just pulling ourselves together when another Andrew 'Shakey' Blakey flew in the door. "Have you guys seen two computers in here?"

We looked at each other and just shook our heads. "No. What would they be doing in here?"

"Well I can't find them anywhere else. I locked them in room 306 last night. They're gone this morning and if I don't get Accounts set up in an office today I am fucked." And with that he was gone.

Adam chased him out the door, but too late. Shakey wasn't wasting any time. "Why are you chasing him? Have you seen them?" I asked.

"No, I haven't been paid again. I was going to ask him if he's knows where Accounts is today."

We had been moved out of our snug bedroom office when it became almost fit for human habitation. We packed up and moved into the unfinished, unnamed fine dining restaurant across from the Breakfast Room. Good features: very spacious, now had carpet. Bad features: no power, no lighting, no security.

The room was accessible from four doors that everyone and their dog had a key for, and one set of windows which were not yet lockable. I thought I would be clever on our first night in our new office. Instead of packing all my paperwork and training manuals off to somewhere semi-secure, I put them inside the closet. It was an otherwise empty room. Who would look in the closet? Well, I never did catch the bastard; but some bugger was off with them.

Accounts were not so lucky either. Their main floor must have seemed like a penthouse suite compared to what they were doing now. I know it's a hotel, but they were living out of a suitcase. One day their office was in bedroom 405, the next it was 207. The day after that it changed again. Every time the workies needed to do some work in the bedrooms, Accounts were sent packing again.

Of course the knock-on effect of this careful planning was that computers and paperwork went missing constantly. People didn't always get paid either; sometimes it was suppliers, other times it was staff. Shakey was swearing up a storm while having to re-wire their network configurations every day. Nobody had the foresight to inform anyone where they had been moved to either, so each afternoon there was a manhunt for the Mysterious Accounts Department. MAD for short.

Shakey had been having a hell of a time. His equipment was being stolen faster that it could be unpacked. There were reports of the workies passing computers down the scaffolding. I for one was skeptical of this. They could have walked out of any number of doors with them, so why would they risk dropping them? Either way, over a dozen had walked out the doors, or windows.

It was approaching 11:30am when I was paged by The Puppet. "Get everybody you have available to room 606 immediately."

Adam, Blair, Timmy and I ran up the nine flights of stairs; the only elevator on this side of the building being stuck between floors with Shakey cursing away inside it. We stopped at the entrance to the room to catch our breath. The Puppet explained: "We need a hand. The first guests are just checking in and we still have some last minute touches to do to their room."

I looked around as the master of the understatement went on: "Timmy, Mike, get up on the bed and hold that picture straight. Adam, there's two small pictures on the bathroom floor. Hang them on the two hooks on the side wall. Blair, hang that small one above the side table in the corner. Where the hell is Andrew Blakey? The DVD player isn't hooked up and the keyboard is missing?"

In the middle of all this stood the mute Creepy Crawly. He swiveled on his outstretched foot, fingers on chin; obviously not liking what he saw. He waved two hands wildly at Blair. Blair glared at The Puppet for an interpretation. "Try another picture. There's two more out in the hallway." Timmy and I stared at each other incredulously as Creepy waved a hand first at me, then at Timmy. This was a little easier to comprehend: up a little; down a little. What was a bit harder to grasp was Creepy's surreal lack of urgency. Even if they had to walk up the six flights, they would be here any second now.

There was no TV or DVD player hooked up. The bed side lights were an unusual feature to begin with. They were like maneuverable garden snakes sticking out of the wall, when they were finished. However they were not going to be finished in this room in the next few minutes; that was certain. Two sets of wires poked through the wall beside our knees as we stood on the bed. I kept my eyes on them, keeping a good distance away in case they were live. As we stood seemingly forever waiting for Creepy's approval on this picture, I envisioned myself going to jail when the cops asked The Puppet who was supposed to be responsible for Health and Safety.

We passed the guests on the way back down, our framed photos in hand. It seems they were delayed at check-in due to the fact that there was no computer system for Front Office yet: those computer terminals being posted as missing also. Shakey had then lent them his laptop to use as a temporary measure. That lasted almost forty eight hours before it too went missing; pretty good by Nam standards! So it was a manual process at the front desk, a very slow procedure.

The next guests to arrive were Mr. Cameron's parents; flown in from direct from Hell for the occasion. After the fifteen minute check-in (which surprised me, since they were paying for absolutely nothing), Cameron took them up to the room himself. I had no doubt that their room would be the only finished room in the building.

So it was quite a surprise to see him back at the desk within minutes: a raging bull. "Get me the Housekeeping Manager and the Front Office Manager. Now!" he screamed at the poor girl on the desk. He obviously wasn't familiar with anyone's name.

Cameron didn't wait though. In fact, he barely broke stride, marching straight past her and into The Puppet's office. Within seconds, the two of them were at the front desk again. Dave, the flamboyant Front Office Manager, stood nervously behind the computer-free desk.

By the time a sweat-soaked Chandler reached the top of the stairs, Cameron had too much steam coming out of his ears to articulate anything. Once again, The Puppet put Cameron's words into his mouth: "There is something floating in the toilet in room 803."

Chandler and Dave stole a glance at each other. Chandler, being older and more experienced said nothing. Dave, much younger and brasher, risked his life: "What's floating?"

The Puppet tried to be as diplomatic as possible, but it was stretching even his patience: "It doesn't matter what's floating. The fact that something is, suggests that a procedure is missing, and it shouldn't be."

The Puppeteer had heard enough and suddenly found his voice: "Bobby Fucking Brown. Get it? Bobby Fucking Brown is in my mother's toilet!"

Blair and I had been hiding behind a doorway near the hotel entrance, enjoying this show. We ducked our heads back in and mouthed to each other: "Who's Bobby Brown?"

"It's a shit!" Fiona whispered from the other side of the doorway. We hadn't noticed her slipping in behind us. "It's a code housekeepers use over the phone so people don't overhear it."

Perfect! I could imagine Cameron's very real pride as he showed his parents around the room, and opened the bathroom door: 'Mom, Dad, I'd like you to meet Mr. Brown.'

"Who was supposed to check the room?" McNeil asked.

Dave seemed to have misplaced his bravado so Chandler spoke up now: "I checked it myself less than an hour ago. And I checked the bathroom," he added almost angrily.

Cameron rolled up his sleeves, smoothed his hair out and casually strolled toward the elevator, which appeared to be operational again. "Read the lock. I want to know who was in there last." With that, he stepped into the elevator and disappeared.

The cast dispersed. The Fire Alarm sounded. The cast reappeared for an encore, minus Cameron, now stuck in the jammed elevator. Luckily Paul, the Chief and so far only Engineer, had also been eavesdropping in the vicinity. He was only a few steps from the Fire Panel. He checked the location of the alarm and ran off. The rest of us just stood there. I held my breath, aware that we were not making the cover of any Health and Safety magazine any time soon…at least, not for anything positive.

Paul was back within seconds. He turned the alarm off and casually shrugged: "false alarm." It must have been hot in the small elevator because when Paul pried the doors open, it was a very red-faced Cameron that stepped out and headed up the stairs, without a word. Ten minutes later, the alarm sounded again, and again five minutes after that. Each time, Paul would check the location, race off to check if there was a fire, and return to reset the fire panel.

Up to now, our fire procedures were: 'meet at the fire panel and await directions.' Unfortunately, The Puppet hadn't quite finished the real fire procedures yet, so nobody apart from Paul knew what they were supposed to do. Technically, this was a moot point since we had not yet received a fire license from the fire department. We were housing guests illegally.

All four of the guests and the forty plus staff met now in the lobby awaiting some kind of direction. The guests from the beleaguered meeting room also made their way up the stairs and straight towards The Puppet. Hands were waving furiously in McNeil's face for a full minute before Richard lost his cool. He jogged to the fire panel to give instructions to Paul: "Shut that fucking thing off for Christ's sake!"

This place was putting the F in Five Star at an alarming pace. Richard jogged back to the meeting group. Whatever he said to them, it didn't work. They ignored his pleas for a seventh chance completely and walked straight out the front door.

The Puppet called Paul and me over to him: "Paul, we'll need to put dust covers on all the smoke detectors. It must be the workies setting the alarms off. Mike, I want you to finish off the fire procedures for me by tomorrow." He turned and walked back to his office.

After a quick lunch break, I went down to Room 399. It was busy. At least, I thought it was busy from the panic in Luca and Roberto's eyes. There were two tables of two guests in the bar: not busy. "Why the panic?" I enquired.

"Can you help us find the Macallan Thirty Year-Old? Start in that corner over there."

This wasn't good. I sensed the problem immediately. Dumb and Dumber had not taken my advice and put a plan together as to how they were going to find each whisky. There was an eerie silence in the room as we searched. After five minutes Luca found it. It was behind the sofa the guests at the only other table were sitting at. He signaled for them to get up so he could move the sofa and get the whisky out. Shaking their heads, they obliged, and then continued on their way out the door. Roberto moved the sofa as Luca fumbled through a set of keys that Fort Knox would have been proud of.

I shifted gears: "Luca, what's going on? Why have we got forty keys on there? It'll take you forever to find the right one each time!"

His hand signals told the tale: "They only put the locks on the whisky cases last night. They weren't even locked until this morning. We've just been locking the whole room up until now. We only got the keys this morning."

This was true. I went back to my first point: "I asked you to list the whiskies on the menu in the order they are lined up on the wall. What happened? You can't search the entire room and ask guests to move every time someone orders a drink!" The current guests were watching with curiosity as we whispered. I decided to take it up with Luca later.

Fire alarms continued sporadically throughout the day. I worked on the fire procedures while Paul trained for the Olympic sprinting event. At eight o'clock in the evening, it was a huge relief to see the four hotel guests go out for dinner. I would not have to wait all night to see if they were going to order dinner through Room Service. Emotionally drained, I headed home at nine o' clock.

'Well, at least the first day jitters are out of the way.' That was the thought going through my head as I made my way back into The Nam at 6am the next morning. I went straight down to the Breakfast Room for a coffee before it opened at seven. A few quick gulps and, with great trepidation, I began my walk round of the F&B areas. I held my breath in an effort to overcome the sense of deja-vu as I opened the Highlands Room. Typical! I cursed my luck. Why couldn't it have looked like this twenty four hours ago?

I was gaining in confidence when I returned to the Breakfast Room just before seven. Adam and Blair were hovering a few feet away from the door, like vultures, as Wilma opened the doors for the first (and her last) time.

I had checked the room thoroughly. She had everything set up just as we had discussed: table settings correct; coffee brewed; plenty of crushed ice in the cold food display…perfect! Maybe there was a glimmer of hope after all.

The cold food display was the one thing Creepy had gotten right so far for F&B. Again, made of Chile's finest, it ran twenty five feet long down one wall near the entrance to the room. A large stainless steel bin had been cut out in the middle of it. This was to be filled with crushed ice each morning to keep the juices, meats and cheeses cold.

We didn't have long to wait for the first two guests to arrive. They were accosted immediately by Wilma when she halted them at the entrance. She drew a deep breath for her high-pitched Jamaican welcome: "Good morning my name is Wilma I am your breakfast supervisor it will be my pleasure to serve you how are you today please follow me to your table."

Stunned, the guests looked at each other and followed her in silence, to their table. Adam and Blair covered their mouths and bolted straight across the corridor to the safety of our temporary office. I could hear them laughing as I stood, rooted to the spot, watching in horror as she took another deep breath: "Can I bring you some coffee or tea we have earl grey English breakfast Darjeeling chamomile orange pekoe peppermint and Assam and would you like milk or cream or lemon with it?" Not even a hint of a pause between a single word!

Just as all this had taken place, Cameron had strolled by the door. He turned to face me in the doorway now. Casually taking a hand out of his pocket, he pointed a finger at Wilma and offered his opinion on her 'different' service style: "To have no further guest contact." With that, he returned his hand to his pocket and slowly continued on his way, shaking his head.

Adam poked his head out of our office now: "Hey, we've got a Room Service order on for Cameron's parents." I followed him through. The parents from Hell had ordered almost everything on the menu of course. And they had asked for it to be delivered through the 'privacy hatch.' I had to admit, this was Creepy's finest invention in The Nam.

Many guests are awakened by their Room Service order being delivered in the morning. In their rush to get to the door, guests have been known to open the door naked or scantily clad. These people tend to be repeat offenders and there is little risk of embarrassment for these guests.

Other guests hastily throw a bathrobe on as they walk to the door, thinking they are safe. All too often however, when they go to grab the tray, their bathrobe opens up and exposes them. If they drop the tray in a panic, you not only have to clean it up, you have to remake the order. This is not only very inconvenient; it's embarrassing for both parties…and also quite common. I wondered if a 'bathrobe incident' of his own had inspired Creepy's privacy hatch.

The hatch was a small door at the side of the room door. The server could just unlock the hatch, slide the tray inside, close the hatch and ring the door bell to let the guests know it had been delivered. The guests, wearing as little or as much as they liked, could then open the hatch from inside the room and remove the tray whenever they wanted, in total privacy…theoretically!

I went upstairs with Adam to see the first one in action. I opened the hatch for him and went to ring the door bell as he slid it in, almost. "It doesn't fit," he whispered.

"What do you mean it doesn't fit? It has to fit!" I grabbed the tray. In sheer disbelief, I repeated his words. "It doesn't fit! Surely they measured it?" We thought in silence for a moment. "Only one thing for it then! You unload everything, I'll hold the tray." We giggled nervously, well aware that we would be getting an earful about this.

When everything was unloaded into the hatch, Adam took the tray and hid around the corner to call the elevator. When it arrived, I rang the bell and ran off to join him.

Sadly, the hatches were not going to be our only delivery issue with Room Service.

It was a much different atmosphere at the nine o'clock meeting this morning. A tight-faced Puppet was seated away from the couch, beside Cameron, who was making his first ever appearance at a morning meeting.

"Someone entered room 803 yesterday ten minutes after it was inspected and fifteen minutes before Richard Cameron's parents were checked into it. We know it was key number one hundred-fourteen. Who has it?"

This was the height of optimism, or stupidity; I couldn't decide which. If they expected someone to stand up in front of Cameron, and thirty others, to say: 'Yes! I left a Bobby Brown in your parent's bathroom,' they were left disappointed. Of course in any other hotel where staff must sign for a key, Inspector Clouseau would have found the culprit in a matter of minutes.

Sensing this was a losing battle, The Puppet moved on. "Mike, Mr. and Mrs. Cameron also complained about their breakfast this morning. It was put in the hatch, but not on a tray. They had to make ten trips between the hatch and the table. The tray is supposed to go in the hatch! What is going on?"

Cameron glared at me as I told the prosecutor: "We tried. The tray doesn't fit."

"What do you mean it doesn't fit?"

"I mean you can't fit the tray in the hatch. It's too big." A collective inhale from the jury filled the room before silence fell.

The two Richards exchanged glares briefly before Cameron got up and stormed out. McNeil continued: "Okay, we'll check that. Now, just one other note: Luca has been let go. Roberto is our new Bar Manager. Anyone have anything else to add this morning?"

I spoke up: "Yes. Effective tomorrow, Wilma will no longer be our Breakfast Supervisor. She will be restocking the minibars for us."

I returned to the Breakfast Room after the meeting to give Wilma the good news. As I ran over in my mind what I was going to say, I thought I could hear her crying. Surely someone couldn't have beaten me to it already! I breathed a sigh of relief as I entered the room to find her lying on the floor with Chelsea and Blair wrapping a bandage around her ankle. "What happened?"

"She slipped on the water on the floor," Blair pointed at quite a large pool of water as Wilma continued to wail away.

"Where's it coming from?" I asked.

Blair dropped the leg he was holding to bend down beside the buffet. "See that pipe hanging down there? That's the drain for the buffet ice. It's not plumbed into anything."

"What!" Why I was surprised was perhaps the biggest surprise of all.

"Yeah. They put the buffet table on this side of the room, but there's no drainage on this side. We'll have to put a buspan under it."

"But you'll be able to see it sticking out. And we'll have to empty it every hour when guests are sitting here watching us!"

"Got a better idea?" he said flatly. I ran to the kitchen for a buspan.

After lunch, we had our first guests arrive in the Drawing Room. Adam, Blair and I went everywhere together now. Partly to see what could go wrong next, partly to have witnesses when it did. However, we had already discovered through a series of mishaps that the Drawing Room required three people for every order.

Adam took the order from the three guests. It was only tea and sandwiches, but if the hotel was The Nam, then the Drawing Room was Saigon. Each order needed a battle plan.

The doors to this room were never meant to be locked as it was considered secure; being located between the Administration Offices, Concierge and the Front Desk. It wasn't secure from the staff however. As far as they were concerned, it was a Starbucks.

Every time we needed something here it was gone: milk, coffee, cups, sugar…you name it! I considered putting a full-time guard in place, or lacing the coffee with arsenic to catch the buggers.

There was a dumbwaiter in the service area behind the curtain / screen in a corner of the room. We renamed this a 'dumbowner' due to its design. Originally, the idea had been for the server to ring the order through the till in the Drawing Room. The order would print in the Breakfast Room kitchen, where the chef would prepare the food and send it up to the Drawing Room in the dumbowner. Dirty dishes could be sent down for cleaning and clean ones sent back up. Easy.

Creepy's oversight here was that after breakfast, when the Drawing Room was open, the Breakfast Room was closed. There was no chef, or anyone else, down there to receive the order, prepare it, or send it up. Nobody was there to remove dishes from the dumbowner and clean them either. Our theoretical one-person operation now required three staff and a map for the order runner to get from the breakfast kitchen to the main kitchen, a good five minute sprint. You couldn't send anyone on their first tour of duty for that job even with a map.

Adam rang the order through the till as I ran downstairs to grab the order slip and run it from one kitchen to another. Blair was sent packing for the milk and the cups. Blair and I returned to the service area ten minutes later as Adam apologized to the guests for the delay, a standard procedure here.

Lucyfer nearly dropped her coffee cup in shock when we ambushed her in the Starbucks self-serve, but she recovered quickly: "Oh, hey I was just looking for you guys. Are you all set for the Fam Trip today?"

"Yeah, no problem," I smiled. I had no idea if we were or not, but that was Barry White's problem.

"Great! Can I just steal a quick coffee while I'm here?"

The 'Familiarization Trip' is a regular sales event. The Sales Team invites 'hotel sellers' from other cities to stay for a night or two so they are familiar with the hotel and staff. The hope is that they will therefore recommend it and sell it more often. Mostly though, they just get very drunk and barely remember who they slept with, never mind the quality of the bed they passed out on. This group of fifteen was being flown up from London. They were having lunch in an awkward location: The Lowlands Room. A floor below the Highlands Room and the kitchens, timing would be crucial.

To help with the timing, the food would have to be placed in an Alto-Shaam (a large mobile device to keep food hot) and moved along the route quickly: from the main kitchen, through the F&B Office / fine dining restaurant, down the corridor towards Room 399, up the ramp opposite the Bar and into the elevator; down one level and into a wide open space. From this area you could access the Health Club straight ahead, the movie theatre to the right, and the Lowlands Room to the left. We set two tables in this space outside the Lowlands to put the last minute touches on the plates before being served.

As we walked the route beforehand, it occurred to me that the only route to get all the banquet food to a banquet room was right through the middle of the restaurant; thereby taking the 'fine' out of 'fine-dining'...if it ever opened.

Once Lucyfer had led the group into the room and they were seated, Timmy started pouring their wine. I phoned the kitchen to tell them to begin plating the cold starters. These came down stacked on a room service trolley. We took the covers off the plates, placed them on the side tables and carried them quickly and quietly into the room. Timmy topped up the wine again and came out grinning: "Fucking regimental man! Regimental!"

Adam and Blair returned to the kitchen for the main courses when Timmy and I started clearing the starter plates from the room. We waited five minutes before concern started to grow. I called the main kitchen: "No. They left here five minutes ago," Graeme assured me.

"Timmy, get in there and top up the wines again. I'll go up and check on them." I shuddered at the thought of them being stuck in the elevator with the food; a very realistic possibility.

The elevator however, arrived within seconds when I pushed the call button. Up I went one level, but I couldn't get out. The Alto-Shaam was blocking my way. "What are you two doing?" I shouted. No answer. I pushed the Alto-Shaam a few inches to squeeze out. Where were they?

I opened the Alto-Shaam when I got out. The food was in there alright. I couldn't wait. I pushed it back towards the elevator again. Thud! I looked around at each side. "Oh Christ no!"

Just then Adam and Blair came screeching down the corridor with a Room Service trolley and some hot boxes. "It's too big. It won't fit," Adam shouted breathlessly. We worked in silence, transferring the plates from the Alto-Shaam to the smaller hot boxes on the trolley.

When we got down to the wide open space, Timmy was in full panic mode: "Where the fuck have you been? Lucy's going to have my fucking nuts for this. Where's the Alto-Shaam?"

I breathed in sharply: "Timmy, where's the prep tables?"

"I don't know. Someone must have taken them away while I was topping up the wines." Great! The plates had been bashed around enough on a voyage Phileas Fogg would have been proud of. Now we had nowhere to even attempt a quick straightening out and wiping of spilled sauces.

We tried to quickly throw down the plate covers and carry them in while they still had a little warmth to them. Timmy just barely caught one of the plates as it fell forward when he opened a hot box door. Unfortunately he didn't catch the chicken breast. It toppled off and landed with a small thud on the freshly laid thick blue carpet.

This was getting ridiculous now! It was at the point where it could not get any worse, or so we thought. We all broke out in a nervous, hysterical laughter. Lucyfer, either hearing the laughter or really needing to go to the bathroom, excused herself from her half-sloshed company to find Timmy trying to wipe the bits of carpet fluff from the chicken onto his pants. The rest of us had had enough. We were bent over double with tears flowing freely while Lucy put both hands to her head, wagged a finger at Timmy, threatened something, and marched back into the room.

It took a few minutes to wipe the tears away and calm down enough to carry the plates into the room. I held my breath the entire time I was in there.

A standard procedure in F&B is to check the quality of the food with each guest a few minutes after delivering it. This was Timmy's show so the three of us watched hysterically as he tried to build up the courage to return to the scene of the crime with a straight face.

Peering straight through her, he somehow managed the most difficult quality check I have ever seen. Without once sneaking a peak down at the untouched 'chicken carpet bleu' on Lucy's plate, he calmly enquired: "And how is the chicken today Lucy?" Who else could we serve it to!

Although the coffee and dessert went out without a hitch, Timmy's ass and nuts were on the chopping block…and he knew it!

A starving Lucyfer could have been no match for The Puppet as she positively flew up the stairs to his office after lunch. Timmy had been preparing himself for the sack after this latest debacle. He was enjoying what we all assumed would be his last coffee, trying to make light of it: "Cheers for your help today guys. Brilliant! Nice working with you." The Puppet came down and called Timmy out, but there was no sign of Chelsea. Nobody ever gets sacked without HR being present. We all exchanged surprised looks.

The Fam Trip wasn't the only site inspection of the day either. From our office we could hear Amanda telling a couple of people all about the Breakfast Room. An hour later, a frantic Lucyfer caught us in the Drawing Room again: "Guys have you seen Amanda anywhere?"

"No…and yes you can have a coffee while you're here," I replied.

"No. Really. We have two groups here for site inspections and I can't find her." Her glasses had fogged up a little from her heavy breathing. She was obviously telling the truth for a change.

"I saw her an hour ago with a small group. She was at the Breakfast Room," I said. Blair offered to take one of Lucy's groups for a tour. In spite of Timmy, F&B was gaining some respect with Sales.

It generally took about an hour to give a tour of the hotel. Blair returned after thirty minutes…but not alone. Amanda was wrapped in a blanket and sobbing heavily. He walked her into the Admin Office where Cameron emerged from The Puppet's office when he heard the commotion. We all listened to the story as it unfolded.

It seems Amanda's first Site Inspection had not been a great success. All had been fine until they had reached the Penthouse Suite with her two guests. They had been hoping to book the Penthouse for a week over the Christmas and New Year's period.

"Relax," said Amanda to her guests, as they shuffled around the huge multi-level suite. They did. They took off their coats and placed them in the cupboard at the entrance. Never shy at being underdressed, Amanda followed suit.

They searched for and played with every little hidden feature and detail in the suite. Finally, they came to the balcony. The large deck had a massive barbecue. Out they all popped onto the deck to check out the barbecue and the stunning view over Edinburgh Castle.

'Click,' went the glass balcony door behind them. Peering back in, Amanda could see her mobile phone and keys lying on the coffee table. The not-so-happy couple could not see their phones in their coat pockets from this vantage point.

And there they waited. For over forty-five minutes. It was minus four Celsius outside…but probably a lot colder and windier up that high. Colder still if you weren't wearing underwear! After about fifteen minutes, with both women crying, the gentleman started to threaten lawsuits. After thirty minutes, there was no talking at all. Just when the never-to-return guest was about to throw pieces of the barbecue through the glass door…in walked Sales' Savior, Blair.

"Where are they now?" screamed Cameron.

"Room 704," whispered Blair, still trying to calm Amanda down. "I thought they could use a hot bath or shower. They'll be down to see you when they're done."

"Christ," Cameron said. "That's the most lucrative week we have. They're not getting a cheap rate on that room!"

Returning to the Kitchen to fill Graeme in on the news, I walked through our office again. In the far corner of the restaurant, was the only chair in the room. Timmy sat sobbing on it; head down in two hands, staring at the carpet. Towering above, McNeil was giving him a good lecture: "This is absolutely your last chance Timmy!"

I walked as slowly as I could to hear more, but it is poor etiquette to watch someone being disciplined…even if it is in a public place …and even if it is Timmy!

Fourteen Days After Opening

The opening party had been a huge success. Of course, we had to wait two weeks after the first guests had checked in before we got the fire license and could officially throw an opening party. Most of the rooms had been finished in time for the extravaganza of the year. Creepy and Co. went all out on the party. Every writer and hotelier from all over the UK had been invited. Massive search lights were placed around the hotel and shot up as far as the eye could see so that nobody in the city could miss the location.

Some of the rooms on show were themed. There was a vodka bar and of course the whisky bar in Room 399. Champagne however, was the order of the day. We had five hundred bottles of champagne ready to go. And it went! Half-way through the two hour party, we had nearly run out. Blair drew the short straw to tell Cameron. He returned with three gold cards. "Let's go. He said to buy every bottle we can find." We did.

Splitting up, Adam and I returned in twenty minutes; Blair roughly ten minutes behind us. All totaled we had amassed about another hundred bottles of champagne. In the panic, Cameron didn't even ask us how much it had cost; let alone demand receipts. He apparently did check his bank statements quite regularly though.

A few days after the party, Blair was called in for questioning. With the extra ten minutes of possession with Mr. Cameron's card, Blair had admitted to purchasing himself a new pair of shoes and a fetching set of cuff links. Perhaps the only reason Blair lived to tell the tale, may have been that Blair reminded Mr. Cameron of himself in his younger days.

We made it through the party with about six bottles to spare. At least, they were spared from the guests. The F&B Team quickly took care of these afterwards.

I don't imagine anyone could give an accurate figure as to how much the whole two-hour event cost, but I did hear a rumor from our Purchaser, Carol, that the lighting, alcohol, food, damage and theft had totaled over two hundred thousand dollars.

From what I could see, the damage was mostly superficial. The theft on the other hand, was quite substantial. In Room 399 alone, there were over a dozen bottles of whisky missing from the walls…and not the cheap ones! Many items had been stripped from the bedrooms and Health Club too.

The obvious solution, it seemed to us, was to touch up the damage and replace the stolen items. However that was a week ago and nothing had been done to rectify these issues. We found out at this morning's meeting part of the reason.

"Richard, they won't do it. I have been asking. Begging even!" Carol wasn't getting through.

"But Carol, if you just ask them really nicely; tell them we are paying our bills…there's just a little problem with the cash flow right now. They'll get paid next week." I'm not sure who Richard was trying to convince, but it wasn't working on anyone in this room.

Carol tried a different approach, spelling out each word very slowly: "We can't buy a thing." She burst into tears for emphasis: "Richard, they hang up on me when I try to order."

I'm not sure who it was directed to, but from the back of the room Graeme added: "They won't deliver any eggs to us for breakfast tomorrow either."

That was enough for Carol. At five foot two, you could have been forgiven for thinking she had been standing all along, but she stood up now, put her clipboard down and walked to the door for her grand finale: "I've had it. Fuck you all!"

This wasn't the kind of hurrah we needed before the Hotel Inspector arrived this afternoon.

Carol wasn't the only one leaving either. Roberto had been sacked the day before. The only surprise being that he lasted thirteen days. He was replaced by an ex-colleague of mine from The Park, where he worked as a Concierge for five years. Other than quaffing down dozens of pints a week, Marcus didn't have a single hour of bar experience to my knowledge. However, experience was no omen of success or failure in The Nam. In fact, there weren't many successes either way.

Joe Anderson had also walked out. He was the best-known Concierge in the city and was a major coup for the hotel when he agreed to move from the hotel on the other side of the bridge. Joe was always dressed immaculately and he insisted that his staff were too. To ensure their shoes were polished every day, he brought in his own shoe shine kit. This was his pride and joy.

The large, not Chilean but very good quality, oak box must have had over sixty different bits and pieces in it; with every color of polish you could imagine. Joe gave his team strict orders: "For Concierge use only. Nobody else ever finds out about it or uses it." They stored it in a small locked cupboard behind concierge where the security surveillance tapes were stored.

Three nights ago, the shoe-shine kit was stolen from the cupboard. Although apparently in a rage about it, Joe replaced it with his back-up: an exact replica.

Also three nights ago, an expensive chair had been stolen from the reception area. I was charged with going through all the tapes to catch the culprit. Knowing this could take a while, I grabbed a coffee and sat in the Concierge cupboard. Before long, a Concierge came in and started polishing up his shoes. Unaware of the history to the sacred kit, and noticing that my shoes were a little worse for wear (a good F&B Manager always has at least one milk stain on his shoes) I asked if I could polish my shoes.

"No problem," says the Concierge.

Adam poked his nose in the cupboard ten minutes later. "See anyone yet?"

"Nah. I'm only half-way through though."

"Hey, can I polish my shoes?"

"Why not," I shrugged.

I could hear Joe's voice getting closer, but not even knowing it was his kit, we just kept polishing and watching the tapes. Joe took two steps inside, boomed: "For fuck's sake!" turned around, and walked out. He changed out of his uniform, returned ten minutes later for his box, and walked along the bridge to his old hotel where he returned to duty the next day.

Also joining the line at the Employment Office was David, the Front Office Manager. David had been on the late shift one evening and was scheduled for the early shift the next morning. I can only guess at the actual conversation, but the facts were as follows:

8:00am: David arrives one hour late for work, smelling of alcohol…obviously hungover.

10:00am: Housekeeping reports to GM that there is a naked and unconscious male, appearing to be in his early twenties, in room 702.

10:05am: The Puppet, on scene, declares unknown guest alive, but extremely inebriated. The Puppet notes that the entire contents of the minibar appear to have been consumed as the room is littered with empties. A short conversation ensues regarding the identity of naked stranger since housekeeping noted the room should have been empty; nobody being registered for the room.

10:14am: Police are called to scene to revive and remove naked stranger from room. Head Housekeeper remains at crime scene.

10:15am: The Puppet returns to Front Desk to check guest register and conduct enquiry as to how the stranger gained entry to the room. David has no explanation, asks to be excused to go to bathroom.

10:16am: The Puppet asks Shakey Blakey to read key lock.

10:25am: Police arrive and are escorted up to room 702.

10:27am: Shakey Blakey arrives in room 702 to inform The Puppet that a key was made for room 702 at 10:48pm last night. The same key was used to gain entry to 702 at 11:12pm.

10:38am: Police are able to get a name for naked male: 'Prince.'

10:45am: 'Prince' insists he was approached outside the hotel and asked if he would like to 'party' in exchange for alcohol and a bed. He had accepted and was given a key for a room and told to meet there in ten minutes.

10:55am: Chelsea follows The Puppet into his office.

11:00am: David, Front Office Manager is asked if he would like to join them.

11:09am: David, ex-Front Office Manager is escorted off-site with Police.

11:10am: The entire hotel knows about the whole sordid affair.

11:45am: Chelsea places ad on website for Front Office Manager.

The Hotel Inspection should have been pretty straight forward for F&B. To ensure that nothing was left to chance though, Cameron decided that they would not take any more reservations for the same night. Normally you are not tipped off as to when an Inspector is coming, so someone had connections. The Inspector certainly didn't seem aware that we had been tipped off, at first anyway.

I'm sure it didn't take him long to clue in though. Everywhere the Inspector went, he was followed by Adam, Blair and I. He knew it too. He entered an empty Drawing Room; we followed him in two minutes later. He went to an empty Room 399 for lunch; we served him. He went to the empty Breakfast Room (which now doubled as a makeshift lunch and dinner room, since there was talk of delaying the fine-dining restaurant opening even further); and we served him dinner.

All, apart from him being obviously uncomfortable with his three stalkers, went as smoothly as possible. The next morning he ordered breakfast through room service for 7:30am. Much to our relief, he did not ask for it in the privacy hatch! He was staying in one of the last bedrooms to be finished, so everything would be perfectly clean.

The three of us took painstaking care of the trolley and everything on it. The hot box was polished up, fresh flowers were cut and placed in a small vase in the centre of the trolley. It looked perfect. Now we had to get it through the maze of rooms, to the elevator up to room 902 in the same condition. Adam came up with the great idea of covering everything that might spill with cling-film. We got the hot food from the kitchen at 7:22 and set off, slowly.

We made it to the elevator and up to the ninth floor at 7:29am. We wheeled the trolley past 903, then 904, and then…a dead end. "Bastard! We came up the wrong side." The hotel split into two spires at level seven. Room 902 was in the spire on the other side. We made our way back to the elevator and down to the seventh floor again; along the corridor to the far side, and up the other elevator to the ninth floor again.

"Okay, we're only five minutes late," I whispered as we caught our breath outside the room. Before the doorway in front of us however, were two small steps up to the door. This was not good. We would have to lift anything that might spill off the trolley completely now. I put the coffee, milk, juice and vase on the carpet as they slowly lifted the trolley up and then back down. We took a deep breath and decided it would be best for Adam to do the actual in-room delivery. Blair and I hid around the corner and waited.

Adam knocked. The door opened. Blair and I stared unbelievably at Adam as he came walking back toward us. "We need to lift it again," he whispered. What our Inspector thought of us creeping out from behind the corner I could only imagine.

As we approached the door, I peeked inside the doorway; more steps. Not just any steps either: a circular stair entrance. Only six steps, but they were tight. This was a challenge I had certainly never come across before. We stood there thinking how we could make this look pretty as the Inspector held the door open for us and smiled. No doubt he was enjoying this.

We decided once again to remove all the spillables to his kitchen table. I held the door open from above, on the third step. Adam, being shorter grabbed the front of the trolley and moved backwards, up and around the steps as Blair held the trolley as high as he could, three steps below, to keep it level. Breathing in deeply so they could get past me, I tried to keep the trolley straight with my free hand until Blair had cleared the doorway. When they finally got to the top, Blair and I made a quick exit and left Adam to set up the table and apologize. There was no doubt he was our best apologizer, with all the practice he was getting in the Drawing Room.

All Managers were called down to the in-house movie theatre shortly after noon. There, The Puppet introduced us to the 'unexpected Inspector.' In a nutshell he found that he liked the staff and that they were all very helpful, although it was the smallest F&B Team he had ever come across.

Unfortunately he found many 'basics' wrong with the functionality of the hotel. In Food and Beverage, he noted the privacy hatch problem (we never found out how he discovered this); and the problem we had with the stairs at the entrance for Room Service trolleys. Warming up, he went on to tell his audience how he had spilled coffee and milk all over his breakfast trolley when he hadn't realized there was cling-film covering them. Blair and I let out a short, but loud, burst of laughter. All eyes turned sharply first to us, and then to Adam, who had his head in his hands trying to figure out how he had forgotten to remove it.

The Inspector had a long list for all the other areas too. The problems with the bedrooms had most of us rolling in the aisles. My personal favorite was the bubble bath dispensers. Another classic Creepy cock-up: Molten Brown bubble bath is very expensive and guests usually take the miniature bottles from the rooms when they check out. To provide as much choice to the guest as possible and reduce the expense of this, Creepy, in a logical move, mounted a secured dispenser on the walls next to each tub. Guests had the choice of six different types of bubble bath, yet they couldn't take them away as a souvenir. Housekeeping could refill the dispensers from bulk bottles to lower the cost.

"I started to get annoyed," the comedian continued, "when I tried to get the bubble bath into the bathtub. Did anyone check these?" Rhetorical or not, everyone looked around. If Creepy was present, he had obviously slunk under the seats by now. "I ended up with large piles of bubble bath on the marble at the side of the tub. The dispensers don't reach as far as the tub." His timing and delivery were superb. Snorts and giggles resounded in the theatre.

The Puppet had heard enough however. He interrupted the show to ask, what seemed to me, a ridiculous question in the circumstances: "Did we get five stars?"

"No. Four stars." Silence fell for a moment. Sensing this was not the hoped for result, the comic continued: "This hotel has some great features. Most of them however, need some finishing touches and some work on their functionality. Room Service, for instance, I have no idea how you can get around some of those delivery issues. Access to every room is completely different, with winding staircases at the entrance to many of them."

I knew I had to start working on a plan for room service delivery. It would have to involve surveying every room to see if a trolley was a possibility and if so, how many staff would be required to deliver it. It would also have to include routes and elevator numbers to reach each room above the seventh floor. Although I already knew the Inspector's room was not even close to being the most difficult to deliver to, I didn't feel like sharing it just now.

As we trudged out of the room, everyone felt sorry for The Puppet. He had tried hard, and that alone couldn't have been easy, working with Creepy and Cameron. We all wondered what would happen next. After all, this wasn't just a blow for McNeil. This was a huge blow for the hotel. The star rating to a large extent determines what prices you can charge. They had overspent in every area possible believing that this would guarantee a five-star rating. I was sure heads would roll.

It was no surprise when I was called in to The Puppet's office two days later. Chelsea was there. I was prepared for it.

Usually HR starts with a little small talk before they give it to you. So I was surprised when The Puppet spoke first: "Mike, we'd like you to go to Leeds for two weeks."

I was stunned. Was this where they do the public executions? "What! Why?"

"Well, you know we have a sister hotel there. They're having some problems with the Duty Manager coverage; and they need some training throughout their food and beverage areas. It would only be for two weeks. You'll stay in the hotel and you can come back on the weekends."

"Great. Sure. I'd love to!" I felt like the noose had been lifted from my neck. I ran back to tell the guys, who were equally shocked.

It was Blair who made sense of it though: "If they move you down to Leeds, they reduce the payroll. I'll bet they're not replacing you here."

After two weeks in Leeds, I no longer wondered why Creepy had made such a mess of this opening. Leeds was every bit a disaster as our hotel, and they had been open for several years.

The payroll had been reduced further when I returned too. Fiona had taken over Housekeeping from Chandler. This was due to health reasons. The poor bugger had lost so much weight in this sweatshop that he was forced to take time off.

Marcus had left as Bar Manager too. Apparently a stickler for order, this was no place for him. The Puppet decided that we didn't really need to replace him: "Adam, Blair and you are a great team. You can manage it between you."

Ninety Days after Opening

The fallout from the four-star rating began to gain momentum.

"A 'Luxury Hotel.' That will be our rating!" Cameron was doing his best, but I wondered if even he could believe what he was telling us now. "Everyone else is in the AA star-rating program. We'll opt out. We'll be different!" And he did opt out. We were soon advertising as a 'luxury hotel.'

Apart from a large part of the Health Club, most of the hotel was open now: dysfunctional, but operational.

It was approaching finishing time on a Thursday when Blair burst into the office: "Holy shit! Did you hear what just happened?" Blair was always the first in with the gossip.

I, on the other hand, have always had a knack for being the last to know. "No. What?"

"They just sacked twelve people up there! One after the other."

Although Blair liked a joke, he was hardly ever the initiator of one. Adam didn't believe him either. We went out to the pub next to the hotel. Two minutes later it was confirmed: Shakey Blakey, ex-IT guy, joined us for a beverage.

I hardly slept that night, knowing what I would be facing in the morning. Twelve staff: gone! Would that be enough? How would the hotel run without replacing people like the IT guy?

I didn't have long to wait. I was in the Breakfast Room with the guys when the call came down from the Puppet's office for me. I shook hands with them and said goodbye. They tried to play it down: "No way. You'd be the last one to go." We all knew it was coming though.

As it happened, I was the first of thirteen to be let go on this day. Chelsea and The Puppet briefly explained the financial issues the hotel was having. The bank was moving in and making some decisions for them…nothing personal. They offered me a job in Leeds, which I quickly declined. Chelsea remarked that if I'd just had a little more Banqueting experience, they'd have let Timmy go. I laughed inside! Somehow, I thought they deserved each other.

They were surprised that I was taking it so well and thanked me for that. I had resigned myself to it overnight, and in truth…it was a relief. We had been working fourteen hour days, six days a week, for the last three months. It couldn't go on. The Puppet added in conclusion: "If there's ever anything we can do for you Mike, just ask."

My only concerns were my fiancée and a house. Carla was due to go on maternity leave from her work in three weeks. We had bid on a house that was accepted; but a bank had reneged on our mortgage loan. I had made an appointment for the next day with my own bank to see about a mortgage. If we didn't get it, we could be sued for breach of contract. This was all causing Carla stress that she didn't need.

I told them about the mortgage issue: "All they need to know is that I am in permanent, full-time employment."

"No problem. I'll have Sarah fax a letter over to the bank today for you," Richard said. We shook hands and parted. I returned to the guys and said goodbye again.

I was making my way up the stairs towards the exit when a salesman stopped me: "Have you seen Blair?"

"Why?"

"He signed a deal with us. We delivered a cappuccino machine to his house four months ago for agreeing to put in two others in your outlets. We haven't been paid and we can't seem to contact him!"

"He was fired yesterday," I told him. "Good luck finding that guy!"

Post Mortem

The next day I went to the bank, hardly confident, but I tried to look it. The Mortgage Officer asked where I was working, which seemed strange. I had told him where I was working (and was still supposed to be working) on the phone a few days ago. I told him again.

"I never received a letter from your work, so I phoned them yesterday. They said you had been let go," he put bluntly.

I had a bad hand, but once again, it was my only hand. Digging up a short laugh, I reminded myself that the F&B Manager is the King of the bluff. I smiled back. "Yeah, we let go twenty five staff over the last few days. Two of them were named Mike, so I'm not surprised there was confusion."

"I asked if it was definitely you. They said they were sure."

My last throw: "Who did you speak to?"

"A lady called Sarah. The General Manager's Assistant."

"Sarah! She was supposed to be faxing you a letter yesterday with my employment details. Didn't you get it?"

"No."

"Well, I'm going straight there now, so if I can get them to confirm by fax in the next hour, will that do?"

"Absolutely. Come right back."

This place was going to haunt to my grave! Near tears, I ran the four blocks to the hotel and went to see her: "Sarah, what happened to the letter you were supposed to send to my bank yesterday?"

"I did send it. I mailed it yesterday morning."

"Mailed it! Mailed it? Are you kidding me? It's four blocks away! I told Richard I needed it faxed yesterday. You told them I had been let go!" I was out of breath now as McNeil stepped out of his office, obviously overhearing it all.

"I'll phone the bank now and fax it right away," he said. This time, thankfully, The Puppet was as good as his word. We got our mortgage and I left The Nam with some sanity still intact.

I kept in touch with Adam, who kept me up to date with the rapid changes going on. It seemed to be common knowledge now that the bank had moved in and demanded the thirty highest earners to be fired. Another five had been sacked the day after me. None of them went as quietly.

Only a handful of these positions were replaced. Blair's fine-dining restaurant was put 'on-hold' indefinitely. Blair and Timmy had come close to blows on several occasions over the last month or so, but now it was an everyday occurrence. With a department that was officially open for business, The Puppet decided to keep Timmy on the books. To avoid the fighting between them, Blair was let go. However what Blair had achieved was something few people would surely ever believe. Blair had worked in the hotel for over ten months as the fine-dining Restaurant Manager of a restaurant that never existed. Quite an achievement and a fitting testament to the owners and the Director of Operations, Richard Cameron!

Adam worked all kinds of crazy hours to try to make it work. Timmy worked even harder at avoiding the work. The Puppet cornered both of them in the Drawing Room one afternoon to give Timmy another good dressing down about his lack of commitment.

That was enough for Timmy. "Well, I can't take this anymore. I'm outta here," he sighed.

"What? You're leaving? Timmy, come back." Timmy didn't come back though. Timmy walked straight out the door, leaving Richard and Adam staring at each other in disbelief. Richard gave it one last loud one this time: "TIMMY!" as the door gently clicked closed behind him.

Scared to move, Adam held his breath. McNeil inhaled, then vented probably a year's worth of frustration with a loud: 'FUUUUCK!' This was followed with a punch that put a hole through the screen dividing the seating and service areas. No doubt drained, McNeil quietly followed Timmy out.

That Richard McNeil could do something like that was shocking; totally out of character. But The Nam got the better of everyone in the end. More shocking to me was that after all the people that had been told when their tour of duty was up in The Nam, Timmy had been allowed to make the decision himself!

Within two weeks of this incident, The Puppet cut his strings. Packing up lock, stock and barrel, he moved back to the hotel he had left a lifetime ago in the South of England. Creepy eventually sacked Cameron shortly after The Puppet left, but only Adam was around to enjoy it: the last man standing. No prize was ever forthcoming.

The phone rang. "Andrew who?" I asked.

"Blakey. Shakey, I believe."

"Oh yeah! Shakey. What's up?"

"I heard you got the axe the day after me. Sorry to hear that, but I have something that might interest you. My wife is the Director of Sales for another hotel in the area. I'm working for them now. They're looking for some good people and I thought of you right away. Interested?"

"Interested? You bet!"

I didn't know it yet, but I was on my way from a hotel of no controls to a group of hotels run by the epitome of a control freak.

Chapter four – The General Manager part I: The Making of a Dictator

As I sat waiting for my interviewer, I watched the replays of the Twin Towers going down on the lounge television. The pressure was definitely on now.

Shakey had been every bit as good as his word. I received the first call from The Grosvenor on September 9th, the day after Shakey's call, to set up the interview. They wondered if I was interested in a Restaurant Manager position. I declined instantly. Although disappointed with the position offered, I was anything but worried. I had been interviewing for several positions at much more prestigious hotels around the city for the last three weeks. A better offer, I was sure, was imminent.

Much to my surprise, it was The Grosvenor that called again the next day; this time to ask if I was interested in an Assistant General Manager position. This was interesting. This was opportunity. This was the move from Food and Beverage to Front Office. I had met only one GM ever who had a Food and Beverage background.

The reason is pretty clear: in most hotels, food and beverage revenue accounts for anywhere between fifteen to thirty percent of the hotel's revenue. Room revenue brings in the rest. Although the F&B revenue can be a substantial amount, the problem lies in the expenses.

The Director of Sales, as they will often remind you, may sign a contract to bring in $100,000 in Rooms revenue. Total labor expense for Sales to do this: their hourly salary. The labor involved for the restaurant staff to serve enough coffees, even at $7 each, to reach $10,000…substantially more. However F&B, although less profitable, is indispensable. You can't run a quality hotel without room service and a restaurant at the very least.

General Manager: the ultimate position of power. In this political arena, they truly are dictators. Some use their power for good. Unfortunately most use their power to create Laws in order to maintain their dictatorship. In the hotel, they are not only above the Law, they are the Law.

As someone under the Law, I was only made aware of some of the Laws when I broke them; memorizing them while serving my punishment.

The Laws of General Management:
1. Put yourself first at every opportunity
2. Never admit you made a mistake
3. Remain completely oblivious to what is really happening beneath you (if it doesn't affect you personally, it is irrelevant)
4. Surround yourself with brown-nosers and incompetents to pander to your ego
5. Whatever Management Skills you may have picked up while climbing the ladder; completely disregard them immediately.
6. Confuse and harass the Food and Beverage Manager at every opportunity

I knew if I was ever going to be General Manager, I had to get Rooms experience. But how? To make the switch means starting over as far as salary is concerned. While money certainly isn't everything to the F&B Manager; I had new responsibilities on the horizon, with Carla now three months pregnant.

Then September 11th happened. After the very obvious fallout, newscasts quickly began to talk about the knock-on effects, turning their attention to the problems that airlines would soon face. It didn't take long to project that if travel was going to slow down, tourism and hotels would too.

I went for the interview on September 12th. I should have known before I even arrived that something was amiss. The first thing that struck me was that the interview was not at the hotel I was being interviewed for. It was at the sister hotel only a mile away.

I was interrogated by Richard, the Assistant GM of said sister hotel, for about forty five minutes. Having an entirely F&B background himself, he approved of me; asking me to wait a bit longer. After what seemed quite a long wait, out came the GM, Laura. She had been doing her hair and make-up in preparation for my interview. The cloud of perfume around her was just settling down as the interview ended. I thought it went well.

As I gasped at the fresh air outside, it occurred to me that the GM from The Grosvenor barely got a mention, and there was no talk of her interviewing me. HR didn't pop by either. Maybe it didn't go as well as I thought!

I started to worry. I called the 'prestigious' hotels back to check on my application status. "Our hiring is 'on hold' at the moment," they all told me. The effects of the attacks on the twin towers had already begun. I held my breath for The Grosvenor.

When they did call, I was certainly in no position for bartering. I would have accepted immediately, but they were adamant that I take Carla in for dinner before I make a decision. Was this another test?

Moments after arriving, we decided it was a test alright: to see if I could stomach the hotel and the GM. The hotel was run down. It was three-star, going on one. The food was terrible and the service a perfect complement. Carla and I stared quietly at each other throughout the forgettable meal.

Sara was not like any GM I had ever come across before. She wore an old blue skirt and matching top that a swarm of starving moths wouldn't have touched. Her shoes were dirty and well-worn. Any dishwasher would have been proud of them; but a General Manager!

Sara would forever change the way I thought about General Managers. Until now, the General Manager position had held a certain kind of reverence. I thought back to the first GM I worked for: Roger Wall.

Mr. Wall was the GM at The Park when I arrived on the scene. He was very tall and slender; although the same could not be said of his wife. They had two sons, which was a bit of a miracle…Roger was reputed to be gay. In fact, rumor had it he was sleeping with the Marketing Manager. At the time, I didn't pay any attention to this. I was too scared of him to even think those kinds of thoughts. Most managers addressed him as Mr. Wall, and I took heed.

I knew that being a GM couldn't be easy. For a start, nobody acted normal when they were around. They obviously had no real friends. Plenty of staff wanted to be their friend, but only for personal gain. Everybody addressed him differently too. I noted that people never know what to call the GM…to their face at least. But you can tell a lot about the GM from how they want to be addressed:

'Sir' is very formal. These GM's have a deluded sense of themselves and their accomplishments so they are easy to manipulate…address them properly and they will sign anything for you without even looking.

Any GM that wants to be addressed on a first-name basis is dangerous. These GM's could slither under rock with a top hat on. They prey on the weak, and any coat-tail riders; pretending to be their friend until they have drawn information out of them. Stay well clear of this GM and any of their hangers-on.

The GM that wants to be addressed on a last-name basis, such as "Mr. Fish," is the most common and the most dangerous of all. This slippery fish endears staff into thinking his is a respectable way to be addressed, without being too scary (like a 'sir') or too informal (like first-name basis). Mr. Fish however, also likes to slip into formality and informality depending on the company he is keeping at any particular time; and he expects everyone to read when those situations are. You will not be told!

So one evening Mr. Fish shows up at the hotel restaurant with company. Panic sets in as he approaches the podium. The Restaurant Manager has only seconds to read the formality of the situation. Is it a client? (Keep it at 'Mr. Fish' level).

Is it a date? (Use 'sir' so the date sees the reverence in which God is held in the hotel…a real show of power. Get it wrong…the date is screwed, and so are you)!

Is it a relative? (Use the first name. If his parents are present he may get an earful about being too full of himself if 'sir' or 'Mr. Fish' are used. Although not as serious an issue as the previous faux-pas, he will not thank you for it).

Nobody that works in a hotel ever calls the GM 'The General Manager.' They are known simply as 'The GM:' a God-like figure that makes less public appearances than the Loch Ness Monster. To Department Heads, they may be called any number of crude things…in private.

The reason for the different outlook is simple. The head of the mafia rarely carries out a hit himself because there are too many eyes on him. But everyone knows who ordered the hit.

In the same way, the GM never tells a staff member they are 'completely useless and should be working in a fucking McDonald's' to their face. When dealing with line staff, even the GM must abide by a few laws. Therefore the GM has to be a talented liar.

From the GM, the staff member is more likely to hear something along the lines of: 'don't worry about that spill. I'm always doing that myself. Hey could you ask your Department Head down to pop down here for a moment?'

Upon arrival at the GM's office, the poor F&B Manager can expect to be shown the stain their incompetent made on the GM's coffee table trying to pour the lazy bastard's coffee. The bigger a deal the GM makes of this is directly proportionate to the number of guests they have in their office at the time.

Mr. Wall was extremely organized and I always thought that this was the key to his success. He was promoted to Director of Operations for the UK shortly after my arrival and headed off to London, taking the Director of HR and (surprising nobody) the Marketing Manager with him.

This is the stuff of dreams for many a Department Manager: the coat-tail ride of a lifetime. The F&B Manager is not generally invited for these unwarranted journeys up the corporate ladder; nor does he want it. The dedicated F&B Manager has principles; they do things the right way. They desire to learn their trade and earn their promotions. So the F&B Manager watches closely and waits for the day when the GM realizes their incompetent has not only set low standards, but has consistently failed to achieve them.

Every time Mr. Wall returned to visit the hotel, he would spend an hour in the GM's office, getting a briefing and checking his notes. Then he would spend an hour or two conducting a hotel inspection. It was here that Mr. Wall's rigorous note-taking became obvious.

In every department he would see a familiar face and ask them a question relating to their personal life. With Barbara in Room Service, it was her son: "Barbara, lovely to see you again. How is little Ryan?"

"He's a spoiled little bastard," I wanted to answer; but bit my tongue.

Barbara would beam for days, and tell everyone what a wonderful GM Mr. Wall was: "Much better than that bitch down there now!" She didn't care that it was the same question every time he returned.

She may have, had she known how many times he had told me to: "Get rid of that two-faced little bitch in Room Service." Other than keeping his name alive in the hotel, I didn't see any real purpose it served him now though.

Barbara was right about the 'bitch down there now' though. Dorta Tinghe had moved in. She was a cold, stone-faced Norwegian woman who would never have to worry about wrinkles around her mouth from smiling too much. Her name provided plenty of smiles for everyone else though.

When the Irish contingent, who worked in Banqueting, tried to pronounce her name, the accent changed 'Dorta Ting' to 'Dirty Ting.' Soon the entire hotel was talking in Irish accents: 'Can you do tree coffees for dat Dirty Ting?'

For the first month, she was staying God-knows where, while her 'apartment' upstairs was being renovated. Every time a new GM arrived, they were given £40,000 to renovate their hotel room into their condo. This seemed an extravagant amount to the rest of the staff on near-minimum wage, especially considering they might only be there for two years. This was only the snowflake on the tip of the iceberg too!

Although the GM had to live in the hotel, it was certainly no hardship. Their room was not the small cramped space that the guests were paying £300 a night for. These were the massive end-of hallway suites. And not just one suite! Two or three of them were connected by knocking down the walls.

Mr. Wall only required two for his family of four; however Dorta required an extra suite for herself and presumably, her large red wine collection. On a side-note, this also reduced the number of rooms the hotel had to sell. All guests at the hotel had five-star amenities and service; but the life of the GM was closer to seven-star. They had few worries, if any.

The GM at The Park certainly never had to worry about their personal cash flow either. They probably didn't know what cash looked like. The Wall's kids (well Mrs. Wall's for certain) had all aspects of their education paid for by the company. This would include University anywhere in the country; although the Wall kids were a few years away from that.

The company paid for their transport to and from their private schools; and this was no ordinary taxi service either. This was a private hire BMW chauffeured by 'Men in Black.' The only missing touches were the diplomat flags and police escort. I'm sure they were sipping apple juice from chilled martini glasses on their way to pre-school.

When Dorta moved in, I thought the air conditioning had been put into overdrive. After her first week I asked my wife: "How long, in extreme cases, can PMS last?" She wasn't even close. I never did check the Guinness Book of Records, but two years without a day off! She must be in there.

Whether it was PMS or a permanent hangover from the barrels of red wine that were rolled up to her apartment, her demeanor was a disgrace. Sadly this attitude was not unique to 'dat Dirty Ting.' I would later discover that Mr. Wall was the exception to what is now widely regarded as the First Law of General Management: 'Me First.'

GM's all say they put the guest first, but that is only because they see themselves as a guest. Not just any guest either: as the longest-staying guest, they believe they are the most important guest. As far as Dorta was concerned, the staff was not there to serve the guests; they were her personal servants. No guest ever came before Dorta.

Every second night at 4:00pm, Dorta would drop off her shopping list for the Head Chef and a wine order for the F&B Manager. The items were to be delivered to her room at precisely 5:30pm the same day. God forbid this was late!

"Hurry up," Barbara shouted down the kitchen corridor. Her arms were waving wildly up and down at her sides. "We've only got ten minutes."

The panic in Chef's eyes said it all. He threw his hat down, not caring where it landed as he waited for Ingo to dig some cash out of his wallet. Chef started to bounce up and down: "Urry Eengo! Urry," he whispered in his French accent as Ingo's fingers fumbled for a fiver.

It was a relay race now. Chef started off on his leg as Ingo finally pulled the fiver out and caught up to him. They handed the baton off just before the Room Service door. Barbara held the door open as Chef sped past her and disappeared out the front door by the restaurant.

Ingo was not happy. Although he wasn't doing the running, he was sweating as he watched the front door, trying to visualize Chef returning quickly. Drew came up behind him: "Ingo. Where have you been? We don't have any Chateau Neuf de Pape!"

"Sheizen!" was all he got out as he took off after Chef and out the front door.

Barbara checked the clock: "Nine minutes." Drew and I looked gravely at each other. It was going to be close.

We needed a game plan. There wouldn't be a second to spare. "Babs, you take the trolley with what we have. Wait right outside her door. Drew, you lock the elevator off on this level. Wait for me. I'll wait at the front entrance for them. As soon as they reach the stairs, I'll run it to the elevator." We nodded silently and ran to our places.

Ingo was back first. The liquor store was less than a block away. Ingo hated that. He knew the closer a liquor store was to the hotel, the greater the likelihood guests would buy alcohol from there rather than from the minibar. He wasn't complaining now though. To be fair, he couldn't have if he wanted too. He was not in the best of shape, and even a block at full pace had him huffing and puffing like the big bad wolf. He handed the bottle over and sat on the top step, fumbling in his pockets for a cigarette.

Chef was in sight now. He threw the brown bag up to me from the bottom step and collapsed beside Ingo. I didn't have time to enjoy the sight. "Time?" I called to Drew as he pushed the level five button.

"Christ. Only seconds."

I held my breath and tore out the doors when what seemed an eternity came to an end and the elevator doors opened. I turned the corner into the final leg and yelled at Barbara from the other end of the corridor: "Knock now!"

I was only a few steps away when the door began to open. "Right on time," Dorta stated coldly as I placed the bottle and bag of ginger root on the trolley. I turned quickly on my heels as Babs wheeled the trolley into the dragon's lair.

I ran back to the front steps to give them the good news, but the steward's inquiry had already begun. Drew was in full song when I was within earshot: "It's not my fault! That wine's a special order. I can only order it on a Friday and she's never ordered that one before."

Ingo turned on Chef now: "How can a kitchen this size run out of ginger root?"

"Run out! Eengo, I don't use zheenger root. Guess how many deeshes we have that call for zheenger root?" Ingo took another puff and stared at the ground, but said nothing. "None. Zero. Nada. Sweet fuck all Eengo. That's how many! Why should I have to run out and leave my orders for her bloody zheenger root? Mon Dieu! My orders!" Chef ran off to whatever orders he had forgotten when he discovered ginger root was on the GM menu tonight.

With nobody to blame, Ingo drew the last puff from his cigarette and carelessly flicked it aside. I turned to go inside with him, but he stopped just before the entrance to let out a large: "Sheizen!" as he kicked over a plant pot.

"But Ingo," I whispered. "We made it!"

"We made it?" A grin started to develop. "We made it?" He didn't…couldn't, believe it. He went to Babs for a second opinion.

Barbara looked at Ingo as he frowned enquiringly at her. A bead of sweat trickled from his forehead, under his glasses and hung from his long nose. He held his breath.

"Right on time," she smiled.

He didn't smile often, but you could have mistaken him for the Cheshire Cat now. As he turned to go, he called back to Barbara: "Oh, and could you call Housekeeping? There are cigarette butts all over the stairs and those bloody kids have kicked over a plant pot again."

Dorta took the Sixth Law one step further than most GM's as well. I was made aware of this Law while conducting Matt's appraisal in a meeting room next to the lounge. Matt had been my strongest Supervisor in F&B for a year now. He was well aware of the GM Laws.

We were about thirty minutes into the appraisal when we were interrupted by a knock at the door. Everyone knew I did not like to be interrupted when an appraisal was being conducted. It had to be important.

It was Barbara. "Dorta wants you in the lounge."

"Me? Why? Does she know I'm doing an appraisal?"

"I told her. She wants you right away. She's having her photo taken in the lounge. Table thirteen."

I apologized to Matt. I couldn't say 'no' to Dorta. It was against the Law! "She must want her photo taken with you. It's your lounge!" Matt said.

I allowed myself a quick daydream as I walked out: "Wow. That would be great. I wonder what magazine we'll be in."

"Stand here and hold this," the photographer said as he handed me a light. I awoke abruptly from my daydream. Dorta said not a word as she sprawled herself out on the sofa. I didn't envy the photographer, and wondered if he was a magician in his spare time. It was a Herculean task to make this shot look good.

It was at this precise moment that it occurred to me for the first time: GM's do not live in the real world.

I had thirty minutes to stand there and think. "Why the hell would she pull me out of an appraisal to hold a light for her?" I looked around. There were plenty of staff to pick from that were equally qualified, if not more so, for this job.

There was only one answer of course. She did it to keep me in my place; in order to uphold the First and Sixth Laws of General Management. She stuck with her task until her final day as well.

At her last Manager's Meeting, she announced: "Everyone must schedule an appointment with me to have their appraisal before I go." Significantly and perhaps not so coincidentally, most companies changed this term to 'performance review' shortly after this. Foolishly, I made my appointment. It was to be done on her last day.

Even the Stewarding Manager took me aside to tell me what a stupid move I'd made. "Billy, how bad can it be? She won't even recognize me unless I pour the tea for her!"

"Good fucking luck. That's all I can say. Good fucking luck! She has a week left and she would have forgotten all about it if you hadn't gone to see her." Billy didn't mince words. His vocabulary was fairly limited to be fair, so he didn't have many to mince.

He was right though. Not only was it a mistake, but nobody else made an appointment and nobody else was reminded about it.

"Just have a seat. Ms. Tinghe is with someone important," the Stamp-Licker (aka Sam, the Executive Assistant) smirked knowingly. What the Executive Ass doesn't know about brown-nosing is not worth knowing. Their self-importance is as unwarranted as it is unfathomable. When my mole in HR told me what Sam's salary was, I nearly choked. I didn't think it was legal to pay that little. I couldn't help giggling every time I saw her.

My only fond memory of Sam was when she complained to the GM that none of the staff respected her. She asked that she be allowed to do some Duty Management shifts. I assumed this was to show others that she should command some respect as a competent individual. I also presumed nobody told her the main purpose behind this position was to handle complaints when guests demanded to speak to the General Manager.

On the day of her first shift, anticipation around the hotel was at a fever pitch. Within a few hours I realized that Sam had skipped the 'complaint handling for dummies' pre-requisite course. Through sheer fortune, the complaint happened to be in my bar. I actually had no idea what the complaint was about. I was extremely busy behind the bar, so a supervisor called Sam up to speak to the irate woman standing beside the bar.

As I watched Sam approach, I knew I had to keep an eye and an ear on the situation.

"Good evening, my name is Samantha." A solid start by Sammy!

"I don't care what you're name is." Samantha's mouth opened very wide. "I have been waiting for…" Probably already realizing she was speaking to an idiot, she asked: "Are you the General Manager?"

I stopped what I was doing completely now, taking mental notes. "Well…well…I am, in her absence right now. I'm the Executive Assistant!" Sam stammered.

"I'm not speaking to some jumped up secretary…" the woman demanded.

Sam, breaking several complaint handling rules in one go, was done with listening already. She cut the complainant off and wagged a witch-like finger an inch from the woman's nose. "Now you listen to me! Don't you dare speak to me like that," she yelled. "Who do you think you're speaking to! Do you know who I am?"

The woman equally flabbergasted now, wagged back as an audience started to grow. "Who you are? Who cares about you? Do you know who I am?"

I have no doubt this would have gone on for some time, but Samantha had had enough. Storming off down the steps, the gob-smacked complainer followed after Sam, who refused to come out of her office. It was a sad end to Sam's era as a Duty Manager.

It didn't deter her from sticking her nose in whenever there was a complaint in any other department though. She harassed my staff for several weeks when she received a complaint letter from someone who was angry that their server in the lounge did not know what the 'soup of the day' was on either of the days he visited.

I insisted at the F&B briefing that this was virtually impossible since, as in all hotels, the 'soup of the day' is more likely to be the 'soup of the month.' Made in massive batches, the Head Chef would scrape off mold and serve it rather than throw it out and take a hit on his food cost.

Every time Sam passed through the lounge she would jump in front of a server and shout: "Quick. What's the soup of the day?" How I longed to throw a steaming bowl of it over her to see if she could guess what it was.

It was now 9:30am. I sat glaring at Sam as she put on her leather gloves and prepared to open the mail. In an attempt to make her lose concentration and stab herself with the silver letter-opener, I interrupted her. "Samantha, how long will she be? Should I come back?" Until a fairly recent incident when my conduct at another hotel (under the weakened influence of an alcoholic beverage or ten) had reached Dorta's ears…and therefore Sam's, I had always insisted on calling her Sam. She hated being called 'Sam.'

She would stop typing, shake her hair, look down at the ground for a few seconds and then slowly bring her head up so the eyes made contact…as if it was beneath her to do so.

"It's Samantha," she would whisper. Sometimes she wouldn't even look at me. I preferred this one; I didn't have to hold in the grin as much. She would just stare at the ground and shake her head again as if I wasn't worth looking at: "It's Samantha." Brilliant!

Before Sam could decide if I was worthy of an answer, the Pearly Gates opened.

Dorta's office was a mess. Half-packed boxes littered the room. "Now we may be interrupted," she began. "I have a lot to do here on my final day."

No sooner had she finished than the door opened again. "Please wait outside again," was all she said to me.

I twiddled my thumbs for another thirty minutes, before the door opened again. "Mike, can you organize tea for two? And you can go. I'll call you when I'm ready for you."

I was grateful to get away, but the butterflies in my stomach only had more time to grow. Several hours after my dismissal, I was called down again; then sent away again, then called back down again. I felt like a yo-yo. At 6:00pm, I was called down for the last time. For fifteen minutes my ears were abused before she finally stood up and rushed out the door, saying she had to catch a flight.

Whoever the new GM was going to be, I knew they had to be a better GM than dat Dirty Ting.

Hanna Berg was a better GM too. German by name; German by nature, she could be summed up in one word: efficient. She had only two down sides: her husband and her son.

Mr. Berg was on the gravy train and he knew it. He didn't work, and certainly seemed to have no inclination to. He strolled around the hotel in his track-pants half the day, annoying staff with stupid questions and just generally looking for something to do. The majority of his time was spent on the phone to room service though.

As with Dorta, Chef and Ingo were duly charged with Hanna's food and beverage shopping list. It was slightly easier for them in that it was weekly, and not every second day. It also seemed reasonable to me that she could run out of a few things over the course of a week. However the items 'Herr Tracky Pants' and son (aka Damien…after the comparatively angelic child in the movie) were pestering Room Service for every day, were household items that I knew they had stocked in their suite.

It started at 8:00pm every night, when Tracky would order a cognac. Room Service delivered the cognac. Herr Tracky would send it back, saying he meant to order a double cognac. It was brought back down (he wouldn't accept the old 'I'll just bring you another shot' speech), topped up and returned. Without fail, he'd already have called down for another one by the time you brought it back up. Without fail, whatever you brought up; was sent back. If it was a single shot, he really 'meant' a double. If you brought a double, he meant a single.

Once the cognacs had been dispersed of, he started with the cigars. Only Cubans would do for Tracky obviously; but after it was delivered, he'd call back for someone to come up and cut it. When it was cut, he'd call back to say he couldn't find any matches. Yet any time he sat in the bar, he had a cutter and lighter in his pocket.

The espresso to finish was the one that really pissed me off. They had a cappuccino machine in the room, and I knew damn well from the weekly food orders, plenty of sugar for little Damien's cereal. Yet Tracky could find endless reasons to send the 'cold' espresso back: it was supposed to be a double espresso; he'd run out of sugar and now it's cold; it's bitter.

Each time he answered the door, the grin got wider and wider. In the morning, it was the same routine with his toast. He would order 'toast,' and send it back when it was delivered 'toasted.' Very occasionally, when really pushed on the phone, he was able to spit out what he yearned for: "Yes, toast…not toasted."

Six months later, when we were still going through this morning toast charade, he admitted openly that he 'had a hard time remembering what 'bread' was in English. There was no shortage of offers to carve it into his arm…or neck.

While Tracky took care of the morning and evening shifts, little Damien worked the afternoons. Three days a week he'd have kids over from school and they'd play video games in his room. "Three plates of French fries; and I mean LARGE bowls of fries. LARGE BOWLS!"

Not once did he ever ask for ketchup. There was no point anyway really. No matter how many fries or bowls of ketchup were brought up…it wasn't enough. For French fries and ketchup, it was a minimum seven-trip ordeal. The little bastard nearly snapped your hand off when he closed the door too. How I yearned to grab his ungrateful little arm and hold it as he slammed the door closed on it.

It took six months but, after much lobbying from myself, Ingo finally agreed that Room Service could not possibly keep up the level of service other guests expected (within budget) when thirty three-percent of the Room Service labor was preoccupied with Herr Tracky and Son.

Hanna did not take the issue lightly. Ingo was seriously reprimanded. It was obvious from his face, but he also told me a few weeks later that I was never to mention it to him again. "She is the GM and that is that," were the exact words he used. But he also gave me a little advice. "If a new GM starts, or if you move to a new hotel, you have only four weeks to lay down the ground rules with them. You have to be ready on the first day."

I knew what he meant. The rules of engagement for this battle had already been established, and he should have gone to her immediately with the problem and, more importantly, how it affected the bottom line. Apart from themselves, that's all a GM cares about!

On a similar note, he taught me that as a Food and Beverage Manager, you have to spend money like crazy when a new GM starts, or if you move to a new hotel. "A new GM is full of expectation about what you can do. If they don't let you buy new equipment; you have an excuse as to why things don't improve. Buy everything you can for F&B! It will improve staff morale immediately, which helps you settle in quicker; and they won't let you buy it after they get comfortable with you."

It took me a few years to confirm this theory, but I had to hand it to Ingo: he was spot-on again. As I kept a closer eye on it, I noticed the GM's did the same thing too.

The GM that is planning on staying put for a while spends money on refurbishment and general upkeep of the hotel. However; a lot of GM's do not invest in the maintenance of the hotel. You can tell if you really look close. The first three things that stand out are the worn furniture, dirty and frayed carpets, and stains on walls because they need paint or wallpaper.

This is done for one reason: the GM is after a promotion. They can proudly e-mail off the Profit and Loss Accounts to their Head Office in Brussels or New York, showing good profitability. Of course, it comes at the expense of the building.

When the new GM comes in (that plans on staying a while), they complain to the same Head Office that the place is in dire need of a renovation from a lack of upkeep. It would look silly to go to Head Office after a year and say the place is run down, so it has to be immediate. Head Office agrees on a budget for it, and they quickly spend it. F&B Managers take note: the same logic applies to food and beverage.

Ingo, perhaps realizing it would be easier to get blood from a stone, started looking to greener pastures. Coincidence or not, the two Germans: Ingo and Hanna moved on only a month apart. Ingo: back to Berlin, and Hanna: back to Hell with Tracky and little Damien.

James Duff was the new GM. He was a short, chubby Irishman with a passion for all things alcoholic. He seemed cheerful enough though; and certainly a majority of staff held this opinion throughout his tenure. This was a remarkable feat; however he couldn't do it alone.

Hans the Henchman arrived only a month after James. Danish by birth, he had spent the last six years in Tblisi, Georgia, presumably chain smoking for a living. We had never had an Executive Assistant General Manager in the hotel before, and it would take years for me to find out that it was only another way of pronouncing 'F&B Manager.'

Hans made enemies easily, and had no moral problem doing it. He had his sights set thoroughly on a GM position himself. So while James was getting pissed in the bar every night, Hans was busy doing James' dirty work.

James treated Hans terribly in meetings too. Any time something went wrong, James went crazy. "Hans! I thought I fucking asked you to do this last week! Are you too fucking stupid to get it done?"

There were at least twelve other managers around the table, but here were the top two, giving us a lesson in politics. Everyone held their breath; except Hans. Hans just stared at the notepad in front of him and answered each question without emotion: "Yes James. No James. Sorry James."

I made a mental note to make sure that anything Mr. Duff asked me for was on his desk before he could finish the sentence. For Hans though, the public floggings continued.

One Friday afternoon, Hans invited a few managers out for a drink with him and his wife. His pal James was strangely missing. Inevitably, someone popped the question: "Hans, why do you put up with him speaking to you like that?"

He casually flicked his cigarette and replied: "What can I do? I want to be a GM, so I just have to put up with it until I get that position."

We all held our breath again. It was scary for me to think that this was the attitude that a GM would have. How was he going to treat his staff if he did make it to GM? It sounded to me like the hallmark trait of the abused perpetuating the abuse. And it was about to get much worse.

His Georgian wife Marina had been sitting very quietly for a long time. I'm sure I wasn't the only one who thought she perhaps didn't speak much English. This wasn't the case however. Hans had started to relax after a few drinks and reached for his second pack of cigarettes, which didn't seem to be in his coat pocket.

"Hey, go and get me some smokes," he called out, barely looking at her. When she returned a few minutes later with his cigarettes, Hans flipped some cash out of his wallet and threw it at her. "Go and get us a round of drinks."

As she obeyed the order, Hans felt obliged to apologize: "Sorry about that. Idiot! She's fucking useless!" To say we were stunned would obviously be an understatement; and it brought about a very sudden end to the night out.

My only other trip outside of the hotel with Hans after that was an unavoidable one. Hans and I had been looking at new minibar systems for the guest rooms. We thought we had found one, but when we called the company to see it, we were told that the closest one in operation was a three hour train journey away.

We boarded the train at 8:00am. Being a work trip, I was surprised that Hans booked first class seats, but held my tongue. We had only just left the station when he excused himself and returned five minutes later with a six-pack of beer. Again, mildly surprised, I risked a 'thank you.'

Upon arrival at Newcastle train station, we were picked up by the developers of the minibar system and whisked off to a small three-star hotel. As the F&B Manager of the hotel was not quite ready for us, we were asked to have a seat in the coffee lounge.

Hans, seemingly deep in thought, sat smoking silently as we waited. One of the developers, clearly unnerved by the silence, asked if we'd like a coffee. Hans nodded, still staring deeply into his cigarette. A few seconds later a woman stooped over the table and said hello.

Without a glance upward, Hans blew a puff of smoke at her. "Coffee, two sugar."

Clearly embarrassed, she replied: "No, I'm the F&B Manager," just as Hans inhaled another lungful.

When he had stopped coughing, Hans stood up, dropped his cigarette on the carpet and stammered: "Oh, sorry. I just expected you to be a man for some reason." He seemed only to open his mouth to change feet.

To her credit, she tried to maintain a smile all the time she gave us a show around.

As the train headed back to Edinburgh, Hans again excused himself and returned with the refreshments. It was our first chance to discuss the system alone. "So," I asked. "What did you think of it?"

'Phhhst' went his can of lager. "Awful. What the fuck does she know about food and beverage?"

I knew Hans wouldn't be with us much longer when he started to feed things back to me in James' actual words. This meant he wasn't scared of retribution anymore.

Construction of the hotel's new spa was moving quickly and a twenty foot drop-off had been dug inches from a well-worn hotel walkway. As Chairman of the Health and Safety Committee, I put it to James that a fence was the least we could do to reduce our liability should anyone slip over the side. James said he would like to think about it and get back to me.

Shortly thereafter, Hans stopped me in the corridor on my way to lunch. "Hey, about your fence; James says you can go and fuck yourself!"

Hans did move on to a GM position only a ten minute drive away. Within three months he was terminated.

Deciding I couldn't do any worse than Hans as an Assistant General Manager, I accepted the offer at The Grosvenor gratefully. One week after my departure, the fence was erected in my honor.

Chapter five - Food, Beverage…and Alcohol

A lot of the F&B Manager's valuable time is spent on the food side of the business: planning times to change menus; reviewing menu sales reports; 'costing' new food dishes; formatting menus; printing menus; programming menus into 'point of sale' systems; changing menus in the outlets, in elevators and on websites.

A lot of money is also spent on creating new food menus: printing costs; training time for chefs and servers; advertising. Factor in food wastage and chef's and server's salaries and you'll see the food side of the business is not nearly as profitable as people might think.

Non-alcoholic beverages are essentially 'food' items: coffee, pop and juice for example. So the 'beverage' in 'Food and Beverage Manager,' is alcohol. Alcohol is the F&B Manager's best friend.

Although the food is a big draw for the hotel, alcohol is more profitable because the costs associated with it are very low. It takes seconds to prepare and serve a drink. People can drink lots of it in a short time too, which keeps staffing costs to a minimum. Training is provided free of charge by the reps and they may also pay for the printing costs in exchange for advertising their products on the menu.

Unlike changes to a food menu, changing the wine list is a joy. Wine reps are always dropping off samples and offering free training for staff. Staff get free training; F&B Manager gets free wine. The bottom line is: no costs. Everyone wins!

The wine reps are usually youngish, flirty women too. This danger separates the Bar (or Restaurant Manager) from the F&B Manager. The Bar or Restaurant Manager falls for the fake blonde's wide smile and cheap perfume the moment they walk out and see the wine rep. A little pat on the knee while sharing a glass of the wine, and the Bar Manager will add any glass of vinegar to his wine list.

The shrewd F&B Manager on the other hand, informs Blondie he is 'just about to go into a meeting.' He sits with her for five minutes to tell her: 'we are still looking at cheaper alternatives for the wine list.' Finally, when his assistant pages him on cue, he jumps up and grabs the bottle of vino from her grasp, and thanks her for her time.

So it would be fair to say I was caught off guard one particular afternoon, when I walked out to meet a wine rep and found a man-mountain in a pin-striped power suit grinning at me instead.

I didn't have time to think as he shot an arm out at me. "Mike Williams," he boomed as I shook the sausages in my tiny grip. "I've got some new wines here you have to try." It wasn't so much of a question. I wasn't going to say 'no' to him, even if he'd asked me for my wallet! I nodded.

Reaching over the bar, he grabbed four glasses and poured…and kept pouring. I got a good look at him now. His suit was definitely not off the rack. He was about six foot five inches and two hundred seventy-five pounds. His thin beard made him look older, but I wouldn't have been surprised if he was anywhere in the twenty-four to thirty-seven range.

I took the pint of wine he held out. Normally a wine rep pours about an ounce in the glass so they can use the same bottle in many places. Not Mike. Mike poured glasses the size he liked to drink.

"This is South African."

I held it up to the light and took a deep breath to nose the wine. By the time I got to a sip, Mike was wiping his mouth with his arm: "Fucking excellent," he put forward as his empty glass went down. He looked at me now. I looked around; we were alone. What the hell was I supposed to do? Gulp it down? I took another sip and pushed the glass away.

"I was just down at Wimbledon for the tennis," he continued as he opened the next bottle. "Phwooaaa…the women down there! They were all over me! Well, it was some party I'll tell you." He poured another two pints of something red. "This is absolutely smashing stuff. Really strong too…if you're on a date?" he winked.

He gulped down half of his glass in one go and nodded encouragingly as I raised my glass again. "Well, I've got a big date tonight. What do you say we do some training for your staff next week?"

"Sure. No problem," I smiled as he handed over his card and strutted out.

I stood laughing for a few minutes as I tried to review what had just happened. A new wine rep comes in; gulps down two pints of wine himself and doesn't even tell me the name of the wines. I did get the name and many sordid details of every girl he'd met at Wimbledon that week though.

It was with a grim foreboding that I waited for Mike's training session.

As it turned out, Mike was a big hit. He certainly knew his stuff about wines; but Mike had a very unusual way of describing them. He was definitely not traditional or politically correct in his delivery though. Mike entertained the staff for an hour with stories about himself, wine and women. It was more like a teambuilding cabaret event than a wine tasting. I thought about hiring him for weekends in the lounge.

We had him back several times by popular demand and it was a big disappointment for everyone when he had arranged another tasting with us and didn't show up. Mike had taken up another job offer and his replacement showed up with some big shoes to fill.

Leading him into the banquet room to set up the wines for us, I asked him if he was familiar with all the wines he had on our list. "Don't worry, Mike left me some tasting notes," he said confidently.

We were nearing the end of the tasting; perhaps on our sixth red wine when he poured The Dead Arm Shiraz for everyone. I loved this wine. A traditionalist may describe it as 'a very big, bold wine.'

As everyone held up their glass to form their own opinion, the rep took a mouthful and pondered Mike's notes. We all watched helplessly as he spat some of the wine out into the spittoon bucket, some onto the floor, but most of it onto the table. It splashed in his face as he choked and coughed for a full minute. When he regained control and wiped the wine from his face and shirt, he laughed uncontrollably for several minutes. A bit unnerved, I walked up to ask if he was alright.

"How well do you know Mike?" was all he said, still laughing.

"Pretty well I think. Why?"

He held out the tasting notes Mike had written for this particular wine. I let out a laugh myself as I read the three descriptors Mike had left for him: 'Big, black cock.'

The F&B Manager loves alcohol because of its profitability. However, it is the poor servers that have to pay the price for guests over indulging.

At The Park, I enjoyed watching people make fools of themselves. As they arrived in tuxedos at 5pm for a banquet, I would watch them going into the ballroom; wondering who was going to punch his boss or insult someone that night. It never failed: you put five hundred people in a room, add alcohol and presto: instant trouble.

I thought I had seen it all when I caught a couple making love under a stairwell between Reception and the staff area one night. As I walked through the door, they stopped briefly. It was dark, but not so dark that I couldn't see anything. They watched me and waited. The alcohol had made them think they were invisible, so I continued through to Reception.

"Mary, there's a couple shagging under the stairs over there." Mary was the Night Manager. A war-horse and self-proclaimed desperado when it came to sex, I thought she would be over there in a split second; either to stop it or join in. She looked at me thoughtfully for a few seconds before continuing with her work.

"Aren't you going to do something?" I asked, surprised.

"Nah. I'll give them a minute to start up again, and then sneak up on them!"

The big problem for the easily led guest at banquets can be the 'free bar.' One large insurance company used to hold three Christmas parties with our hotel every year. It came to a stop after one particularly bad year of festive binge drinking.

At party number one, five men were involved in a punch up in the bathroom. One of them had made a comment about his co-worker's wife's choice of dress while the gentleman was in a cubicle. Overhearing the comments, the gentleman washed his hands and battered his soon-to-be ex-co-worker at the urinal with a soap dish.

Not to be outdone, a middle-aged lady fainted just after dinner on the second night. Having sampled plenty of wine with her dinner, she collapsed on her way back from the bathroom, beside the bar. The large crowd gathered around her and was held off, giving her room to breathe. Paramedics were called immediately. One of the company Directors, claiming to know a little about First Aid, stuck his finger in her mouth to make sure her airways were clear.

Silence fell as he stuck his finger in. Suddenly, she awoke. Totally unaware of who she was, where she was, and why someone had a finger in her mouth. With the crowd staring down at her, she must have decided she was a dog. She started by trying to bite the Director's fingers; gnashing her teeth at his fingers several times, catching him once. Then she got on all fours and started growling and barking. The crowd quickly dispersed as she began to chase after the owner of the finger; all the time gnashing her teeth!

She was jumped and held down by four co-workers before the paramedics came and stretchered her off to the nearest vet.

The third party was brought to a brief but dramatic halt when an exuberant drunk told the CEO what he thought of his leadership, at the bar. When his drunken demands for the CEO to buy him a drink were ignored, the drunk grabbed the CEO by the coat and swung a wild punch. Missing completely, he popped his intervening friend clean in the jaw. After a brief wrestling match, the drunk agreed to go up to his room in the hotel for the remainder of the evening.

It would have been bad enough had he just stayed there. However, there is an interesting phenomenon that can occur to hotel guests when one has fallen victim to the host bar. This is my 'theory of the missing bathroom.'

When the inebriated hotel guest is drunk and passes out on their bed, they will hopefully awake when they need to go to the bathroom. However, they are not fully awake; they are in a drunken stupor and, a bed being a bed, believe they are at home. So if they normally get up in the middle of the night and turn left to go to the bathroom, they will (in their drunken state) turn left in the hotel room.

If they are lucky, they walk into the bathroom, or a closet. When they are not so lucky, they walk out the room door and into the hallway. If they are lucky, they are wearing underwear. When they are not so lucky, they are wearing nothing. As the door locks behind them; they are usually jarred from their drunken stupor to realize their nightmare is just beginning. This particular guest was wearing nothing as his room door slammed behind him.

He decided, quite rightly, that the only way to get back into the room was to get a manager to let him in. Unfortunately for him, he made two fatal errors in judgement about how to find the manager. First, rather than use the phone by the elevator, he decided to go down in the elevator to the desk himself, to blame the manager for being locked out. Second, he got off on the wrong floor.

His timing was sublime. Perhaps three hundred of the five hundred party attendees were making their way from the closing ballroom to the lounge bar as he walked out of the elevator between the rooms. He walked straight out and into the middle of his three hundred co-workers.

There was a sudden silence before a huge roar of approval and laughter filled the bar. Non-plussed, but realizing his error now, he turned and gracefully returned to the elevator and down to the ground floor where a blushing Beverley grabbed a concierge to escort him up to his room.

It was a rugby weekend when the next 'missing bathroom' phenomenon was attributed to a guest making a wrong turn.

I was on the night shift in Room Service, and the Irish were in town: massive drinkers. I didn't mind working Nights during a rugby weekend. It beat the hell out of working behind the bar. The only down side was you were basically bartending to the already incredibly intoxicated until 5am. Two drunks are hard work, two hundred were a nightmare. This night, there were two left in the bar at 5:30am. They had fallen asleep on the couch, but I managed to carefully shake one awake. He knocked over a table with about ten empty glasses on it as he staggered off towards the elevators.

The last one wasn't waking up for anyone. As a last attempt, I slammed the room service door behind me as I walked down the long corridor toward the kitchen to get a shovel and brush to sweep up the broken glass.

On my way back, I rounded the corner beside the room service office to find the last drunk standing before me. His left hand was grabbing huge amounts of nuts and stuffing them in his mouth; his right was leaning high against the closed fridge door as he urinated on it. His eyes remained closed and he continued to shovel peanuts into his mouth as I reached for my walkie-talkie.

"Diego, you better get up here with security. I've got someone standing in room service, pissing all over the place."

I waited as Diego finished his mouthful of ice cream. "Can you repeat that?"

"Diego, someone is standing here pissing all over the room service fridge. Get up here now!"

Diego and Michael walked him back out into the bar where they sat him down and interrogated him. At least, they tried to find out which room he was in. In the end, they couldn't get any information out of him. He had stuffed so many nuts into his mouth, and had so little saliva due to dehydration, that he just chewed and chewed...and chewed. After twenty minutes of chewing and waiting, the police arrived. He couldn't tell anyone his name and his wallet had no ID in it, so they took him to a less comfortable bed for the night.

"I'm not cleaning that up Diego. I don't have time! I've got fifty pre-orders for breakfast at 7am and I have to throw out everything he's just pissed on."

It was pure joy to watch Diego bleaching the entire area. "Cheer up Diego. You should be grateful the guy didn't need a number two. God knows what he would have done if he'd opened the fridge door!"

At least these two gentleman had the decency to make an effort to get to the bathroom. Mr. Shitey-Pants did not.

Mr. Davidson was a regular in the hotel for two weeks every summer. A rep for a large distillery, he was charged with entertaining clients his company flew in from all over the world to watch the Edinburgh Military Tattoo. Mr. Davidson had a group of twenty new people every night. They would stand at the bar for two hours before the Tattoo and return about 10pm. Sometimes they would have a few drinks and be in bed by twelve.

More often than not though, they were up until at least 2am; and he had to stay up until they were ready to go to bed. I used to think this guy had the best job in the world; but after about the third night, you could see the toll the alcohol and sleeplessness was taking on him.

He could have had a juice or pop of course, but Mr. Davidson enjoyed it once he got started. It was the mornings he had a problem with.

"Mike, pot of tea mate…and put the fucking teabags in the pot will ya?" That was his room service call each morning. An hour later he'd call back to order breakfast.

Guests who stay in the hotel for a long time get to know the staff very well. The more personal it is for them, the more they feel like they're at home.

I usually took the tea up and Barbara would take his breakfast up later. That was our arrangement; because Babs refused to take the tea up. I'm not sure if he answered the door naked at his home, but he always did when his tea was brought up. By the time his breakfast was ready, he was usually dressed.

In fact, one morning, he wasn't there at all. Barbara went up with his tray, but when she knocked on the door, there was no answer. A moment later, a housekeeper answered the door. "Babs, look at this," she whispered as Barbara put the tray down on the coffee table.

"Oh my God! That's disgusting," Babs wailed as the housekeeper lifted the sheets.

The elevator doors had barely opened before Wee Blabs was spreading the word. "Mike, he shouldn't be allowed back here. He shat all over the bed!"

And from the time Wee Blabs had finished her shift, everyone knew Mr. Davidson as Mr. Shitey-Pants.

I smiled as he appeared at the bar the next evening to do it all over again. "Bottle of bud Mike…and don't worry about a fucking glass mate."

Of course…they don't all make it to bed either. I was enjoying a quiet night at The Grosvenor as I made my way up to my first floor office. Rounding the first corner halfway up the stairs, my route was suddenly blocked. The body was lying almost entirely upside down. Her feet were on the top step, her head on the bottom landing, but her neck was lying at an impossibly acute angle against the wall.

"Brian, call an ambulance," I yelled down to the front desk.

Brian popped his head up. "What happened?"

"Look at her! Didn't you hear anything?"

"Nothing." Of course not; he'd be too busy selling his toy soldiers on e-bay.

I was too scared to move her because of the angle of her neck. It must be broken! I could get no response from her at all, and could not see or hear her breathing.

The ambulance arrived quickly. They hovered over her for a minute or two, trying to get a response; then one turned to me and asked: "What room number is she in?"

I remembered her checking in. She had come down from Aberdeen to attend a retirement party at a financial institution across the street. "Four hundred nine."

They nodded at each other as one counted out: "One, two, three, go." They hoisted her up quickly and carried her up the stairs as she made some hand gestures and opened one eye now, perhaps involuntarily.

I opened the door and let them in. Squeezing through the door, they dumped her rather unceremoniously on the bed, turned and walked out.

"You're just going to leave her there?"

"She's drunk. As long as she can't get out the room, she'll sleep it off." Without another word, they left.

They were right too. She no doubt awoke only moments before she checked out at the stroke of noon, but I noticed her neck seemed to be almost straight again.

Alcohol was not only the downfall of single over-indulgers. Couples could also provide entertainment for the whole hotel. One couple from Glasgow was always good comedy. They would stay in the hotel every couple of months. I was always alerted to their imminent arrival in the bar by a phone call: "Room 415. Stick a couple of Buds on ice for me; your fridges aren't cold enough." Mr. Sharp was a class 'A' asshole.

He always got his money's worth out of the staff too: being rude; ordering them about and making them listen to jokes that weren't the least bit funny. I'm not sure how much money he had, but after years of serving and working for millionaires, my theory remains: if you have to tell everyone you have money; you probably don't. If you think being rich means treating staff poorly; you probably aren't rich.

During each visit, in order to warn other staff they had returned to the hotel, Concierge called each department to pass the code: "The Weegies are back." 'Weegie' being a derogatory term for a Glaswegian!

But the worst thing about Mr. Sharp was his love for Glasgow Rangers football team. He would always wear the same blue blazer in the bar and talk loudly enough about 'the 'Gers' to piss off everyone within earshot. And he did piss off everyone: staff, guests...but especially his wife!

Mrs. Sharp was rough too. 'Mutton dressed as lamb,' was how most staff referred to her. She was a staunch supporter of Rangers' fierce rivals, Celtic. So after Mr. Asshole had

had a few ice-cold Buds, it was a given that they were going to end up arguing about who supported the better football team.

Their legendary fights did not always end in the bar either. There were always numerous complaints from the bedrooms next to them. I was in the escort party one night as Beverley took two of us to their room as reports of a 'domestic' poured in from adjacent rooms.

We could hear them as soon as the elevator doors opened on their floor. It seems ridiculous to try to creep up to a door while such a racket is going on; they were hardly likely to hear, but sneak up we did.

"Hello, hello we are the boys in blue!" Mr. Weegie sang his team's chant.

"Rubbish, Rubbish, shut yer face! They've never won the European Cup like the famous Glasgow Celtic," Mrs. Weegie shot right back at him, before bursting into her own little song. "Hail, hail, the Celts are here…"

This was getting serious now. How would he respond to her taunt? It didn't take long to find out. He went straight into a rousing rendition of 'the sash my father wore' (Rangers' fans anti-Catholic sectarian song of choice). It really was top entertainment listening to them trying to sing over the top of each other, but Beverley had heard enough. She knocked just as the first crash came.

Wasting no more time now, Bev opened the door and we all stepped in to see Mr. Weegie standing on the bed, swinging his blue blazer around his head like a scarf. Presumably this is what had knocked the lamp over. Mrs. Weegie, green shirt-scarf raised high above her head too, broke into 'You'll never walk alone,' as she didn't see us come in behind her. Who says you can't buy class!

If class could be bought, Angus Reid could have afforded it; although I doubt he would have wanted it. Angus Reid was easily summed up: stinking rich and, more often than not, stinking drunk. Angus Reid was entertainment personified, but it did take me a little while to warm up to him.

"Oh no, Angus Reid's here." Shelly warned me behind the bar.

I looked at the short, rotund man that was making directly for me. "Who's that?" I whispered back.

"He's a pain the arse," she squeezed out before he got within earshot. "Good evening Mr. Reid," she smiled at him and walked away, leaving me to serve him.

"What can I do for you sir?"

"Ah, another bloody American," he gasped in horror.

"Scottish actually, but my accent is Canadian since you're asking," I spat back.

His demeanor warmed instantly. "Good heavens man! Canada! My brother is an MP or something in Canada. A large gin and soda for me my good man; and get that fat little thing over there to bring it to me." He waved a finger in Shelly's general direction as I looked over at her red face.

"What did he say?"

I went about making his drink, chuckling to myself and pretending I didn't hear either of them.

Ten minutes later, he sauntered away from his company and made his way back to the bar. "A glass of champagne my fellow Canadian." In the time it took me to open the bottle, he had turned to the table closest to the bar to endear himself to the four ladies that sat there. "I say! That's a funny looking animal on your head."

He was right of course. This woman was obviously looking for attention wearing a leopard skin hat that was shaped like a boot. I was sure I had seen one similar in a Monty Python film. She would have anticipated the stares from everyone, but not the attention she and her friends were now getting from my new friend. They did their best to ignore him.

Turning to me again, he ordered: "A bottle of champagne for these peasants my good man." They heard that all right; they had to! The 's' in his 'peasantsssss' seemed to hang in the air forever. It was a kind of whistle through the small gap at the front of his teeth.

The toe of the leopard boot turned towards me; the eyes below it glaring at me; waving the bottle of champagne away.

This didn't put off their host in the least however. On the contrary! Pointing at a bottle of Tia Maria behind the bar, he waved it toward him. Reluctantly, I handed it over. Mr. Reid banged it down on their table with great aplomb and wandered off to annoy someone else on the far side of the room. The ladies looked at me in disgust, wondering what they were supposed to do with it. None of them were even drinking Tia Maria!

The bottle remained untouched on their table after they left. I raced around and grabbed it back, replacing it on the shelf. Twenty six shots of Tia Maria were added to Mr. Reid's bill.

Mr. Reid wandered around the hotel with his drinks while his wife sat on the far side of the lounge with another man. They were supposed to be attending a dinner in the ballroom; but I could see Mr. Reid wasn't the type to sit still for long. I kept an eye on him as he wandered into the ballroom and returned fifteen minutes later. Then he made his way through the lounge to the restaurant; ordered a drink, and returned to the lounge again.

"Another glasssssss of champagne my good man," he slurred on his next visit to the bar. Every 's' dragged on forever now. As I poured the bubbly, he reached inside his jacket, and pulled out a solid gold swizzle stick.

"What's that for?" I enquired casually.

"A swizzle stick man! Good heavens, have you never seen a swizzle stick? It gets rid of the bubbles!" Reaching for a cocktail napkin, he put his head down and peered over his glasses, carefully wiping the swizzle stick and returning it to his pocket.

Just then the ballroom doors flew open. The speeches had finished. Most of the guests coming out headed to the bathrooms. A few came to the lounge bar for a drink. Two sidled up to Mr. Reid.

"I take it you didn't like my speech?" one ventured.

Mr. Reid was definitely the worse for wear now. "Tosh! A room full of peasants man!" Mr. Reid then made a 'shh' gesture with a finger over his lips, before stumbling away.

What the packed ballroom had witnessed inside was Mr. Reid's loud entrance to the room as the orator was being introduced. He took a seat for a few moments; decided he didn't like the company at his table; got up and left. Even with five hundred people in the room, a whispered: "Such nonsense! Poppycock and tosh!" can travel quite far when they are all quiet. As far as the stage itself apparently.

The speech giver was obviously not amused. They were grumbling about him at the bar now.

"Why was he invited?" I asked. It seemed obvious he didn't like anyone there and didn't want to be there.

They looked at each other and took a sip of their whisky before the other gritted his teeth. "He owns the company," he replied. With that they turned and headed back to the ballroom.

I later found out, he didn't just own one company. Mr. Reid owned several large companies, and had recently sold three others. Multi-millionaire!

His night wasn't over either. He was only just starting to enjoy himself, walking around making suggestive and insulting comments to almost every table. In fairness, he had to keep walking…when he stopped, he would almost topple over. His red face would stare at the floor as he rocked back and forth on his shoes: toe to heel. Shelly walked beside him for the next ninety minutes trying to keep him away from other guests.

It was approaching midnight when a young Spanish couple came down to the lounge. Most of the other guests in the lounge had left by this time, having had enough of him. He was onto them the moment they sat at the closest table to the bar.

Mr. Reid leaned heavily on the bar now, directly across from them. He waved his hands magically in the air: "A bottle of champagne for my Spanish amigas!"

I don't think they were too sure what he was ordering for them, but they clearly didn't want anything from him…other than to be left alone. That they were not going to get! And they figured it out pretty fast too.

After one minute of arguing: 'yes champagne, no champagne' they got up and walked back towards the elevators.

As a parting gesture, Mr. Reid decided to show off his knowledge of Spanish phrases. With both hands held up triumphantly in the air, he exclaimed: "Buenos Aires!"

With nobody left in the lounge to annoy or chase away, it was nearing time for Mr. Reid to go. He made a gesture for the bill, his words almost completely unintelligible now. I printed it for him and pushed it across the bar with a pen.

He lowered his nose and tried to focus on the bill as he slowly rocked from heel to toe. Reaching inside his coat for another pocket, he brought forth his own pen; the quality of the hotels' obviously below his usual standard. With a swooping motion the pen managed to make contact with the bill on the third attempt and form some sort of squiggle. Good enough.

Good enough for me anyway. I wrote 'Angus Reid' at the top of the bill and went to file it away when Shelly stepped in. "You can't sign it Mr. Reid. You don't have an account here." I blew out a sigh. Was this night never going to end?

He completely ignored her. "My chauffeur boy! My chauffeur!" He was looking at Shelly, but talking to me.

Shelly, sensing she had the upper hand of sobriety now, tried to throw her Supervisor's weight around. "Mr. Reid. You have to pay cash; you don't have an account."

"Tosh!" was all he said, but he reached inside his magician's coat to produce a wallet now. He pulled out a £20 note, crumpled it up as tight as he could and threw it across the bar at me. Shelly crossed her hands in front of her. Another £20 note appeared. It too was crumpled. This one he dropped on Shelly's toe as he walked straight past her.

She picked up the £20 and stormed off past the bar. "Wanker!"

"That's not going to cover his bill," I reminded her.

"It's not supposed to. That's how the little wanker tips every time. You have to pick it up off the floor!"

I chuckled as he weaved towards the stairs. "Hey Shelly, how do I get his chauffeur?"

"He's sitting with his wife over there."

The chauffeur, overhearing me, jumped up and doffed his hat. He grabbed Mr. Reid's arm to ensure he didn't roll down the wide staircase. Feeling partially responsible for his current state, I offered to walk him down while the chauffeur brought the car around.

"No thanks, it's right at the entrance," he replied.

He was spot on. I looked out the revolving doors halfway down the staircase. A blue Jaguar was almost blocking the entrance doors. He had driven right up onto the entrance walkway which was about forty feet from the drop-off driveway.

I mouthed at Wayne who was watching from the safety of the Concierge desk: "Is he allowed to park there?"

He shrugged his shoulders and smirked.

Whether or not it was permitted, and despite the numerous complaints, it was to be the norm. And with good reason too. On his next visit, Mr. Reid had to be picked up and carried down the grand staircase on the shoulders of Ken Ancram, the F&B Manager, and a few quickly chosen Concierge. He remained completely parallel to the floor on his ceremonious journey from the lounge to the back seat of the Jag. It looked like a funeral procession. All that was missing was the box!

They didn't want to be looking around the parking lot with that weight on their shoulders. The front door of the hotel opened as the back door of his final resting place, the Jag, did the same. The pallbearers lowered him, slid him in and said their final goodbyes.

Several months later, Mr. Reid appeared to make a miraculous, if brief, recovery. It was another dinner in the ballroom that he didn't want to attend. On this occasion though, he was not the only one carried down the staircase.

I have never seen a contract between Mr. Reid and his chauffeur but I'm sure there was a breach of contract somewhere on this night: something to do with a 'drinking on the job' clause perhaps.

The chauffeur was smashed. At least there was no danger of him drinking and driving. He was the first one stretchered into the Jag.

A bloodied Mr. Reid was spotted an hour later, stumbling beside the bathrooms. Someone had popped him a good one when there were no witnesses about. It could have been any number of people he had insulted on any given night. But he had a good cut now, right on the bridge of his nose, where his eyeglasses once rested.

Mr. Reid was soon propped up beside his paralytic driver an hour later. Now we had a problem: nobody knew what to do with the car. It couldn't be left there until the morning!

It was the F&B Manager to the rescue. Ken agreed to drive him home, albeit before he found out where Mr. Reid lived: Perth. At least an hour from Edinburgh…even in a brand new Jag!

Ken was as good as his word though, and even stayed at the Reid mansion overnight.

After each Reid visit, I was paid a visit by Accounts. This time was no different. "Angus Reid does not have an account with us. He can't just sign his bill!"

We went through the same routine each time: "What do you do with his bill then?"

"We send him an invoice."

"Does he pay it?"

"Yes, but that's not the point. He hasn't set up an account with us! You have to tell him to set up an account with us before he signs another one."

Usually I countered this with: "Have you ever met Angus Reid? Nobody is going to tell him anything. He does what he likes and nobody is telling him otherwise."

Usually, it ended there and the accounts rep du jour, would storm off to start on the invoice. This time however, the etiquette was broken. This time they added: "…or you're going to be paying his bill!"

This was personal. I said nothing and went down to see Ken about this. "Come in," he called.

A semi-conscious chauffeur had just delivered him back to the hotel. Ken kept his back to me as I related my accounts problem to him, pinning something up on his wall.

As I finished my griping he turned and sat, grinning at his wall. I looked up to see what he was admiring. There, dangling from a blue pin, was a pair of eyeglasses. They were bent very acutely at the bridge and one lens was missing. "Angus Reid's?" I laughed.

He smiled and nodded: "I found them in the bathroom after I heard the he'd been popped." And there they remained, in the F&B Manager's Office, for as long as Ken did.

"Don't worry about Accounts, I'll speak to them," he reassured me.

I never heard from Accounts again about Mr. Reid's bills. Mr. Reid's alcohol consumption, not to mention the company dinners he brought with him, were worth hundreds of thousands to the hotel. No F&B Manager was going to let that go to pot because Accounts felt belittled by Mr. Reid's refusal to beg them for an account.

Money leads people to do a lot of things in a hotel they would probably never attempt in the real world. It was a good thing Mr. Reid never bumped into 'The Tranny' on one of his visits. That would have been interesting.

I hated The Tranny. It was a test of professionalism in the extreme. I was sure I was going to blow it one day. Although it was always the same routine, it was a shock every time.

The client was a regular guest at the hotel: a financial advisor with a very large and well-respected firm. He would sit in his suit at the table closest to the bar and order a brandy...Martell Cordon Bleu. So far; so good. Minutes after receiving his brandy, The Tranny would join him at their table for two.

The first time I saw it I panicked. It was a 'he,' no doubt about it. I watched and tried to look away as it approached the bar, but I couldn't. It had obviously shaved early in the morning; a shadow beard was growing back. Its thick red lipstick was perfectly applied to the lips, complementing the pin-striped, knee-length dress and high heeled shoes.

I gasped a sigh of relief as it sat just before it reached the bar. Now I knew for sure. It obviously hadn't had 'the operation.' I could see the crotch in his dress. I looked in vain as every server in the lounge seemed to disappear. The Tranny and Co. waved me over.

I tried to keep my cool as I approached. I knew I wouldn't laugh…I was too scared! Before I could ask, The Tranny's huge adam's apple bobbed up and down: "I'll have an Armagnac.' If you closed your eyes, you'd have sworn it was Barry White.

They kept entirely to themselves; sitting very happily for a couple of drinks before heading off towards the elevators, amid many funny looks from others. They were a difficult couple to figure out. Was he trying to pretend he was a woman? I didn't think so. He would have at least shaved. Probably just a cross-dresser we all agreed in the end, but it was very uncomfortable serving them.

There was no mistaking what Mr. Barnes was after though. I was bartending one night when Mr. Barnes sat at the bar. I had been getting quite chatty with a gorgeous blonde at the bar, maybe five years older than me. She was asking pretty leading questions: where do you live? Do you have a girlfriend? How much money do you make?

That all changed as soon as Mr. Barnes sat beside her. I thought he was blind at first; his hands worked her over like he was feeling for a ripe avocado. He certainly wasn't blind though; his eyesight was obviously pretty good. Hers was much more suspect. She was ignoring me completely now for this fat grocery inspector. He must have been twenty years older too.

Then the penny dropped. He was wearing a ring; she wasn't. She was a pro! She had been asking me questions to see if I was a potential client! I felt like an idiot. She was totally focused on her paying customer now, who was equally enamored.

They sat at the bar for quite a few hours before they disappeared upstairs. She turned out to be quite a frequent guest at the bar; about as frequent as Mr. Barnes, coincidentally. I became pretty good friends with Mr. Barnes' paid mistress, in a professional manner of speaking (my profession at least). She would always arrive early and sit at the bar to chat with me for thirty minutes before Mr. Barnes would arrive; and then she would forget about me again.

Then one day, they didn't sit at the bar. They sat on the far side of the lounge, close to the elevator. It must have been some sort of anniversary for them; they were drinking a bottle of champagne.

They were clinking glasses as another couple strolled through the bar and did a double take at him. They stopped, looked again, and then continued walking away. Even from the bar, I could see the sheer panic in his eyes. For a man his weight, his leap out of the deep lounge chair was nothing short of breathtaking.

He quickly drew a few things from his pocket, emptied them onto the table and ran after the couple. His mistress grabbed the contents from his pocket, the champagne bucket and glasses, and disappeared in the elevators.

Mr. Barnes stood talking to the couple for a few minutes before the three of them returned and took a seat at the bar. It must have been hot in that corner where they'd been talking, Mr. Barnes was not only sweating, he was very thirsty.

"I still can't believe it myself," he explained to his friends. Well, his wife's friends actually. The real Mrs. Barnes' friends were celebrating their own anniversary in the shape of a get-away weekend in Edinburgh. She had told them where her husband was staying on business. Mrs. Barnes suggested they try to surprise him in the bar, as he gets lonely on his many business trips. Mrs. Barnes needn't have worried.

"I had no idea she was a prostitute. She brought a bottle of champagne over and just sat at my table. Well, I thought she worked for the hotel! It's disgraceful that hotels like this allow prostitutes to solicit guests on the premises."

It sounded very weak to me, but the couple both shot me a disgusted glance; they seemed to believe it. The three of them sat at the bar for almost four hours. It was 1am when a very inebriated, but much relieved Mr. Barnes made his way up to join his mistress…who would surely be asleep by now. I was quite sure Mr. Barnes wasn't going to get his money's worth that night, whether he was paying by the hour or not.

I definitely did not condone Mr. Barnes' behavior; that was crossing a thick line. However, strippers were a little different; that seemed more like a little harmless entertainment. At least, so I thought. And so, ten years later, I didn't see a problem when a group of fifteen guests asked me: "Is it okay if we use a banquet room for twenty minutes? We're on a stag and we've arranged for two strippers to come at 6pm tonight. They'll just do a little dance around him, nothing rowdy."

They would be drinking too! "Sure," I said, "but I'll need to be in the room as well. Just in case anything happens, I'll be held responsible." They seemed like a reasonable bunch of guys, not like some of the nutcases you get on stags.

It started out great. They got two beer each and headed jovially into the banquet room. Fourteen chairs were arranged in a semi-circle in the middle of the room; one chair at the front, facing the others. I stood at the entrance door as the first stripper came in dressed as a nurse. She sat the soon-to-be groom down on the lone chair and started her music box. She danced around him for ten minutes, taking off her top briefly for a photo opportunity for the boys. Pretty tame stuff; and I had to admit, very enjoyable entertainment.

The nurse walked out the door as the boys applauded and had a good laugh. The Dominatrix was next. She wore skin-tight leather. Actually, her top looked like it was cutting into her skin! She wasn't smiling like the Nurse either. This one looked like she meant business. I could see the music she started with put a worried look on the best man, who had organized this, it was just a weird screeching noise.

The groom kept up a smile though as the others laughed and cheered. By the end of the first song, she had stripped him down to his boxer shorts as he sat on his chair.

The second song started. Standing him up, she tied his hands together with a rope and reached into her bag, taking out the cat o' nine tails. Silence now, apart from the bizarre sounds squeeling from the boom box, filled the room. Everyone held their breath. Surely it was just for show! She wasn't going to use it?

The first slap was a relatively light one. Relative that is, to the quick series of lashes she threw next. On his back, his chest, his legs! I could see the blood trickling from some of the welts instantly. The groom, visibly shaking, was trying in vain to hold back the tears. I stood watching, like the fourteen others…my mouth open in horror at what was going on.

At last a high pitched yelp seemed to wake them up. Three of them jumped up at once and pushed her away, shouting: "That's enough! Get out of here. Fucking psycho!" Very calmly, she grabbed her music box and walked away quietly. I noticed she had a big grin on her face as she walked past me and out the door.

I ran to the nearest pantry and grabbed a couple of towels for the poor bastard. They were all gathered around him now, apologizing. I had a feeling they would be doing it all again soon…to his bride. It brought about a rather quick end to the stag night out on the town.

The groom, ably assisted by the best man and two others, retired to his bedroom for the remainder of the evening. Their night out ruined, the rest of the group sat in the bar for an hour or two, shaking their heads before they too called it an early night.

Although over indulging can be a major factor in turning regular guests turning into nightmares for staff, it's certainly no guarantee. Sofia didn't drink any alcohol at all. She drank coffee…lots of coffee. And not just any coffee either. It had to be fresh!

"Oh Mike, Mike, oh thank you dahling."

"Good afternoon Sofia." The sweat from my brow dripped onto the table as I tried to wipe it clean. I was breathless.

"Some fresh coffee please dahling."

The rugby crowd, all six hundred that had almost drunk the bar dry, had just collectively headed off to the match. The lounge looked like a bomb site as Sofia swept up the stairs and showed her disgust that her regular table…make that her only table, was not cleared and polished for her royal arrival. She stood at the side of her table; fox coat in hand, waiting for it to be cleaned.

Perhaps a long time ago it was called table number two; but certainly not in my time there. It was known only as Sofia's table.

I wiped the sweat from my brow with my soaked shirt sleeve as I walked away. She was busy fanning her face when I returned with her coffee. "Oh I work so haaaard dahling!" she exclaimed.

Sofia was hard work; she certainly didn't work hard. In fact, she wouldn't know what hard work was. Her daily routine was simple:

9:00am: wake up
10:00am: drive to hotel lounge for coffee and shortbread
11:00am: sauna for sixty minutes
12:30pm: lounge for coffee and shortbread (possibility of a sandwich)

2:00pm: sauna for thirty minutes
3:00pm: lounge for coffee and shortbread
5:00pm: drive home

As far as we could tell, she had never worked a day in her life. So I didn't discount it out of hand when she claimed to have once been in the Greek Royal Family. The hardest job she had now was squeezing her body into the ridiculously tight leather pants she insisted on every day. They were hardly flattering either.

"There you go Sofia: fresh coffee."

She eyed me closely. "Are you sure it's fresh? It came out awfully quickly dahling!"

"It's very fresh Sofia." I got a good look at her skin as I stared her down. Nobody would hazard a guess as to how old she was. She had spent so much time in the sauna over the years that her skin looked like old, worn leather: dry and cracked.

She poured the coffee. This was the signal that I was permitted to leave her presence. I wasted no time and went to brew another pot immediately.

Evan came back before I had even pressed the start button. "Sofia says the coffee's not fresh."

"I'm already on it!" I shouted back at him. "I only brewed it ten minutes ago! How's the shortbread?"

"She didn't say anything about it."

"No, she won't. You need to ask at the same time she sends the coffee back or it's another trip," I advised him. "Can you put the bill down on the table while I bring her another pot?"

I put the pot on the table. "The coffee was very fresh Sofia, but here's a new one for you."

"It didn't taste nice dahling. And Mike, the shortbread…can I get the light shortbread? This is too dark dahling. You know I like the light shortbread."

"Yes Sofia. Sorry Sofia."

She meant 'light colored' shortbread of course, not calorie-light. We bought the shortbread in bulk. It arrived in large boxes, which we emptied into containers in the room service area. Sometimes the box had light colored shortbread; sometimes it was darker. Often you would find both 'types' in the same box. There was absolutely no difference in recipe or taste. Sofia of course, was having none of it.

130

I could hear Evan getting it now as I tried to slip the shortbread in unnoticed. No luck.

"Mike, why do I have two coffees on here?" She waved a finger at the bill, refusing to touch it.

"Well Sofia, the first one you ordered was over two hours ago. I'm sure this is your fifth pot."

"But Mike, I am a regular guest!" She gave up. "Take the bill away. I don't want to see it." We were dismissed with a flick of the back of her hand.

She was chancing her luck, hoping that Evan wasn't aware of the new 'Sofia charging policy.' This time she was out of luck.

The policy had to change. Sofia was drinking about three pots each morning, three in the early afternoon, and two in the late afternoon. At least eight pots a day, not including the ones we had to throw out every time she didn't think it was fresh. With this of course, were countless plates of shortbread. Her total bill for the day was £4.00 for one coffee.

Before Sofia left her table, she waited until a staff member put a 'reserved' sign on it. She never headed to the sauna until it had been secured. When she returned, she therefore insisted that the next coffee was really just a refill. She had been allowed to get away with it once at some point, and it could not be reclaimed now.

I brought it up with Ken one day. Ken didn't like it either. "With regulars like this we'll be bankrupt. Who does that lizard think she is?"

I felt great. Finally someone was going to take some action against this obvious abuse of generosity. Ken hatched his solution out. It sounded good to me.

"Great. I want you to tell her first thing tomorrow. Good thing you brought this up. This is ridiculous!" Ken finished.

"Me?" I was shocked. I didn't expect to be sent to speak to her.

"You're the Bar Manager," he replied calmly to my dazed look. I couldn't argue that.

I knew exactly what was going to happen as I approached Sofia. All eyes were watching me as I tried to explain, not quite in layman's terms, that she was actually costing us more money than she was bringing in; and that because there was no policy, we had to have one. Ken's solution to charge her for a pot every time she left the table for over thirty minutes was not well-received.

She wept. Not just as I spoke; for the rest of the day…and every time I saw her for the rest of the week. She'd curl her feet up at her table and dab at her eyes with a handkerchief every now and again. The staff, while trying to show her some empathy, were clearly enjoying it. Finally some payback for them!

Many times Sofia tried to rush back in forty minutes and claim it was thirty, but nobody gave her the benefit of the doubt. The precise time her leather pants left the couch was whispered around faster than one of Wee Babs' secrets.

Sofia gave me her pitiful 'death wish' look for several weeks, but eventually she came to terms with it. She decided to try to get her money's worth by sending the coffee back every time now. At first, it had only been if the coffee was brought out too quickly: she suspected you were lying. The staff knew it was better just to spend an extra minute in the back listening to Babs' latest and give Sofia the stale coffee that was already brewed. That was never detected! So really, when she sent the coffee back now, she just got the same pot back, topped up with more of the same 'fresh' coffee.

Her distrust had always extended to new staff though. They had to get it right every time, coffee and shortbread, for an entire week before they had earned her trust. Only then, would she not send the coffee back automatically.

I don't know why she would sit there all day. It seemed a pretty sad existence. I suppose that's why she was such a pain: for the attention. She may have imagined she was living the existence of a Greek Royal, holding court in her palace instead of a five star hotel.

The first Royal visitor was usually her daughter. A very somber looking lady in her early thirties, she was always close to tears. Sofia enlightened me a little one day…before the price of her coffee went up. "Her husband left her recently."

You would have thought she wasn't sitting at the table. It wasn't like I had even asked! "Oh, very sorry to hear that," I offered. Feeling like I had been made to intrude, I gave them a few extra pieces of shortbread that morning, the light stuff too.

I could understand the temporary depression, but her demeanor never changed in the next six years. She came in every morning, cried a little through her coffee and left. That's when the bag lady generally arrived.

Had she walked in and sat on her own, I would have asked for the cash up front, had I let her in at all. Her coat probably could have walked in on its own too. It was filthy!

This was Sofia's royal servant; a maid or something. At least sixty, she was very short, maybe five foot three, and plump. I assumed she was picking up the daily shopping for Sofia before joining in for a coffee. Sometimes she arrived before Sofia had returned from the sauna. I could tell she preferred this scenario.

She would drop her two bags at Sofia's table, ask for a glass of tap water, and relax. You can tell when someone is relaxed: their arms clutch the side of the chair, then slowly slide forward. Their feet stretch straight out in front of them, off the ground, until they quickly drop and rest where they fall. They push their back deep into the seat and raise their head skyward until it lolls to one side, and they fall asleep.

While she was snoozing one day, Evan snuck a quick peek in the bags: junk and clothes. "All my worldly possessions are in there," she informed him as she suddenly woke up. Luckily, he was only peering in the tops of them and not rifling through them. "Is my darling Sofia back yet?"

She adored Sofia. She was constantly asking the staff that passed her by: "Isn't Sofia wonderful?" Evan was the only one that dared answer this question.

"Oh yes, she's absolutely wonderful!" he would exclaim loudly. He seemed to believe it too.

Befitting a Royal's attitude toward the hired help, Sofia clearly did not reciprocate this adoration. Instead, Sofia would often fan her hands flamboyantly in front of her nose when her bag-lady trundled off to the bathroom: "Oh, what a smell!" she would shout to anyone passing by.

In fairness, she was probably sleeping on the streets. Sofia wouldn't buy her so much as an occasional coffee, so she would usually just ask for a glass of tap water instead. Occasionally Sofia's kindness did extend to a piece of free shortbread though. No wonder she had such a small entourage!

Only very occasionally did Sofia's husband make a brief appearance. It would always be just before she left for the day. He was a chain smoker who spoke very little English; very little anything actually. About six foot five, with very long arms and a large thick moustache; he was a monster. He looked like the strongman in a circus; all he was missing was the black and white striped vest.

Evan was Sofia's favorite member of staff. Sofia would always pay cash, when she had to part with something, and would usually look for Evan to hand it over to as well. He wasn't bothered that she never tipped, and he never seemed to get annoyed at her sending everything back and demanding so much time from staff. Although I always thought that he didn't so much enjoy it, as put up with it very well.

He was swapping Sofia's dark shortbread for the light shortbread one day when I asked him: "How do you always keep so happy when you're serving her? Doesn't she ever just drive you nuts?"

Evan picked up a piece of light shortbread, held it up high, stuck out his tongue and licked all the way along the bottom of the shortbread finger. "No. Not at all," he chuckled as he put the shortbread on a plate and carried it out to the lounge.

'Surely not,' I thought as I followed him out a moment later. There he was, dropping the plate off with a large smile on his face. He even went back a minute later: "Is that shortbread better for you Sofia?"

"Wonderful dahling! Wonderful!"

Chapter six - The Bradburn Files

There are many trials and tribulations one faces on the long and arduous road to become a Food and beverage Manager. Perhaps the biggest challenge is one's ability to overcome their worst nightmare.

"Hi, I'm Mark…Bradburn. Welcome to the team!"

"Thanks," I replied as I shook the long and bony, almost weightless hand that stretched out to mine.

It was my first day at the hotel and, although I didn't know it at that moment; I had just met my biggest challenge on my journey. Years later, Jane in HR would tell me: 'everyone is someone else's nightmare.' However, eight year's hard time with 'Bradders' as he was most commonly known, nearly put me in another line of work…and on the end of a rope.

I took a good long look at him. Anyone looking at him had to stare, even if only for a few seconds. He was thin; very thin. Soaking wet he would have struggled to tip the scales at a hundred pounds. He had short, black, almost spiky hair; what was left at it at least. But the trademark of Mr. Bradburn was his glasses. The large round frames had tinted lenses…rose tinted aptly enough. He looked like The Fly. In fact, not long after this meeting I mentioned this to a few people and they immediately burst out laughing, nodding their heads. 'The Fly' was to become one of Bradders' many nicknames.

Of course, frames this large needed support; and Bradburn's got more than enough from his absolutely enormous ears. They really were huge. I couldn't help thinking he could be blown down the street if a gust of wind caught him unexpectedly.

Dangling from the top of his shirt was a bow tie that accentuated perfectly the size of his tiny neck. Despite its small size, he certainly managed to stick it out far enough on too many occasions. How many times I would dream of that frail neck; my hands with a firm grip on it!

My first two shifts were spent bartending with Mark as my trainer. This was a stern test of patience right off the bat. I had been used to bartending in a large restaurant and lounge. It was very busy, and I had to be sharp every shift. The Fly was slow...very slow; with equal portions of methodical and pedantic thrown in.

"Okay, now put the ice in the blender and cover it with the lid. Good. Now flick the 'blend' switch. Watch out! It's a bit noisy. Blend it for thirty seconds, pour it in the glass. Perfect. Not quite to the top. That's it, two straws. Good."

There is always one village idiot in every hotel. I took an educated guess that this hotel's was training me. Pre-Bradburn, it had always been my theory that it was more difficult to deal with village idiots if they worked in another department because you had no control over their fate. So I thought it might be a good thing to have this idiot in our camp.

He was speaking to me as if I was a three year old; yet the extent of his knowledge on cocktails wouldn't have challenged a thirteen year old. Some of the serving staff were watching and laughing too. I wondered if the servers were having a laugh at my expense; but soon realized it wasn't only me he spoke to like this. He spoke to everyone in a bizarre, condescending tone. He was trying to be helpful, but he just couldn't sound normal.

The effect was that people thought he was trying to make fun of them. In time, I learned this couldn't have been more wrong. However, staff enjoyed watching to see how much the guest could take before exploding. It didn't always take much.

On my second shift, an American gentleman foolishly sat himself at the bar. "Good evening suh."

After indulging himself in a ten second stare at his bartender, the American remembered what he had come in for. "Yeah, what's a good scotch?"

I cringed. It's never a good idea to ask a self-appointed expert an open question. "Well suh, my personal favorite is the Taliskuh (Talisker) suh. Quite smoky suh, and peaty too. Or if you'd prefuh something a bit lighter suh; pehaps Glenmorangie suh? With a hint of apples and oranges it is really quite nice with just one drop of water suh.

Realizing his error, the American listened patiently for a full five minutes. As Bradders turned to reach for a sixth bottle to show off, the guest seized his opportunity. He stood up to leave, leaned over the bar, and with his face bright red, offered some advice to Bradders: "Get a fucking life!"

Bradders turned and gave me the look that will haunt me to the end of my days. His sad childish, blank stare seemed to say: 'it wasn't my fault.'

This was to become his catch phrase and, I was sure, my epitaph. Every time a question was asked or a complaint came in, Mark would call out: "It wasn't me," before I could finish reading it out. Thus endearing himself further to everyone else present!

The second annoying habit I noticed about Bradders was that whenever he was in the bar, he developed an English accent. He was Scottish, and no self-respecting Scot would ever do this on purpose. I asked him why he never pronounced his 'r's.

"Well, this is a five-star hotel and people expect a certain level of education. So I try to sound like I was in a private school. They all speak with an English accent."

I drew in a long breath and made a mental note: nutter.

The Outlet Manager, Peter, put me a little more at ease halfway through this shift. "Yeah don't worry about him. He mainly restocks the mini bars so you won't see him much. He usually only comes down to cover breaks, or if we're desperate."

The next week was bliss.

It was about eight days later I saw Bradders again. Frosty was giving me a brief overview of how the mini bar system worked. At least, how Frosty thought it worked. Richard Frost could be summed up in three words: young, cheeky and likeable. However, he wasn't giving anyone a run for their money in the 'employee of the year' voting. Nor did he care.

Frosty was not exactly the most productive member of staff. To his credit however, and unlike The Fly, Frosty had learned how to make friends. Concierge were always using rooms that are 'out of order' for one reason or another. Sometimes large groups are departing but don't leave until late in the day. Concierge would put a room 'out of order' and store their baggage in it until they departed. Sometimes there is a big football match on.

I am sure that, in the UK at least, this is the most common delay in concierge service.

Frosty was always being invited out with Concierge. I thought this seemed liked a good gig. After all, they got a lot of perks, including free dinners around town and by-passing the line-ups at clubs. I immediately put out the feelers to join the club. Wayne was the head concierge. We supported the same local football club, so I had an easy in…no 'hazing' necessary. I soon started getting strange, anonymous phone calls from Concierge on weekend afternoons: "Mike, the minibar in room 426 needs checked. They asked for you personally to do it right away." Click.

I took the keys for the minibar trolley and made my way up to 426, expecting to find an empty room. I had to double check the room number I'd written down when I got to the door. It sounded like a carnival going on inside. I knocked. "Minibars."

Wayne opened the door and led me in. Frosty was lying on one bed, Concierge David on the other. Neither of them so much as glanced at me. Wayne quickly took his place again on the floor right in front of the TV. The English FA Cup Final.

"Someone called me to check the minibar here," I mumbled. Nobody was interested. I stood for a minute or two, watching the game. At a break I ventured again: "Someone called me to check the minibar." They looked at each other blankly.

"No," Wayne, the spokesman for the group, went on: "We called you so you could watch the game."

"There is a couple of beers that need replaced though," David piped up, laughing as he held up a can of lager.

I watched for a few minutes, but my conscience got the better of me and I made my way back to the bar.

This was small time for Frosty. It was only months after starting that I received an urgent call to check a minibar in a room. Nobody could find Mr. Frost, who was supposed to be covering minibars that day. I took the spare minibar keys and ran up to the room. I didn't knock. If the guest was waiting at Reception to check in, I figured I shouldn't need to.

I zipped in and kneeled down by the minibar when the bed started to move. I jumped up in panic. "I'm so sorry, I'll come back later sir," I stammered as Frosty's head popped out above the sheets.

"Frosty, what the fuck are you doing? Everyone's been looking for you!"

"I'm really hungover. I needed to crash for a couple of hours man." Rather than show remorse, he glared at me as if I should be apologizing for the intrusion.

"You better move it, someone's supposed to be checking into this room right now."

"Fucking hell man! Concierge said they'd put this room 'out of order' for me. Can't anybody do their bloody job right?" The irony passed him by. He just reached over to the phone. "Reception? Yeah, you can't check anyone into this room, it was supposed to be out of order." Problem solved.

This wasn't a one-off for Frosty either. If he turned up at all, one could fairly regularly find him tucked up in a bed that had departed early, particularly on a Saturday or Sunday morning. Even the Housekeepers covered up for him. They would just leave the room dirty and clean it after he'd had his beauty sleep. Bradders couldn't even have dreamt about what Frosty got away with.

We went looking for Bradders one day. He was leaning forward over the trolley, head down. He turned slowly toward us. "Oh I feel sick," he mumbled.

I tried to contain my laughter as I watched him lurch toward the next door and knock.

"I think I drank too much last night," he continued when suddenly and, obviously unexpectedly, the door opened. "I'm going to be sick," he got out when he realized the door was open. "Oh, sorry suh, uh housekeeping, er room service, I mean minibars suh. Would you like me to replenish your minibar suh?"

All Frosty and I could see was the door close on Bradders' pale face, with no reply from the guest. The tears dripping down our cheeks turned into a river as Bradders put his big lip out for sympathy.

"Bradders you are a fucking numpty!" was all the sympathy Frosty had for him.

Peter didn't do anything about the conduct of Bradders or Frosty. He was having a pretty good time himself and wanted no hassle from anyone. After two years I was promoted to Supervisor. Over the next two years, Bradders applied for the position four times, unsuccessfully. There were five Supervisors in the department and things were running smoothly when Peter broke the news that he was leaving.

We all waited to see who was next in line for the job. Tim Donnelly came out on top. He had been a Banquet Supervisor for a few years, but knew little about the outlets he was taking over. In return, we knew little about him; other than a rumor about his body odor.

Wee Babs was on the case immediately. She cornered me by the laundry room as I arrived for my shift on Tim's first day. "Oh my God, Mike. It's disgusting! Somebody needs to have a word with him. Don't go into the office." She wasn't exactly being covert about it either. People halfway down the corridor were listening.

This was how Wee Babs' grapevine worked. She didn't always whisper in a lot of ears. She had so much gossip that she didn't really have time to. So the really juicy stuff, she shouted out, loud! It served two purposes: a) it saved time whispering in many ears individually; and b) when confronted about gossiping, she could always say: 'I didn't tell so and so anything. They must have been eavesdropping.'

For the poor bugger she chose to 'shout the goss' to though; it made them look like an accomplice. "Babs," I tried to laugh as I walked away, distancing myself from it: "It can't be that bad!"

Woe betide the fool that called Babs on her gossip too! That was a fight that just wasn't worth winning. That's when Babs would run off crying to HR to say you embarrassed her and called her a liar, telling everyone she met on the way there as well obviously.

I had seen a few Managers fall for this trick, and poor Tim was to be no exception. Of course, HR knew Babs was lying each time. But Babs also had the ear of my pal, Samantha in the Executive Office, who at least made out that the GM would hear about the plight of poor, helpless Wee Babs. HR were loathe to tackle this one. Tim would have to play the game.

Wee Babs, for her part, took Sam down a tray of tea and cookies every morning at nine o'clock precisely; no doubt dropping the latest gossip to her at the same time. It wasn't for no reason that Wee Babs was often referred to as 'The Poison Dwarf.'

Tim, rightfully claiming that Babs was too busy at nine o'clock, tried to cut off the morning tea service to Sam. Such foolishness! Tim did not pass HR, but was sent directly to the GM Office for a little reminder of who the GM was...and was told to bring a pot of tea for two down with him for his trouble. I offered to fill the sugar bowl with salt for the bitches. Looking back, it was probably a good thing he declined.

When he returned from his lesson, I was sitting in the office, working on the next schedule. Tim walked past and took off his jacket, draping it over the back of the chair I was sitting on. "I think this coat needs a wash," he casually commented.

He stood outside the office making himself a coffee, as I leaned back in the chair. "How's it going?" I asked.

With his cup in his right hand, he stretched his left hand up and leaned against the doorway, blocking my exit. "Pretty good," he affirmed as he took a sip.

Now I could see the massive rings of sweat on his shirt, but it didn't prepare me for the smell that emanated from them. My stomach turned instantly. I bolted from the chair and under the offending arm in one giant leap. I reached for the large bin under the coffee machine and pulled it out just in time.

When I felt confident I could make it without being sick again, I ran for the safety of the changing rooms underneath us. The hundred or so lockers of clothing offering an ironic solace from the one piece of clothing adorned directly above me.

For a change, Wee Babs was bang on. It really was disgusting.

Never again was I caught in such a vulnerable position. Whenever I heard Tim's voice, I would spring from the office like a salmon.

For months, the staff clawed at me to speak to him about our problem. It was a double edged sword though. Not only was it an uncomfortable conversation to have with your new boss; but it would also rid us of what was, after all, and endless source of comedy.

I approached the Banqueting Manager: "Steve, Tim worked for you for three years. Did you ever notice any BO at times?"

"At times? No. All the time? Yes. A bit stinky in that small office is it?"

"Did you ever say anything to him?"

"No. We'd send him for coffee to get rid of him. Anyway, there's only one of us here at a time, so I didn't have to work with him much. Why don't you just tell him he's a smelly bastard?" he grinned. I had a feeling I'd be wasting my time. Steve was never very helpful.

It was the ironically-monikered 'Fast Eddie' whose badgering eventually prompted me to speak to Jane in HR about Tim. After their quiet chat, Tim spruced up a bit. We put the vomiting incident behind us and became friends.

So it came as a gentle surprise when he told me in private that he was going to promote Bradders to Supervisor. "Are you fucking nuts?"

"Well, he's been in the department for six years and I think he deserves a chance."

'Deserves a chance.' Note it well future F&B Managers! When you hear these words it is HR speaking. I cringed.

"No. He's been doing minibars for six years because he's hopeless down here. Nobody in this department has an ounce of respect for him. And nobody's going to have any respect for you either if you do this! How's he gonna run a shift?"

"He's a tryer," was all Tim could muster as he squirmed uncomfortably. I was careful not to put him under too much pressure at this point, lest he sweat.

Fearing a backlash from staff at me for having any part in the decision, I did make a formal complaint to Jane in HR. Rather predictably, she smiled and regurgitated it for me: "Mike, he's a tryer and he deserves a chance."

"That was good. Tim's lips didn't even budge," I snarled on my way out. As I left I spared a thought for the poor buggers that Bradders beat out. What a disgrace. I should have really called the Samaritans to have them on suicide watch.

A large dose of the ridiculous was added to the Bradders look when he strutted out for his first shift in the black Supervisor's jacket. Obviously he was not on the seamstress' Christmas card list either. His sleeves were about two inches too short. I thought Wee Babs was going to need resuscitated when Jenny eloquently summed it up: "He looks like Lurch."

Unfortunately, many of the younger crowd in the department had to be told who Lurch, of The Addams Family, was. To make it easier for them, he got another nickname: Dracula. His collection of bizarre body piercings ensured this nickname stuck.

Bradders loved it! Much to everyone else's amazement, whenever someone called him this he would show his teeth, put his hands high up in the air and hiss: "I want...to suck...your blood."

Whoever really made the decision to promote him, it was Tim's legacy that took the beating. I wish I had a dime for every time I heard someone say: "Who made that idiot a supervisor?"

Everybody within earshot would let them know: "Tim Donnelly."

After a year of self-imposed torture from Bradders, Tim resigned. I was announced as the replacement a few weeks before Tim left. At his farewell party, I sarcastically thanked Tim for promoting Mr. Bradburn. He turned serious for a minute: "You know, if you just give him a chance, he really is a tryer." Then with a huge laugh that was obviously therapeutic for him, he announced to all: "He's your little project now!"

I laughed. But I knew, sadly, that he was right. I would need to support this idiot now. Publicly at least!

What Tim or HR thought was Supervisor material in Bradders, remains a mystery to everyone else to this day. But I knew if I could get rid of The Fly, this department would not only have the highest morale the hotel had ever seen; I would have a much easier climb up the ladder to the next rung.

My plan was as simple as my antagonist. I would document everything. Dates, times, quotes and my notebook became my weapons of choice.

And thus opened 'The Bradders Files." Not the only Bradders File obviously. "HR's file on him is longer than Charlie Manson's," Tim once told me in disbelief. I guessed Tim, and Peter before him, were not very good prosecutors, since he was still running free. I would sort that out.

As always for HR, every mistake has to be treated as a 'training issue.' Therefore all cock-ups must be treated as a 'training opportunity.' I listed the basic skills a supervisor needed in order to start the re-training process. This was done by examining each of his last few 'training opportunities.'

A Supervisor must be a good listener and must be able to provide feedback effectively. I looked again at Jenny's appraisal and shook my head. 'How on earth could anyone screw this one up?' I wondered.

I had given each of the Supervisors four appraisals to do; except The Fly. He got one: Jenny's.

Jenny had been with us for three years now and was our star employee in the department. She could have been a Supervisor, in fact she was better than most of them. However, she had a fear of authority that held her back at first. When she first joined us, she was so timid that I didn't see her sticking it out. Any time a Supervisor or someone in a position of authority came near, she would literally shake with fear. She would get so nervous that she would drop trays and cups. At all other times, she was nothing short of brilliant.

I finally decided that the only way to get her over her fear was to have her order me about. I would do absolutely nothing unless she asked me to do it. Guests would sit down at tables. Jenny would look at me. I looked at Jenny. Rather than ask for help, she went to all the tables and took all the orders. She would try to do all the work herself until she just couldn't keep up.

Then she cracked. "Can you just take coffee for two to table eighteen?" She was too busy to worry about it now. Shift after shift, she got more comfortable with it and eventually I could hardly keep up with her ordering me around!

She kept all the staff in line and I never had to worry about service when she was on duty. I was proud of my work with Jenny.

Bradders had just gone through the 'Conducting Appraisals' training seminar, and I reviewed with him my expectations: "I want to see all your notes before you go into it and she must have at least twenty four hours notice." I felt I had covered all bases, so it was with no real worry that I asked Bradders to do her appraisal. "Just tell her how wonderful she is." What could go wrong!

A few days later, Jenny came flying through the bar doors. She silently and quickly collected her coffee mug and headed for the exit. "Jenny are you okay?" I asked. She wasn't usually quiet.

"I just had my appraisal," was all she said.

My blood pressure went up slightly. I hadn't seen his notes yet and he hadn't told me when it was happening. "Oh, everything good?" I asked.

"Fine." 'Bang' went the back door and she was gone. I knew it wasn't good.

"Where's Bradburn?" I called out.

Shrugs all around. Thirty minutes later, The Fly strolled sheepishly past the office.

"Mark, you were supposed to tell me when you were doing Jenny's appraisal."

"I couldn't find you."

"What do you mean? You were supposed to give me, and Jenny, twenty-four hours notice. When did you tell her?"

"This morning." The fact that he seemed totally unrepentant was not helping me.

"How did it go?"

"Fine."

"Show me your notes."

"I'll have them typed up tomorrow."

We were interrupted by a phone call. Jenny…crying. She did not want to come in for her shift the next day because: "Mark made me feel useless and worthless." I stared at the ears and glasses across from me, nodding my head and trying to keep my cool.

I eventually convinced her to come in the next morning to talk about it. She brought with her a six-page complaint letter detailing everything he had said in the appraisal. I immediately took the letter to HR. Jane could not believe it any more than I could. She called Bradders down immediately. "Mark, read this," she said handing him the letter. We waited.

When he finally looked up, she continued: "Did you have any idea that this wasn't going well?"

"Well, when she started crying the second time, I kind of…"

"What! Mark, this is your star employee! You made her cry twice during an appraisal that should have been 'outstanding' across the board?" Jane was warming up now, so I sat back and enjoyed it. At least, I tried to. The unnerving thing was that he not only showed no remorse, he looked like he felt he was being picked on. "Do you realize how much effort Mike has put into building Jenny's confidence up? This is a major setback Mark, because of you!" I didn't think Jane had it in her.

No more appraisals for Mr. Bradburn. One more Written Warning in the Bradders Files.

A Supervisor must have a good knowledge of standards, and command enough respect to be able to enforce them. From personal experience, I knew Bradders had reached ground zero on training skills. That didn't stop him from digging though. The day after he had been on a 'train the trainer' seminar, I walked through the lounge. A large bag of candy was lying open on the bar and I could see several staff chewing away.

"Whose candy is this?" I whispered so guests at the bar couldn't hear. Nobody said a word. I don't think they could have…their cheeks puffed out like hamsters. A few eyes wandered in the direction of The Fly though. That was good enough for a conviction.

I picked up the candy, threw it in the garbage bin and pointed Bradders through to the office. "What the hell are you thinking?"

The sad eyes and pouting lips spoke: "I thought it would be a good way to introduce the new girl to the department."

This didn't make sense to me. "You are aware that you are supposed to be enforcing the rule that states nobody eats or drinks in front of house areas?"

"You told me I needed to build some rapport with the staff." This was another classic annoying habit of Bradders: he tried to hang you with your own words.

"I told you to build rapport, not hand out fucking candy!"

No need for Jane on this one. No more training trainees. Written Warning in the Bradders File.

The next entry in The File was 'the case of the missing Louis Thirteen Brandy.' It had taken me a long time to convince Drew in Purchasing that this was a worthwhile investment. The outlay was several thousand pounds for one bottle. I assured him it would be looked after and that the return on investment was worthwhile. It sold in the bar for £150 a shot.

Everyone was under strict instructions that this crystal decanter was not to be touched unless purchased.

Not two days later, I watched in amazement and horror as Bradders took the bottle from the display 'island' in the centre of the bar. Removing the decanter top, he held it across the bar for the guest to smell. The guest was drinking a pint of beer, so I wasn't convinced he had actually enquired about investing in a measure. As I pondered that, the crystal decanter slipped while in the Defendant's care. I froze as the liquid gold flowed from the decanter in slow motion. About £450 worth of brandy was wiped up from the bar in a soggy cloth.

When taken in for questioning, the Defendant blamed the guest for asking the village idiot: "What's that in the expensive-looking decanter up there?" I couldn't give the guest a written warning, so it was another yet another entry in the Bradburn Files.

I didn't dare tell Drew. I had actually forgotten about it until the first day of the next month: inventory day! "Hey, you sold a few King Louis!" he exclaimed. I had to come clean. He was going to notice once he'd done the calculations.

"Fucking numpty!" was all Drew had to say about it. I wasn't sure if it was directed at Bradders, or me for letting the idiot near it. I didn't ask.

Of course, spilling drinks across the bar was hardly a new trick for Bradders. What he couldn't cock-up wasn't worth cocking up! Six-Nations Rugby Day had arrived again. I always looked forward to this for the revenue, but it was three days of sheer hell in the hotel. An average beverage revenue total in the bar on a busy day was maybe £1,000. An average Rugby Day was at least £14,000.

It was torture trying to keep up with these people. Standards went out the window. Rather than wait in the line for another drink, people would order a case of beer at a time over the bar...with a bottle opener. Warm beer too! It didn't have time to hit a cooler. It didn't matter...they would drink anything. We had five staff behind the bar. Two others simply re-stocking. Every hour we would swap roles and give the bartenders a break from the verbal abuse. The stockers would go into the front line of the battle, behind the bar.

This was tough. The bar top was u-shaped and perhaps thirty feet around. From behind the bar, all you could see was a sea of faces, five deep, yelling at you to get their order in next. I tried the 'orderly line' routine. No chance. These were beer-wolves, not our regular five-star crowd. The orders were sometimes twenty drinks long. Large groups would send someone for another round of drinks as soon as the last person returned with one, thus ensuring a steady supply. Pandemonium was King, from 8am until 3am the next morning. It wasn't finished at 3am; just quiet enough to see the carpet in the lounge again.

The only rest was during the actual match itself. Eerily, the lounge emptied only minutes before kick-off. Then, ninety minutes later, the first few drunks returned. Five minutes after this, chaos reigned supreme again.

In all this mayhem, we had one Micros Point of Sale till behind the bar for five people!

It was 8:30am. Bradders had just arrived on duty and the bar was filling up nicely. "Bradders, you start on the stocking duties," I called to him.

Ignoring me perfectly, he took the first order he could find at the bar and started pouring pints. As he reached over the bar to put the first two down, he spilled half of one directly onto the Micros keypad. I stared at Bradders incredulously as a sinking feeling hit my gut.

The screen went blank. I held my breath. 'Okay, don't panic,' I told myself. My extensive IT training kicked in automatically: I turned the power off, then on again.

Nothing.

"Mark, what the fuck!" was all I could get out as my rage and frustration took momentary control.

One totally oblivious set of rose-tinted eyes looked at me bewilderingly through the Elton John-like lenses. I was tempted to turn them black, however I was vaguely aware that every other set of eyes was glued to me, looking for direction: 'what should we do with the wads of cash being thrown at us?' they pleaded.

No use calling IT; they didn't 'do' Saturday's. I grabbed the price list off the wall. "Keep serving, go manual until I get back," I shouted back as I ran off to Accounts. I grabbed every calculator I could find in the Accounts office as the copier made six copies of the price list.

My heart pounded as I returned to the bar. It was five deep now and I could see signs of panic. I called a quick huddle behind the bar. "Okay, grab a calculator and a price list each. Add £3 to any orders five drinks or under. Add £5 to all orders over five drinks, just in case. Guess as close as you can, don't underestimate. Go. Bradburn, you're on re-stocking duty all day. Got it?"

I waded into the front lines without waiting for my obligatory: 'it wasn't me.'

No thanks to Mr. Bradburn, we managed to top £15,000 for the first time ever. I have no idea how much was actually because of the staff 'overcompensating,' but it was an excellent inventory that January!

The only ones not impressed by our great one-day total were Accounts. I overheard Ron in the lunch room on Monday: "Some bastards broke into our office over the weekend and knicked all the calculators!"

The need for Bradders to build up some respect with staff was reaching fever pitch. I had an inkling it may be a hopeless case when everyone fell about laughing each time he told us he had been knocked off his bike again. Bradders rode his bike to work every day. He had now been hit by a car and knocked flying three times. A good excuse for being late, I agreed. Great entertainment for everyone else apparently! Fortunately, I had an alibi on each occasion.

The staff also had a good laugh at his expense on social occasions. Every Friday night, in fact most nights, a large number of hotel staff could be found at the pub right across the street. If Bradders was there impressing anyone with his whisky knowledge, someone was charged with discreetly calling his cell phone. It was too loud to speak on the phone in the pub, so Bradders had to go outside to field the call. Thus allowing whoever he was annoying to escape.

I believe the record in one night was thirteen trips outside before he switched his phone off. Everyone in the pub was in on it and laughed hysterically each time he'd venture outside. After several months, he eventually caught on when the caller, Drew in Purchasing, had had too much to drink.

Anyone receiving this many calls from one number is bound to call them back at some point to ask what's going on. The trick is to turn your ringer off, so they can't hear your phone ringing, answer the call and hang up discreetly. An inebriated Drew put Bradders' return call straight to his voicemail. The gig was up.

A teambuilding event was the next effort to make Bradders seem respectable. At this point, Bradburn was personally eating up close to twenty percent of the hotel's training budget. Quite an investment with no return!

The first teambuilding event was a personality type indicator: Myers-Briggs. I have done many of these personality-type indicators since then. 'Belbin' is a quick and easy one to administer. 'Insights' focuses on personalities as 'colors' so it is less personal and easier for some to accept their 'opportunities.' Myers-Briggs is very detailed, but needs someone very knowledgeable with it to administer it. I have found all of them useful as a teambuilding event and as a management tool. However, this was my first brush with them and it did not fill me with confidence right away.

I was sure Bradder's test would come back 'negative' for personality. Ingo, our F&B Manager, had once suggested that perhaps I had a personality clash with Mark. "Ingo, he doesn't have one to clash with," was my response to that.

Ingo had had no dealings with The Fly himself. Then one day a training opportunity presented itself to Ingo.

I was off one Sunday when our regular pianist called in sick. Rather than call anyone for advice, Bradders decided that he would flip through the 'entertainment' file in the office for a replacement. This file contained letters and brochures from various bands that were available for hire for catering events.

Bradders, in all his wisdom, called a jazz quartet and asked if they could make it on short notice. They could.

They came. They played. They invoiced.

Ingo called me down to the office. He was staring out the window. This was always a bad sign with Ingo. It meant he was too angry to say what he really felt. He normally used the weather as an escape. "Rain. Always it rains here. In Germany it never rains this much." I waited.

Rather than saying anything, he handed me an invoice. "What's this?" I asked. I knew what it was…I just didn't know any more about it than him.

"I am asking you." He stared out the window again.

"I wasn't here last night." He looked at me and didn't need to ask the question. "Mark," I answered.

Ingo snatched at the phone and called him down. We sat in silence until The Fly knocked. He sat across from Ingo's desk as I sat on the side, near the door.

Ingo passed him the invoice. "What's this?"

The Fly's glasses hovered over it for a minute or two. "It's from the band we hired last night."

"We?" Ingo wasted not a word when his face was red.

"Well the pianist called in sick last night, so I called a band in."

"You?"

"Yes."

"Mark, what do we pay the pianist?"

Shrug. The blank stare turned to me. "£80 for three hours a night," I offered.

"Mark, how much is that invoice for?"

I felt like I was watching a cartoon as the adam's apple dropped slowly and then squirmed back up with a loud 'gulp' sound: "£600."

"How did we arrive at that price Mark?"

"I just told them to charge us whatever they normally charge. I got their number from Mike's 'entertainment' file in the office." Mark looked smugly at me now. This was his 'it wasn't my fault' refrain. I sat silently, visualizing my hands around that tiny neck…squeezing.

Ingo's glare woke me up. "That's info on bands for banquet enquiries."

Bradders gulped again. Ingo changed tact and smiled at him. "Mark, you didn't know how much you were paying or how much you were supposed to pay. I just want to know that if this was to happen again, you would not do the same thing again." He was letting Bradders off lightly.

Bradders looked straight at Ingo. "Yes. I would." Was I hearing right? All he had to say was: 'No Ingo. Very sorry Ingo,' and he was off scot-free.

Ingo leaned forward now. "Mark, if this was your business, would you call someone out without knowing how much you could afford or how much they were charging?"

"Yes."

"Mark. You would call someone out to your own business? Your own business Mark…without knowing how much you could afford or how much they were charging?"

Mark did not even blink. "Yes."

This was too much for Ingo. He stood up, pointed at the door and screamed at Mark: "Get out of here."

The door had barely closed when Ingo wiped the saliva from his chin and screamed at me now: "Just get rid of him!"

I waited until he sat and turned a few shades paler. "Ingo, I am trying to! I have him on five final written warnings. Jane keeps telling me they're all for different things, so we can't do it."

He picked up the phone instantly and called Jane for confirmation. Jane confirmed that this was another new 'training opportunity.' Another written warning in the Bradders Files.

I read through my results from my Myers-Briggs test again. It seemed accurate. Very accurate! I was impressed. As we shared our results, one anomaly stood out to me: my result had the same basic result as Bradders'. This couldn't be right!

I was about to demand a recount when Bradders exclaimed from behind me somewhere: "Hey, Mike and I have the same personalities!" We all looked at the instructor, Jane, for the meaning of this.

"No, you have scored in the same four quadrants. But look at your scores Richard, they are really quite extreme, while Mike's are all near the middle; a more moderate range."

Much to my discomfort and everyone else's enjoyment, it didn't stop him going around telling everyone we had the same result. That wasn't the only gossip he was spreading these days either.

It was a generally held opinion that Bradders couldn't find a date with a fistful of pardons in a women's penitentiary. So a great many of us were caught off guard when he broke the news that he was going to be a father.

It was one of those moments, like when Kennedy was shot or when you first saw the planes of 9/11 crashing into the World Trade Centre. I will always remember exactly where I was and what I was doing at that moment.

I was enjoying a rare quiet moment with a latte in the office, working on the next week's schedule. I peeked out as I heard the bar door crash into the wall. Wee Babs almost took my nose off as she rounded the corner. "Oh Mike, Mike! You are not going to believe this one. I can't believe it!" she squealed as her seemingly detached hands flapped wildly at her side.

I'd never seen her so excited. "You got a £20 tip?"

"No, no, no!" If she flapped any faster she would have taken off.

Money and gossip were the only things Wee Babs cared about. Two days after every Christmas, she'd tell me about every gift she received: the item, the giver, and its price. "My aunt got us a new duvet set. £30 at Mark's and Spencer's. But she has a friend that works there. I know she got twenty-five percent off. What a cheeky bitch leaving that label on!" Babs knew the price of everything, and the value of nothing.

Now she had piqued my attention. For once it wasn't money. My mind raced. "What is it?"

"Bradburn. He's going to be a dad!"

My jaw dropped. I was stunned. Jenny, returning from her break, read my mind: "That'll be right! We'll see in eight months," she casually commented and continued through to the bar.

"No," I thought. "Impossible." I tried to picture the poor monster that could have had enough alcohol to drown a small army. Her hangover would be horrific, but nobody deserved that.

Babs was enjoying watching my facial contortion show when she reached for her cleaning rag. "Here he comes," she warned as she assumed her position. If the conversation went long enough, she could wipe through a steel counter until her eavesdropping was done. Totally conspicuous, she cared not a bit.

Babs was our hotel and reigning world champion gossip. What she didn't know, she could make up with breathtaking speed. It was always my take to let her eavesdrop, thereby giving her the real information. She would still make most of it up when 'spreading the goss,' but it was dotted with the occasional fact.

"Did you hear the news?" Bradders grinned from massive ear to massive ear.

"Yes. Congratulations." I meant it too. It was quite an achievement. Unfortunately I hadn't been able to find a bookie that would take the bet, such huge odds involved. It would certainly put a few of them out of business if he could provide DNA proof in a few months time!

We waited. When he finally brought the photo in, there was no doubting it. 'Dumbo' was definitely a chip off the old block. We never got to see him in person though. The mother, in all her sobriety, decided that Bradders' only influence would be a monthly paternity cheque and occasional visiting rights. Bradders seemed happy enough with this.

Of course, even Bradders had his good points. He provided endless entertainment for everyone…even if it did take me a few years to see the funny side of some of these things.

However his main contribution came in the Supervisor role: looking after 'The Dead Thing.'

"Someone at table nineteen wants to speak to the manager," Jenny shouted from the bar door. I put my coat on. I hated this feeling. It's either a wine rep or a complaint when someone asks to see the Manager. Since these days, I have always insisted that staff ask their name and why they want to see me. If it's a wine rep, I'm in a meeting. If it's a complaint, I can think about solutions on my way out there. I grabbed my coat.

As I approached, a small man in a tweed coat stood up from the table. "How do you do sir?" He shook my hand furiously. "I just wanted to make sure it was okay with you."

I took a step backward. He was spitting as he spoke. Not an occasional spit…a steady stream. Disgusted, I took another sharp step back. He stepped forward and continued: "You see, I need to conduct some business around the corner. I want to leave my mother here. She'll be okay and I won't be long. I have ordered her a drink and a sandwich. I'll pay now or when I come back, whatever you like sir."

I looked down, first at my jacket. It was going straight to the dry cleaners when he finished. It was soaked with spit. I felt nauseous already as my glance turned to his mother. If he had told me she was ninety six years old, I would've said it was a conservative guess. She sat in her wheelchair, a shawl draped around her neck and shoulders, staring at me.

As I peeled my eyes away from her, he spat at me again: "So would you like me to pay now or when I come back?"

She wasn't going anywhere fast. "When you come back is fine."

He dawdled off out the door as I looked at his mother again. I thought she was staring at me again, but as I moved in front of the table, I realized she wasn't. She was just staring: straight ahead; not even blinking.

Jenny waited for me to come back to the bar: "Mike, I've got the sandwich and drink for that dead thing, but I honestly can't take it over. She's giving me the creeps."

I couldn't blame her. She was giving me the creeps too! But I took them over and placed them in front of her. She didn't budge. For ninety minutes. I could see other guests staring at her, no doubt wondering if she was dead. I considered briefly pulling the shawl up over the staring eyes and open mouth.

Fearing she'd been abandoned, I breathed a distinct, but short sigh of relief when her doting son returned. I watched in horror as he stuffed the entire sandwich into his mouth and made his way toward me.

He would have talked as long as I could stand there. Most of what he said was unintelligible due to the amount of food in his mouth; and he was soon spraying it onto me. "I will need to come back a few times over the next few months. Who should I ask for?" was all I caught before a piece of something landed on my cheek.

I was nearly sick. "Ask for Michael," was all that I could get out before I had to run into the back. This guy was rivaling Tim's BO in the 'offensive habits' sweepstakes.

From that day on, Jenny would always try to give me the warning to disappear if she saw them first: "Mike, the Dead Thing's here."

If a member of staff ever came in saying someone was here to see 'Michael,' I sent Bradders. Nobody ever called me 'Michael!'

Over the years, I lost count of the number of verbal, written and final written warnings bearing my signature that had been placed in The Bradders Files. I did have him on five final written-warnings at one time though. Surely a record! On three occasions I was sure I had his neck in the noose.

"It isn't technically the same thing," was the company lawyer's opinion on two of these occasions: "Not dismissible." The other time I was doing cartwheels around the HR office until Jane informed me that the year had expired for that one. Written warnings are removed from your file if there are no further violations in one year. I had missed him by eleven days!

The lesson here is easy: don't be over-specific with your documented 'warnings.' Jane had originally opted for specific warnings like 'timekeeping.' If she had stuck to 'general performance,' she could have saved the company millions in compensation for guests and therapy for management.

After I left the hotel, I would drop in now and again to see Wayne and Drew. Bradders was still there. One year in the restaurant; the next year in Banqueting. As far as I know, Bradders is still at the hotel; no doubt challenging other potential F&B Managers.

I thought back to what Jane had told me long ago: 'everyone is someone else's nightmare.' I'd supposed she was right at the time. Now I wasn't so sure. Here was Bradders: everyone's worst nightmare. So that freed up a few thousand people immediately.

Chapter seven - VIP's

To the untrained eye, the Hotel is dotted with hundreds of people carrying out menial little tasks. While it seems obvious that most roles pale in importance to the F&B Manager's, it is imperative for the F&B Manager not to neglect these lower ranks.

Stewarding, Purchasing, IT, even Maintenance; managers of these departments can be vital to the success of the F&B Manager. They are his VIP's: Very Important Pals. Being smaller departments, they are usually cheaper to buy out too. Sometimes as cheap as a cappuccino.

Perhaps the biggest bunch of misfits ever assembled by choice was the stewarding team at The Park.

Old Tommy Dorans was slow. He had to be. A year off with a double by-pass saw to that, but it didn't stop him from smoking two packs a day. He was reliable when he was there though. After Old Tommy, it was all downhill. Although I'm sure he didn't want to admit it, Tommy had a multi-talented son in the department.

Wayne Dorans could start a fight in an empty room. So bars, football matches and hotels were child's play for him.

There were about thirty of us that went to every Scotland football match in Glasgow. The hotel subsidized a bus for us, so it made getting there and back a lot easier. Twenty minutes before the bus would leave the hotel, we'd empty out of our local pub, buy a bottle of pop, empty half of it and top it up with a half litre of vodka. The drivers didn't mind if it was 'concealed.' We'd sing songs on the way there and sleep on the way back. Despite the results, we always had a good laugh.

Why Psycho Wayne, or just 'Psycho' as he was affectionately known, even signed up one day was a complete mystery. He was a devoted supporter of Hearts, one of the two Edinburgh football teams, and given any opportunity, would let you know it. He also made it perfectly clear that he did not care in the slightest about the national team.

Against everyone's advice Concierge Wayne, who organized the bus, allowed Psycho to come along.

We managed to get to Glasgow without too much trouble and headed to the same pub we always went to before the match. As I got closer to the front of the line for a drink, I could hear voices shouting at the back.

After ten minutes of pushing and squeezing, I reached the corner of the bar where the others had gathered. There was Psycho, proudly wearing a Hearts shirt. He had concealed it under his jacket until he got here. I glared at Concierge Wayne: "I thought you spoke to him?"

"I did. Bloody wanker!" Although it was only a gentleman's code and not a hard and fast Law, wearing your club's team colors was not accepted at Scotland matches. Everyone was there to support the national team and this antagonistic display was guaranteed to start trouble.

This was of course, why he had done it. Psycho laughed as the irate eyes bored through him: "What's the matter? Jealous of Scotland's best club mate?" In the squeeze to get out of the pub, someone emptied a beer on him. He was lucky the bottle didn't follow it, but he didn't seem to care in the least.

During the match, Concierge Wayne and I had bumped into a couple of boys from Aberdeen that we had met at a few away matches. As we had a couple of extra seats on the bus, Wayne offered them a ride to Edinburgh, where it would be faster for them to get a train home than in the exodus with 50,000 others.

No prizes for guessing who was last to arrive back at the bus for the journey home.

When he causally strolled aboard, Psycho overheard Wayne and I chatting to our friends about our football clubs, Hibernian and Aberdeen. We weren't two miles from the stadium before he started chirping in comments about Aberdeen supporters and their sexual affinity towards sheep. Our friends turned to see this idiot pointing at his shirt and the matching tattoo on his arm, laughing at them. Wayne and I were used to it; the two Aberdonians tried to ignore it, but Psycho really was relentless.

One of our friends walked back to Wayne's seat to ask him politely to shut up. Old Tommy tried in vain to grab his son's arm to keep him seated, to no avail. As he was approached, Psycho threw a punch. A flurry of punches ensued as the other Aberdonian soon joined in. Psycho came out of it with a beautiful shiner and a ripped shirt as the bus pulled over. Instead of kicking Psycho off the bus, Wayne decided to move him to the back of the bus, where his shouts could more easily be ignored, by the ears they were intended for at least. And shout he did, all the way home.

Only weeks after this, Psycho was kicked out of his beloved Hearts football stadium, for starting a fight in the stands…amongst his own supporters. Even they couldn't stand him!

What any girl could ever have seen in Psycho I could not imagine; but one did. There were two Aussie girls, sisters, working at the hotel on one year visas. Somehow, one had fallen for Psycho. In a surprise move, Wayne decided to move back to Melbourne with her when the visa ran out. It was a shock, but everyone at the hotel was delighted to see the back of him. Alas, it was short lived. He was back working at the hotel in less than ninety days.

The details took a little longer to make it back, but the other sister kept in touch with some staff in the restaurant and e-mailed them eventually. Psycho had been permitted to stay at her parent's house for a month. They kicked him out when he punched their daughter, leaving her with a black eye and several other bruises. Having nowhere to go, he slept in the airport for an entire week until Old Tommy could wire money over for a flight.

Wayne turned the Psycho levels up a few notches now. He shaved his head and rumor had it he had joined a neo-nazi gang. I was enjoying lunch with Jason, the Aussie concierge, one afternoon when the skin-headed Psycho sat on the far side of the lunch room. It was Jason's birthday and he was excited about the big night at the pub he had planned.

Overhearing this, Psycho chipped in again: "Hey, I'm celebrating today too!"

Jason and I looked at each other. I wasn't about to ask, but Jason's morbid curiosity got the better of him. "Okay, celebrating what?"

"The anniversary of Hitler becoming Fuhrer of Germany!"

I checked the date too. He was right.

Psycho usually worked the day shift with Tina. Tina was a psycho of a different sort. Some might describe her as 'a sandwich short of a picnic.' The chefs preferred a different term: half-wit. She was rough around every edge and a king among drama queens.

Greasy Dave, on the PM shift, was not only shagging her, he was telling everyone about it. Of course, Greasy was no catch himself. None of the Stewarding Team looked particularly flattering in the one-piece burgundy overalls, but they seemed to suit Greasy perfectly. I saw him on his day off one day, strolling around downtown in it.

Rounding out the squad was Old Jimmy. He was only a year from retirement when he joined the crew, and it was a surprise that he lasted that long. He was short; about five foot three inches, with short red hair, thick glasses (often taped at the bridge), and half an index finger missing on his right hand. He had a perpetual limp too. It was actually quite comical when he was in a hurry, which wasn't often.

What really cemented this group as a unit was their unilateral disregard for hygiene. So who better to be responsible for all the cleaning and disinfection of F&B areas; and putting out the staff meals?

It was a packed lunch room one day when Tina could be heard screaming down the corridor. No big deal, she often did this. The last time was at the Staff Christmas Party. She had approached Chef Adam and his wife in the middle of dinner to inform Adam's wife that she was sleeping with her husband.

Nothing could have been further from the truth. Adam was cheating alright. But like everyone else in the hotel, Greasy apart, he was disgusted by the thought of Tina. Adam stood up. "Get the fuck out of here you stupid, lying bitch."

That was too much for Tina. As it was my first year in the hotel, I had to work during the event. I had the best view in the house as the ballroom doors flew open. "Waaaaaaaaaaahhhhh," she wailed as she ran down the stairs and away from the hotel.

So it hardly raised an eyebrow when everyone realized it was Tina again. Jane in HR had no choice but to investigate though. As she left, Old Jimmy quickly limped into the staff room, looking a little rattled. Jane popped her nose in a few minutes later, signaling to Old Jimmy. He limped back out again...considerably slower than he had come in.

I eventually got the story from Jane. Old Jimmy had been putting the garbage away. He had loaded up the trolley with garbage bags from the F&B areas and took them to the compactor room by the staff entrance. The smell in the garbage room seemed to have taken on some strange aphrodisiac qualities that overwhelmed poor Jimmy. Tina had walked in to find Old Jimmy behind the compactor with his pecker in his hand, concentrating furiously.

Somehow this had only constituted a final written warning. It seemed to me the definition of gross misconduct! As Jane had told me in extreme confidence, I could only make a silent protest of boycotting the lunch room when Old Jimmy was putting the food out.

I didn't have to keep hush for long though. Tina told the gossip machine and before long Wee Babs had half of the staff verbally agreeing to a boycott of the canteen. Old Jimmy was removed from lunch food duties and restricted to cleaning dishes and removing garbage. Hardly a fall from grace, and he certainly didn't let it bother him.

Between the missing finger and the compactor room incident, he really was the leper of the hotel. He still had one friend though. I overheard Greasy consoling him: "What's the big deal man? It's natural!"

Even a band of morons needs a leader; and Billy was a fitting leader for this bunch. Cappuccino Billy, as Babs called him, was lazy in the extreme. He was six foot tall, with a large red moustache, and a massive beer belly. He was talented too. He could literally fart on demand…and he demanded it a lot.

It always seemed like Billy had a lot of spare time. Few people passed his office because it was suitably isolated in a far corner of the hotel. Every time I passed, there was Billy with his feet up on the desk, next to a cappuccino. He was either on the phone or reclining with a newspaper in his hand.

Jean-Phillipe, the Restaurant Manager, had the closest office to Billy's. He saw first-hand how little work Billy did, and this angered JP. Being French, JP didn't mind telling Billy what he thought of his productivity level. Billy didn't like being called lazy.

JP should have been more careful though. He was correct in assessing that Stewarding have a relatively minor role in the overall success of Food and Beverage. But I knew that only two people had access to all the goods in the hotel: the purchasing controller and the Chief Steward.

Any time there was a large surge in business, for a rugby weekend for example, more supplies were needed for each department: cups, glasses, plates and cutlery. All of these items had to be requisitioned from Billy's storeroom. The department is 'charged' for the requisitions, so it affects their profitability.

I was able to take advantage of this situation simply by offering Billy free cappuccinos. Billy was one of my VIP's. My departments never ran short of anything. This was carefully orchestrated with Babs as my accomplice.

Billy and I would stand outside the room service office sipping cappuccinos. Babs would interrupt to ask me if we had ordered more coffee cups.

"No, I knew we were getting short, but how many do we need?" I would ask.

"Fifty."

'Not bad' I thought. I had actually told her to say forty, knowing she would bump it up when I was in no position to contradict her. I winced towards Billy: "Oooh that's expensive. It's been pretty quiet this month. I don't know if we can afford that."

Billy didn't like to be asked. That was putting him under pressure. He didn't mind offering to help out his friends though. When Babs left, Billy would raise a leg, let one rip and say: "Leave it with me. I'll see what I can do."

What he could do was issue the cups thirty minutes later, and charge them to JP's restaurant.

JP's restaurant on the other hand, was always scrambling. Cups, saucers, cutlery, glasses…you name it. The crockery and cutlery in each department were different styles too, so they couldn't just borrow from another department. At least, they shouldn't have.

Thus began 'The Teaspoon Incident.'

As we filed in for the 9am meeting, it was clear trouble was brewing. Ingo was staring out the window again. "Bloody rain again!" Billy was the last to arrive. As soon as he sat, Ingo held up a teaspoon. "Dorta was in the restaurant last night with two friends. This is what she got with her coffee." We all stared silently at the weapon. It was a lounge teaspoon.

JP wasted no time. "Eengo, we ave no teaspoon. I gave Billy a requisition three days ago and still I ave not got zem!"

Billy did not handle pressure well. His face would go bright red when he was angry, but he would say nothing. He clearly didn't trust himself to keep quiet, so he put a mental zip on his lips. They turned white now as he took the Fifth Amendment.

Ingo spoke for him. "JP, you cannot just go and steal teaspoons from other departments because you need them."

"Me? Eengo, They are not for me. They are for ze guest! What will I do with feefty teaspoon? We ave no teaspoon for ze guest!"

This was JP's lament. He always insisted everything was 'for the guest.' It always worked too. How could any F&B Manager let the guest suffer! He went for the throat now…Billy's: "I keep asking for our order. He's too busy drinking cappuccinos in room service."

Ingo turned to Billy again: "Did you get a requisition?"

No answer. Billy's red face just stared straight ahead and out the window.

"Billy, why didn't you give him his order?" Still no answer. "Billy!" Nothing.

Now it was Ingo's chance to turn various shades of red. JP settled back in his seat, completely satisfied. Ingo waited a few seconds before letting loose: "You are all stealing. I warn you right now: if I find anything in your departments that shouldn't be there, there'll be consequences!"

Ingo eyeballed everyone all the way around the room. "Yes Ingo," everyone whispered. Almost everyone. Billy continued to stare straight ahead.

"Do you understand Billy?" Still nothing. That was it. Ingo stood up and exploded into action: "Billy do you understand anything?"

Billy stood up now too. His fists were clenched as he took two steps towards Ingo. JP and the banqueting tag-team of Steve White and Simon intervened just in time, physically restraining them somehow.

As we took our seats again, Ingo went on: "Well, we were supposed to do our employee satisfaction meeting just now, but I think we'll recess for an hour." With that, he got up and left his office.

When we reconvened, the red mist still hung heavily in the air. Billy was still fixated on the window too. Ingo tried to clear the air. He threw his hands up and brought them down heavily on his desk as he boomed: "We need to relax!"

To say the meeting was unproductive would be an understatement. We all left the meeting with our heads down and our tails between our legs. Billy headed straight to the room service office to let loose his feelings on JP and Ingo. I listened, saying nothing. Wee Babs wanted in on the gossip, she came through with a cappuccino for Billy, to keep him talking here.

Just as he lifted the cup to his lips, Ingo walked past, duly noting JP's comments. "Instead of drinking more cappuccino's Billy, why don't you go and get JP's order."

As soon as Ingo was out of sight, Billy threw his cappuccino down the sink…cup and all. "Bastard!"

Ingo was on the warpath. While Billy went for JP's teaspoons, Ingo sniffed all around room service and the lounge bar for any hidden or 'misplaced' crockery and cutlery.

Finding nothing in my areas, Ingo moved on to the next department. Billy's tight, white lips passed me moments later, on their way to Stewarding along with several boxes of spoons.

He returned five minutes later. His face wasn't red any more. It was purple. He stood by the cutlery bins holding aloft one single teaspoon. There he stayed, perfectly still for a full five seconds. Then the volcano began to erupt.

The head started to shake first, then the teaspoon hand, then the entire body convulsed. The inevitable explosion followed: the spoon was lifted slightly higher before being slammed down into the cutlery bin with enough force for it to bounce three feet back up into the air. A tremendous 'FUUUUCK!' filled the air as the teaspoon landed back in its bin. Billy walked away silently.

Apparently Ingo had found another lounge teaspoon in the restaurant.

It didn't occur to me until many years later. Was this JP planting one to get back at Billy?

Billy's run of bad luck continued for several weeks. It seemed every time he lifted a cappuccino to his lips, Ingo would walk past, glaring. Billy would shake his head in disbelief, throw the coffee down the drain and storm off to his office…presumably to put his feet up and read the paper.

My other VIP did not have the luxury of time on his hands. Drew had been the 'controller' at the hotel for as long as I had been there. Then the Purchasing Manager left and Drew was unveiled as the 'purchasing-controller.' Although he was allowed to hire a 'storeman' who did the daily issuing of goods, Drew's paperwork had effectively doubled.

Every day I had to requisition food and beverage from his 'store.' Whenever I picked up my orders, Drew and his storeman were always drinking and nibbling something. I also knew that he was conducting the inventory count every month, which included his storeroom. Drew wasn't going to have a shortage in his own storeroom, so whatever he was eating or drinking, he was charging to someone else's department. I immediately decided Drew had to be one of my VIP's.

My cunning plan was easily executed. Drew had all the same interests as I did. When others were out socializing on Friday nights, we were often found working late into the evening; scouring bars to sample new beer and wine trends for the benefit of the hotel.

Amazingly, there was no extra pay for this work; although I was rewarded in other ways every so often. There were three separate bars in the hotel. Banquets were responsible for their own. It was quite isolated and as it was not in daily use, it was usually locked. JP's restaurant was responsible for one, and I ran the other, serving room service and the lounge.

On the second day of every month, I would walk past Drew's office at 7am. He always had to pull an all-nighter on the first: inventory day. This was when he was at his most vulnerable. I'd grab him a coffee and knock on his door. "Hey Drew, you look like you need this." I'm sure he just wanted to finish up and go home, but when you work twenty-four hours straight you are easily distracted. He took my bait every time.

No point beating around the bush. "Hey how's my beverage stock result looking?"

"Well, I'm still working on it, but I don't think it's looking too good. Your liquor cost is quite high. Looks like you're missing a couple of bottles."

It was entirely possible that someone stole it, but unlikely. More likely, a server from the restaurant needed a few shots of something that had run out in their bar. What they should do at this point is fill out a 'goods transfer' form and give it to the bar in exchange for the alcohol they need. Drew would then move the cost of the item from the bar to the restaurant.

Each bar had a different color code for their bottles. When it was issued to your department, a sticker with that color was put on the bottle so in theory at least, it couldn't just be taken from one bar and placed in another.

In reality, when the bar and restaurant is full, the server grabs the bottle, yelling: "I'll bring it back with the paperwork later." Later, of course, it is forgotten about in the rush to get out.

Unlike Ingo, Drew didn't go around searching every outlet for the one bottle that may have the wrong colored sticker on it. Drew trusted me.

I shook my head. "Bloody restaurant staff are always stealing from us!"

"I'll tell you what," Drew pushed his chair back and stretched out fully now. "We'll just transfer over a bottle of vodka to him from the bar. He never even tidies his bar up for his inventory count. Fuck him!"

"Cheers Drew. Another coffee?" I made a note to myself here too: make sure my bar is spotless before the count; and get someone to mix up all the bottles in the restaurant bar.

The overall food and beverage inventory results were pretty good. My beverage cost usually came in ahead of budget; JP's was usually under. The trick here is to keep it close and stay under the radar…but err on the side of caution.

Trouble was brewing when Drew was having problems getting a reliable storeman. It was no longer just inventory days when he was pulling all-nighters and it eventually started to take a toll on him. This was bad news. If he went off sick for a while, it might be Drew's boss, Dave Stacker, doing the inventory counts. This wouldn't do.

The news got even worse for me. As I was passing by his office I saw a large bottle of antacid on Drew's desk. I opened the door to find him bent over double, holding his stomach and gasping for breath. I wondered if Billy had just paid him a visit, but the air smelled clean.

"I have an ulcer," he gasped.

After a week, the bottles of Milk of Magnesia were getting bigger. They must've cost him a small fortune. "You should take the Tums antacid tablets," I advised. "That liquid stuff can be really heavy on your stomach. It'll burn a hole right through you."

I wasn't sure if the Milk of Magnesia was going to beverage cost or food cost, but I wasn't taking any chances. If he was charging the hotel for them, at least the tablets would go toward the Chef's food cost!

Like his ulcer, the bottles of Tums got bigger by the week too. At one point there were so many bottles of them in his office, I thought we were going to be handing them out at 'turndown' instead of chocolates.

Stewarding and Purchasing are quite similar in that the advantages that can be gained from them benefit the F&B Manager at work. This is definitely not the case with Maintenance. Making Maintenance a VIP mainly benefits the F&B Manager outside of work.

This was brought home to me long before I ever even dreamed of being a F&B Manager. Gordon, the Chief Engineer at The Park, was also a football fanatic. His brother once played for my local club, Hibernian.

It was a busy day in the lunch room when I first met Gordon. The only seat left was at his table. I asked if he wanted a coffee while I was getting one myself. He shot me a surprised glance, or a suspicious one, but slowly nodded.

We got chatting about football. The big game was coming up this weekend. Hibernian versus Hearts: the Edinburgh derby. I asked if he was going. "Nah. I've got two staff off this weekend. You going?"

I shrugged: "Still can't get tickets. I guess I'll be listening to the radio."

He said nothing else about it for two days. Then he pulled me aside by a boiler room door on the Friday. I didn't recognize the man in the beige overcoat as I approached him. Only when he raised the fedora slightly and gave me a 'pssst,' did I stop.

Carefully looking all around him and down every corridor, he put a finger over his mouth and whispered: "Still looking for tickets for the match tomorrow?"

I nodded.

He reached into the overcoat. I took a step backwards. He produced a slip of paper with a name and directions. I stepped closer. Handing it over, he gave me the instructions: "Arrive at the East entrance, the players entrance, at 1:30pm. No later. Tell them you're with the Ray Party and that Gordon sent you. Wear a tie...and don't tell anyone at the hotel."

I took the note from his hand and stared at it as I nodded again. "Thank you so..." He was gone. He had slipped away through a boiler room door and into the maze, leaving no trail. I looked around to find Babs walking towards me. What had she seen?

"What are you standing here for?" she asked.

"Nothing. I...have to go." My chest was pounding as I left her standing there and raced to my locker to secure the valuable slip of information.

I arrived at the stadium the following day as instructed. I was led into a room where a glass of champagne hit my hand before I could get my coat off. After a three course lunch and a few drinks, I felt more ready for bed than a football match, especially one with the bragging rights to the city at stake.

I had to admit, the box seats were much more comfortable than the cold, crowded stand. Even before kick-off I thought to myself: 'I could get used to this.' And that's when it hit me: how could I get used to this?

Gordon obviously didn't like to get close to people at work. I had to make an effort though. If this was the reward for getting him a coffee, what would I have gotten for a cappuccino!

As it happened, Wee Babs threw a spanner in the works. She developed a crush on Gordon. I was angry; after all, I had spotted him first!

She started to tell people that Gordon was hitting on her. Everyone knew of course that this was nonsense. Gordon had a beautiful wife and unless he needed a garden gnome, would never set eyes on the Poison Dwarf.

Sensing that nobody paid heed to her lies; the lies got bigger. "Mike, he cornered me outside the smoking room and told me he wants to leave his wife for me! What am I going to do?" she exasperated.

It's one thing to spread rumors about other people, but what kind of lunatic spreads rumors about themselves? I had two options. I thought a minute while I played them out.

"Get a good psychiatrist," seemed the appropriate response, but she would take this personally and respond in the form of a sick call the next morning. Not good.

I plumped for option two: "Babs, you better keep that quiet. If he's going to leave his wife, you should stay away from him until it happens. You don't want to be blamed for it."

I felt smug. This would surely end the stupid rumor she was spreading and keep her away from my supply of comp tickets.

It was Drew that woke me up out of my football fantasy the very next morning. I parked the trolley in the storeroom and started loading my food order. "Hey, I heard Gordon's leaving his wife?" It was a question.

"What! Where'd you hear that?"

"Wee Blabs. She said you told her."

I stood there stunned. How had she turned the tables around on me so quickly? If word got out that I was spreading this, A-list seats would be the least of my worries. I had a feeling it was already too late though.

Although it was never confirmed that he heard about the rumor, I never saw Gordon in his trenchcoat again. Babs had evened up the score.

It was easy enough for Gordon to avoid me in this large hotel too; unless he was interviewing. He had to do that in the lounge. I rubbed my hands together each time I saw him walk in with his clipboard and notes. I'd also quickly send Wee Babs on a break to keep her out of the way.

I brewed him extra-fresh coffee for his interview. Gordon spent forty five minutes interviewing a plumber on one occasion. Near the end, I overheard the plumber enquire about the salary. Foolishly, Gordon told him.

The interviewee simply said: "Oh! Is that right?" Then, taking a sip of coffee, he got up and walked straight out the front door. I tried to console Gordon, but it was no use.

The failure rate for maintenance interviews is very high. Tradesmen are paid the same as other staff in hotels…poorly. They could earn much more working on their own. They also have to work hotel shifts: early mornings, late evenings and weekends. So the maintenance staff in hotels are generally either too lazy to work for themselves or so bad at their trade that nobody else will employ them.

The interview procedure for maintenance staff goes like this: the interviewer lures them to the lounge and tries to impress them. Tradesmen are used to coffee in a paper cup, so hopefully fine china will impress them into thinking this is where they come for their breaks.

Then the interviewer tries to 'hard sell' the hotel to the interviewee as quickly as possible. They note all the benefits: subsidized meals, cheap hotel rates when they're on holiday, free coffee…anything he can think of to keep the interviewee quiet in the seat. The interviewer must not allow silences where the interviewee may ask about salary or working hours. For this reason, HR usually interview with them. They must act as a tag-team to shout down their opponent when he looks like he may ask a question.

If the interviewee is allowed to sneak in a question before the half-hour mark, the game is up.

The irony is that so much effort goes into getting maintenance staff, because they are so lazy or inept that everyone except HR and the Chief Engineer wants rid of them. However, it is almost impossible to get rid of them unless there is a death…either theirs or someone else's.

I came to this conclusion one day when a vacuum with a frayed wire was brought to the maintenance office for repair. Stevie fit the hotel maintenance profile perfectly. This pseudo-electrician removed the 'frayed wire' label on the vacuum, wrapped some tape around the wire to hide it and returned it to the Banqueting department.

Judging from the steam coming from Katie's hair as she flew ten feet across the carpet when she plugged it in, Stevie would have been better replacing the wire completely, or using electrical tape instead of masking tape. Katie handed in her notice and returned to Australia as soon as she was discharged from A&E.

Stevie was quickly suspended while an investigation ensued. He got a shock too…the next day when he was sacked. He really was surprised! The judge at his tribunal wasn't surprised though, and agreed that it was not a wrongful dismissal.

Stevie was certainly no 'China,' that was for sure. Several years later, when I started at The Grosvenor, I was told there was only one maintenance man: 'China.' Real name Alan. Nobody knew why he was called China, and he wasn't telling anyone either. But he answered to nothing else.

One maintenance man for a hotel was unthinkable as far as I was concerned. However; I thought: 'This is a smaller hotel. Let's see how it works.'

He was older, in his fifties. Most maintenance guys are in hotels. He was very thin too. I must admit I was worried he wasn't going to be up to the job. "What's your specialty?" I asked.

He chewed his gum as his hands never budged from his hips: "Everything mate. Everything!"

'Here we go! Another know it all,' I thought. But China actually was as good as his word. He did everything, and anything. He was thin, but he was as strong as an ox. This hotel had struck gold.

There were two down sides to China though. First, he obviously couldn't be there all the time. China worked mainly day shifts. When Adam finally threw in the towel at The Nam, I snatched him as Restaurant Manager. Adam would be working mainly evenings, and I would cover his evenings off. Adam and I would have to tackle the maintenance issues when China had gone home.

In theory, we were to call Ian, the Chief Engineer at our sister hotel two miles away, for assistance should any maintenance emergencies arise in China's absence. Our problem was that there was a Grand Canyon between what Ian and I considered an emergency.

When a brick smashed through the restaurant window one evening, I called for help. "Ian? Listen, a bunch of punks just threw a brick through the restaurant window down here!"

"So? What do you want me to do about it?"

Did I have the right number? "Arrange someone to come down and replace the glass; or at least board it up. The restaurant's freezing and there's glass everywhere. We're trying to re-cook twenty main courses to make sure there's no glass in people's food."

"Listen, I've got two engineers off sick and one on holiday. I don't have anybody to send down there."

"What do you suggest I do then?"

"I don't know. Call a glazier."

"You are responsible for this place when China's not here, right?" I gave up and slammed the phone down. He had picked up his office phone on the first ring, so he was hardly being run off his feet up there. We went 'al fresco' for the rest of the evening. As soon as we closed the restaurant, which didn't take too long; guests choosing not to eat in sub-zero temperature, I called SD.

"Steven, someone threw a brick through the restaurant window."

"Jeeeeesus! Were there people eating? Did we have to compensate?" Money was everything to Steven; health and safety a very distant second. "Anybody hurt?"

"Nobody's hurt. Not too much in compensation either. We're probably losing more money in the heating going out the window. "

He cut me off: "Eh? What time did this happen?"

"About two hours ago."

"And you haven't done anything about it? Call the bloody Police. Call Ian and get it boarded up. Do you know how much we pay in gas bills down there?"

It was my turn to cut him off: "Steven, the Police have been already and I called Ian. He said he was too busy to get someone down here."

"Call you back."

"Sorry Mike, I thought you were someone else. You should call me for these things right away. Why didn't you say it was broken?" Ian was standing in front of me now, staring at the window. Whatever Ian had been preoccupied with when I spoke to him had been dropped when Steven Duncan called him. Ian made it down in less than ten minutes of my call to SD. "I know a glazier not far away. He'll be here in five."

My phone rang. Ian held his breath as I answered it. "Hi Steven. Yes, he's here now and he's got someone on the way. Thank you Steven." It was the same every time.

Leaks in the restaurant also did not constitute an emergency in the eyes of Ian, at least until SD was called. Although the sound of the drips did have an eerie, soothing quality for a few minutes, it soon took on all the comfort of a water torture treatment: each drip in the scattered buckets becoming louder and louder. Although some guests turned away as soon as they saw the buckets, some did not. They still wanted to sit and eat around the buckets.

This always amazed me. Some people would rather stand in the line of fire during an emergency than let their coffee go cold. Leaks in this hotel were a monthly occurrence, but the one and only time it happened in The Park, it was a real tsunami.

I tried to remain calm on the phone: "Ingo, you better get up here. There's a lot of water coming into the lounge."

Four ceiling panels had blown out and water was flowing down in a slow, but steady stream. Luckily, all of the leaks were above the walkway that split the lounge in half. We had placed large bins below the panels and they were clearly going to fill in no time.

By the time Ingo reached the top of the stairs, panels were popping out like tic tacs. It was like a waterfall scene in the Serengeti. Ingo put his two hands on his head. "Sheizen!"

Within two minutes, over thirty staff were on the scene. Large bins were arriving from every direction and being thrown under the cascading waterfalls. The fire alarms had been triggered now too. I placed one bin under a torrent of water that was splashing less than three feet from an occupied chair. "Excuse me ladies. I'm afraid I will have to ask you to move outside; the fire alarm is ringing." I had to shout it. They shot me a short, disgusted glare as they packed up their belongings.

Six other tables enjoying their coffee and shortbread had to be asked to move; in the nick of time too. As the last two tables left, a panel blew out directly above me, soaking me from head to toe instantly. That wasn't the only shock either. I thought it was warm water from the splashing, but it was scorching hot.

"Clear the area!" Ingo hollered. Twenty or so of us had remained, trying pathetically to stem the flow. I looked around me now. It now resembled a scene from the Titanic, as we too jumped ship.

Gordon, also soaked and scorched, stood beside me huffing and puffing as the fire engines lined up. "A couple of gaskets blew on the fourth floor. It's draining all the way down to the first available outlet: your lounge." This insurance claim would be over £350,000.

Sensing opportunity, I nodded. "Hey Gordon, big match coming up next week. You going?"

Thank God Ian wasn't on that job! I hated to think what may have constituted an emergency to Ian. It certainly wasn't a leak anyway! Leaks through the ceiling and into guest rooms were so common at The Grosvenor that even I grew to score them off my 'emergency list.'

It was quickly apparent to me that in smaller hotels, the F&B Manager must have some maintenance experience. If he doesn't, he soon will.

"You just eh, take off the thing there and screw it off, right. Yep, and then twist the other thingy off and replace it with the new one. Then seal it and that's you done mate. Call me back in a half hour if you can't get it." The second down side to China was that he wasn't a great trainer.

"Another shower in 306," Brian giggled over the pager. I ran from the restaurant to sort it out. This would be quick. I didn't understand how it was so difficult to turn a shower on and off. The directions were quite clear on the tiled shower wall. I had traveled all over Europe, and apart from one football trip where I fell out of a bathtub (although alcohol did play a minor role), I had never found it difficult to turn a shower on or off. If I didn't get hot water, I kept turning until I did. Yet showing guests how to use a shower is by far the most common function a Duty Manager performs. The Duty Manager should really be re-named the 'Shower Assistant.'

The real hassle with these shower calls wasn't that the guest didn't speak English. Some didn't, but this should hardly be cause to call someone to do it for you. I suggested re-writing the directions: instead of 'turn knob' it should read 'turn, knob.' Then we'd find out if they could read them or not.

The real hassle was that you ended up getting soaked half the time; leaning over and showing them how to turn the tap all the way around. Maybe they didn't want to get wet until they were actually in the shower. Their embarrassment was always obvious when I'd shown them too: "Oh so you turn it all the way around for 'hot.' Got it! Sorry." Nobody had ever asked me to show them again, or wait outside until they were finished so I could turn it off for them.

I paged Brian back now: "What was the tone?"

This was important. Fixing the problem was sometimes easy. Fixing the guest could be another matter completely. You never knew which way it was going to go. Some guests just lost the plot when the first thing went wrong. In that case, it's always best to call them first and let them blow off some steam on the phone before they strangle you in person. I had developed this theory when I walked in to the command centre at The Plaza one morning.

Lisa was holding the phone at arms distance away, trying not to chuckle. Everyone in the room could hear the happy customer on the phone loud and clear: "This fucking thing has ruined my fucking day."

Lisa braved a few words: "Yes sir, the shower is a little tricky…"

She pulled it away from her ear just in time. "A little fucking tricky! A little fucking tricky? This is the worst fucking shower I have ever fucking seen in my fucking life; and my day is totally fucked!"

I checked my watch: 7:35am.

Lisa tried again. "Sir, I am trying to tell you how to turn it…"

"Hang the fuck on!" he interrupted again. We all looked at each other…and waited. If we started laughing, this guy was surely going to jump out a window. When he hadn't returned to the phone within five minutes, we sent up an Engineer, the Security Chief and a First Aider…just in case.

He didn't sound happy on the phone, so I can only imagine he wasn't cheered up by the sight of three staff bursting in to ensure he was enjoying his shower after he had finally figured out how it worked.

"He didn't sound too bothered," Brian replied.

So I made my way confidently up for this call. "Good Evening. I believe you have an issue with the shower?"

I could hear it running, and nearly turned to go away when he nodded. "Yes, it won't turn off."

"No problem." I had had this one before too. They forget which way they turned it on and can't figure out how to turn it off. Idiots!

I opened the door as the steam enveloped me instantly. I could hardly see the shower stall as I groped my way to the tub and got my hand on the knob. Quickly, I rolled up my sleeve and tried to turn it. Nothing. The guest poked his nose in through the doorway. "Yeah, it doesn't seem to be catching anything. I'll need to call our maintenance guy."

"Okay, we're going out for dinner now anyway."

Thank God! That bought me some time. Not much though. I slammed the bathroom door closed as the steam built up in the bedroom, and called China. If this went on too long, the fire alarms would start ringing. It was a race against time.

"China, screw what thingy off and twist where?"

"Under the knob…"

"Okay, how do I get the bloody knob off first?"

"Just get my tool kit from my office."

"Anything else I need from there?"

"Nope."

"Call you back in five minutes. Don't move."

I raced down to reception where China locked his keys up. Brian said nothing as I stood there raking through the key box, dripping wet. Racing around the back of the kitchen, I opened up Pandora's Box and started the search.

I suppose China believed there was a system to where he kept things. If there was, it was oblivious to everyone else. He later told me, he suspected Nights staff were stealing his tools and batteries, so he would hide them; not only to inconvenience them, but to try to catch who it was.

The funniest part about it was that it was more likely China was giving his tools away to guests than anyone stealing them. I had often been in empty rooms, to find a hammer or screwdriver lying on the bed. When I'd give it back to him, he'd say: "Well, I was fixing something when I got called away for something else."

A lot of guests actually called reception to say they'd found a tool in their room. It was an unusual welcome amenity, but no doubt they would find a use for it. I felt like telling them: "Hold on to it, you'll probably need it for something in there!"

A few expletives later, I found the toolkit locked in a cupboard at the back of the office. China's phone was already ringing by the time I opened the door. The sweat was pouring off me again by the time I had the toolkit out by the tub.

"Okay, now unscrew the wee screw under the knob, then twist the knob off," China continued.

I was working nearly blind as the water and sweat streamed down and into my eyes. The water was scorching hot now too, so I had to be careful. I could feel my heart racing as the knob finally twisted off. Something small behind it fell off too, and washed straight down the drain. "Okay China, I got it."

"Right, now be careful: right behind that is a small washer that can fall out. Take that off carefully."

"What? Fuck China! It just washed down the bloody drain. Why didn't you tell me that at the start?"

"Don't worry about it, I'll get some more. Now, the rotor is stripped. Get the pliers and twist the rotor 'til the water stops."

Relief and joy rolled over me in waves as the water slowed to a drip. One last twist and it was done. I reached for the phone. Okay China, that's it off. Now, how do I fix it?"

"You can't. I'll need to replace the rotor and the washer tomorrow. Can't do anything until I get those parts. I need to replace five other ones anyway, so I'll get them first thing in the morning."

"What? You've got five others that have been stripped?"

"No, well, they're stripped, but I haven't changed them yet. But they could go at any time." No sense of urgency whatsoever.

I should have been grateful that only the one went on my shift, but I wasn't. I suggested instead that China conduct a weekly training course with Adam and me. He would show us how to fix something 'imminent' each week, so we had a fifty-fifty chance of resolving the issue ourselves.

It paid off instantly in many ways. I taught China how to be a more effective trainer, and China became the centre of attention for a while. Up until this time he had worked basically on his own. Now we were a small team of three in maintenance really, with China as our leader. He enjoyed it. Adam and I were still no experts when it came to big things like floods, but we could cope with leaks and we could change a toilet seat hinge in thirty seconds flat.

The toilet seats were a pain because it was embarrassing for the guest to call down for. Therefore, they were always angry when you got up there to fix it. The problem was the type of hinge being used. We used plastic because they were cheaper; of course.

That was the Managing Director's way. SD was the tightest man in Scotland. The plastic hinges snapped easily and Adam and I were changing at least one a night; with China doing a couple each day. China had suggested changing the hinges to a ceramic type. SD laughed it away as ludicrous. They were twice the price.

I told China just to order the ceramic ones anyway. Would the Managing Director know if we had spent an extra six dollars per hinge? I doubted it. We changed a few at a time over the next few months; and Adam and I never had to change another toilet seat hinge again. Long-term thinking is essential in the F&B Manager's role; if not the Managing Director's.

China was happy with this change for two reasons. One: he liked to feel like he was saving the company money and therefore doing a good job. Two: he felt he was being listened to. Not by the Managing Director; but by someone who believed in his idea enough to stick his neck on the line by over-ruling the Managing Director.

To China, loyalty was King. I had earned a lot of points with the training and the toilet hinges. It was time to cash in!

"Hey China, do you have a tile cutter I can borrow?"

"Sure, no problem."

"Now, what type of grout should I use for a bathroom?"

He eyed me suspiciously. "Is this for your home?"

"Yeah, it's really expensive to hire someone so I was going to take a crack at it."

His eyes narrowed. "Ever done it before?"

"No. I read a book about it though." This was the crucial line. I had to make it appear like anyone could do his job, without being over-insulting.

China laughed. "Listen, it's not that easy mate. I'm free on Saturday for a few hours. I can do it for you for a few cups of tea."

I laughed last: "Are you sure China?"

"Hey, not just anybody can be a tiler. It's not that easy you know."

Sold: hook, line and sinker.

Of course, this was only job number one. When he arrived on the Saturday, I had bits and pieces of all sorts of other jobs ready to go as well. Every time I asked a question, he'd grab the tool out of my hand and finish the job. He did the tiling and grouting, then some painting, and he finished off with a bit of plumbing: the shower. What else?

Carla inspected the work when he was gone. "That was nice of him."

"No kidding. He saved us a fortune."

"No, I mean to leave you some tools as well."

Sure enough, right in the middle of the bathroom was a beautiful screwdriver and pliers set. No doubt Nights would get the blame for this.

It wouldn't be the last time China popped around on a Saturday to do some work for us. He came out of it quite well too. When the opportunity arose, I voted him 'Employee of the Year' at the hotel. Nights weren't too happy about it, but at the end of the day, when the chips were down, he was faster and cheaper than calling out a plumber.

The IT Guy is a similar animal to the Maintenance Man. The F&B Manager must therefore remember that they have similar needs. But where the Chief Engineer likes to be left alone and remain hidden in their cave; the Maintenance Man and the IT Guy crave attention. Show them the attention they feel they so deserve, and their skills are at your disposal.

With the IT Guy of course, the tricky part is not actually showing that you are interested in the mundane; it is maintaining a certain interest level. If it drops, the attention you receive will drop too. This is called the 'IT Engagement Scale.' It runs backwards from 4.5 - 2.5 (everything in IT counts down).

4.5 – 4.0
If the IT Guy walks past you and asks for directions to room service, you are in this range. Your department is obviously not important to him. You have no chance of receiving any favors, work or personal, from this IT Guy. Try leaving a Geek Monthly magazine on your desk to see if he will ask to borrow it.

3.9 – 3.0
If the IT Guy walks past you admiring only the pen collection in your shirt pocket, you are in this range. He would know your name only from your name badge. The IT Guy may occasionally feel obligated to fix some of the work-related IT issues you have…in his own time. Most staff fall in this range.

2.9 – 2.6
If the IT Guy responds to your e-mails within three days (without follow-up); and mentions your name in a meeting in a positive fashion, you are making great headway. Feel free to start lining up your 'how do I do this at home' enquiries…slowly.

2.5 – 2.499
You will know you are in this range when the IT Guy actively asks you how his IT set-up is working in your department. He trusts you like a father because if there is an issue, you give him time to fix things before others find out about it. You are King of the Geek Squad. IT Guy's services are at your command.

And like the internet itself, the IT Guy's services have no boundaries. They benefit the F&B Manager both at work and at home. They are truly top VIP's.

The good news is that the IT Guy usually lets everyone know who or what's pissing them off. Most people turn a blind eye to it. They have enough on their plate already. Most people don't understand what the geek is talking about anyway; so conversations with the IT Guy focus more on a 'telling' strategy: 'do this' or 'fix that.' They feel left out and become the Loners of the hotel.

To get into the IT Guy's elite list, the F&B Manager should ask them questions. Nothing technical, just the basics: "How's it going? What's the matter now? Who? Why? How much?" Pretty quickly, you will build a profile for communicating with the Hotel Loner. You will know what he likes and dislikes from the stories about what's bothering him each day.

Keep this up for at least four days, and he will soon be seeking your ear again, mistaking you for someone who cares. After a week, he will have made a note of your name and department in an electronic journal somewhere. You have made it.

Now the F&B Manager can slowly start asking questions about IT to feign interest. Keep it work related and simple at first. One slip here and you could be quickly relegated back up the scale. Phones are a good starting point as there are usually few issues with them; but do not mention the phone log…ever.

Beware the phone log. Every IT Guy in every hotel is charged with monitoring your calls. If you happen to spend over ten minutes on a phone, expect a tap on the shoulder from IT.

If you need to make a ten minute call, use someone else's phone. At the Park, I used to use Billy, our Chief Steward's, phone. Extreme caution must be observed when utilizing this technique. Make sure you know the victim's whereabouts at all times. Meetings are tricky. If your victim is in a meeting with Senior Management, they have an alibi and this is not a good time to call. However, if they are in a meeting with anyone else; close their door and dial. Do not lock the door…this is an admission of guilt if caught, and make sure you have an excuse ready in the event of anyone opening the door.

To avoid getting caught, do not tell anyone your important dates. Relative's birthdays are a dead giveaway if others are aware of the date. Even Mother's Day can hold danger. If your family live in another area code, or another country, be creative. Risk a ten minute call only after you have laid some groundwork with either HR or IT…whoever you have a more personal relationship with. Hint that your mother has been sick. Build a little sympathy. They will think twice about a disciplinary with some background information. Even IT has a little empathy once in a while.

You also need to ensure your own phone is covered when you are out of your own office. Rest assured, if someone has been pulled in to HR for an 'IT Policy' chat, they will lash out at anyone. This is natural. They have been violated after all. Do not take this personally. Do take precautions: appoint a watch dog - someone you trust to cover your phone when you are out of the office. This works better if there is a bribe in it for them.

It doesn't have to be much. An extra five minutes for their lunch break can be enough for most. Wee Babs was my watch dog; more like a pit bull really. Even I was scared to use it when she was around.

Unplug the phone. The wall jack is usually in very hard to reach areas, and behind heavy desks. Nobody will want to risk being caught on all fours in someone else's office. They will also never incriminate themselves by asking someone where the phone jack is or for help to move the desk.

Put a sign on the office door: 'Back in five minutes.' Do not put the time of leaving or return on the sign. If they don't know what time you left, they will not risk a ten minute call.

If you have played your cards properly you should get, at the very least, a few days notice in the event your phone extension shows up in an IT report.

When the F&B Manager is confident enough with the phone log, they may progress to blocked web-site surfing. There is no log for this. What gets reported is at the total discretion of the IT Guy. Hotmail is a good one to try out. Most companies block this, but you can get through if you're savvy enough. I always have my excuse ready: "I have a spreadsheet on there from an old workplace. I really needed it." I've never needed to use the excuse, but I always practice saying it before I log on.

The last time I got to this stage, the IT Guy sent me a little test. It was an invite to nominate him for the 'Rockstar IT Guy of the Year.' I had obviously never heard of this competition, and a lot of people were talking about how arrogant he was for sending it out when he hadn't fixed their phones that broke over a week ago. They certainly weren't voting for him.

I did. Quickly too. And it was a good job I did. The web-site sent him a reply with all the names that had nominated him. Others were shaking their heads wondering why they hadn't got their phones replaced, when Rockstar IT Guy was hooking up a new set of speakers for my computer the same day I'd asked about some.

I had made it to the 2.5 – 2.499 range. I'm sure I could have got Dolby Surround Sound hooked up if I had asked.

IT Guys are like computers though. A newer, better model is always coming soon. I had put a lot of time into building this computer and had to make the most of my investment before it was thrown out. I knew the clock was ticking down only three days after he got his 'Rockstar IT Guy' nominee t-shirt.

Suddenly he was arriving late for the nine o'clock meeting. He'd walk into the GM's office: shades on, Starbucks coffee in hand. I shuddered at the sudden show of overconfidence.

"Tomas, I need a new computer at home. Know any good deals on at the moment?"

He peered over his shades at me. "Come back in an hour."

When I returned he had three options. "Well, do they all come with software?"

"Software?" Clearly I had insulted him. "Software? What do you want?"

I handed him the list. "No problem." He handed me a printout of a computer on sale a few blocks away. "Buy this computer here and I'll double the RAM for you. I'll build it here for you in one afternoon!"

He spent most of the next day on it and by his third Starbucks break, it was ready for pick-up. But the service did not stop there. There are always issues with new computers, especially when an IT expert has loaded it up. I didn't know what the hell most of the stuff on it was.

No worries: Super Tomas to the rescue. He gave me his e-mail address to invite him to dial in from his home to fix a few things.

The Chef caught me sneaking out the door with my new computer. I came clean, but asked him to keep it quiet. The next week, Chef was bringing up his own computer for some 'rebuilding.' Chef hadn't laid the groundwork it seemed though.

Several weeks later Chef asked me: "How long did it take for Tomas to build your computer?"

"Half a day," I whispered.

"Bastard! He told me to bring it in for him three weeks ago. He hasn't even taken it out of the box. My wife's going nuts!"

I laughed. "Did you vote for the 'Rockstar IT Guy' thing he sent out?"

I later heard Tomas apologizing to Chef as he collected the still-unopened box from the IT office: "Chef, I just really haven't had the time."

Tomas may have been okay if he had just kept going quietly about whatever he did. Instead, he marched into the GM's office one day and asked for a raise…a large raise. He also asked for some time off as he was about to become a father. He wanted to work from home. The money wasn't forthcoming however and the GM started worrying about his stability.

The problem for the GM was that she didn't have a clue what he did, so she couldn't measure if he was any good at it, or if he was making progress on anything. I didn't see any difference if he was at home or at work. She still wasn't able to tell what he was doing, if anything. To the entire hotel, all he seemed to do was build 'new and improved' internal websites (intranets). Nobody ever used them. Nobody had the time to be honest, but this seemed to be his chief mission.

When she kept asking what he actually did with his time, he would speak in so much technical jargon that she was sure he was making it up. Something had to give.

Finally, Super Tomas was given the six months off, as he requested. On his last day before leave, he was told he would not be getting paid for any of his time off though, and that he was not 'on-call' for emergencies. This was a huge blow for Super Tomas. He wasn't given any time to 'plant' something to go wrong, thereby proving they needed him on-call. All staff were banned from contacting him.

I had done alright out of the bargain. All my IT needs had been satisfied at this stage; in the office and at home, so it was the perfect ending for me. I wasn't even allowed to pay him attention any more. All my bases were covered; and that was the most important part. If he did come back, I would still be in the 2.5 – 2.499 range…and I'd have a new list waiting for my VIP.

Chapter eight – The F&B Team

In order to get to the F&B Manager position, the pilgrim will always have to 'learn the ropes' in the food and beverage outlets. This is the tried and tested method to see if the pilgrim can withstand the rigors of what is to come. Some people do go to college 'management training' courses. I have never seen any of these staff make it in F&B.

Over the years I have taken on many of these wannabes for their practicum work experience. Although it was free labor, I felt I was ripped off every time.

Their significant experience would basically amount to brewing coffee and preparing plates of shortbread and biscuits. Waltzing around the department on their first day, they clearly thought this was beneath them. I surmised that they were expecting to be brought in as supervisors judging by their attitudes. One of them actually said to me once: "I don't need to do this. I'm going to be a Food and Beverage Manager when I graduate."

"Well, every F&B Manager needs to know how to plate the biscuits," I laughed. I didn't waste any more time trying to train any of them up to serve coffee either. From then on, they were all promoted to the coveted position of biscuit-plater for the duration of their term.

I don't know what they were being told in college, but it wasn't humility, or how to serve guests. I could have saved a lot of my time putting a stamp where my comments went after their two weeks: 'poor attitude toward service - would not hire. Might be more suitable for Front Office Division.'

The stark reality is that most F&B Managers have worked their way up through the ranks. The dedicated pilgrim therefore has to distinguish himself from the other F&B staff, in the UK at least. In North America, a server only has to ask HR to join the management team. This is strictly theoretical of course, since no server in North America can reduce their greed for tips long enough to see a long-term future in management. In the UK however, serving tables is seen as, well...subservient. Competition for promotion is fierce.

Since only a few of the staff at The Park were particularly strong candidates, I decided all I had to do was keep my nose clean and not make any mistakes.

Wee Babs had already over-achieved as a Supervisor, so I only had to keep on her good side. This was easier said than done, but she wasn't winning any IQ tests. Every time my birthday rolled around, she'd ask how old I was going to be. The answer was 'twenty-five' for five years running. She never caught on.

Her Room Service side-kick was Mohamed. He was as greedy as Wee Babs, but he was a lot sharper in bringing the money in. Keeping it was a different issue. An Iranian Celtic supporter with a badly-hidden gambling problem, Mo had his own way of doing things.

When Celtic were playing, Mo would bring in his three hundred year old radio and plug it in beside the room service trolleys. He would polish the trolleys for the entire match if he could get away with it. You knew when Celtic were having a bad day though.

I heard the smash from the bar one day and ran through to see what had happened. "Mo, are you okay?"

Mo was walking around in a small circle, red face staring intensely at the ground, where the pile of broken crockery lay.

"Is everything..." Mo shot up a 'stop' hand signal.

'Goal!' the radio declared. Mo lifted a dinner plate and brought it crashing down just in front of his feet. "Fucking Rangers. Fucking penalty bastards!" Celtic had lost on a penalty shot with the last kick of the match. I wondered how much he had lost on his bet.

Mo had a few issues but when it came to service, he could turn on the charm like no other. At the start of each shift he went around every outlet, changing all his bills for coins. I had always wondered why until I helped him carry a couple of trays up to a room one day.

Once entering a guest's room, Mo would bow down low, almost at their knees, and apologize profusely for the delay, regardless of whether it was late or not. Professional it wasn't; but I could see what he was doing. He was maximizing the guest's feeling of superiority, so they would feel sorry for the 'poor little foreign servant.' Mo played the part of Manuel in Fawlty Towers at every delivery.

When he'd set the tray down, he would hand the guest the bill to sign and put his hands in his pockets. That's when the unmistakable jingling started. His two hands worked furiously; they had only seconds to register. It always did.

The guest would sign their name, write their room number; then stop and look at him when they heard the jingle bells. "Can I just put the gratuity on the bill?"

"Of course sir. No problem sir. Our Manager will thank you for that. The Manager thanks you sir."

This wasn't true of course. The tips signed to a guest's room were split between all the Room Service staff, but cash tips were kept to themselves.

The guest, feeling obligated now, normally felt bad for poor Mo. "Hang on, I think I have some change here somewhere."

Mo did alright. I checked his bills several times. Ninety-five percent of the total Room Service tips were signed to the guest's room. Mo had less than thirty percent signed to his rooms. He made a note of all the good tippers too. He would rip the tray from your hand if you grabbed a tray for one of these rooms!

Apart from his gambling, Mo had a reputation for being pretty tight with his money. As he ran around the outlets changing his bills for coins, he would also collect any newspapers that were lying about. At the end of his shift he handed them in to his local fish and chip shop on the way home. Rumor had it he got free fish and chips every Friday in return.

After a few other rumors of frugality had made the rounds, I began to wonder if there was anything Mo wouldn't do for money. I soon found out there was one thing.

I took an order for a bottle for champagne one afternoon. Well aware that champagne orders were always good for at least a five pound tip, Mo hovered over this order like a vulture.

He knocked at the door twice, with no answer. Hearing movement in the room, Mo knocked again.

"Come in," someone called. He opened the door.

Mo took four steps into the room and discovered why they couldn't get to the door. He wasn't sure if he was a little early or a little late with the champagne, so he just apologized for catching them in the middle of their love-making embrace and tried to walk out quickly.

As he put the tray down, the gentleman grinned at him. "Would you like to join us?" he asked.

"No thank you," Mo answered. "I only brought two glasses."

With the help of another couple of colleagues, I cunningly deduced the effect alcohol can play in determining how far someone climbs up the corporate ladder. I found New Year's to be a great separator of F&B Managers and Pretenders in particular.

I dreaded New Year's at The Park. New Year's Eve held the promise of at least a sixteen hour slog, culminating at 2:00am when we had sorted out hotel residents and non-residents from the emptying ballroom.

On one Eve I waited forty-five minutes for a taxi home; stepping back into the return cab at 7:00am. I always marveled at the number of bodies piled high in the bank cash-machine cubicles on New Year's morning. Thirty this morning: the most I'd ever seen.

Giving up on getting a taxi home, groups of revelers would stagger into these make-shift hostels and pass out in front of the door so that nobody (police included) could get in to kick them out of the heated bedroom.

I vaguely felt Wee Babs chewing away at my left ear: "This is bullshit! Why didn't they do more prep for me last night?"

'Wee Nags' would have been a more appropriate name for her. I poured myself a coffee and briefly considered answering: 'They were run off their bloody feet for ten hours solid, that's why.' Deciding instead to conserve my energy, I walked through the ballroom and past the maze of sleeping bodies.

The banquet staff did this every New Year's. By the time they had kicked all the revelers out of the ballroom, cleaned it up and reset it for the NewYear's Brunch, it was close to 5:00am. Most of them just took their uniforms off and crashed out on the sleeping bags they brought until 10:00am; when a well-rested, but hungover Banquet Supervisor would awake them for work again.

I tried to read some of the name badges as I passed them by. This was one of the better games in the hotel: 'fool the Engineer.'

Banquet staff were extremely transient mainly because of the amount of work available. If banqueting was quiet, they got no work; so they looked for other work. When banqueting picked up again, anybody that had applied in the last year was called up and hired instantly. The banquet supervisors then had to get them name badges.

The names were written on a 'name badge form' and handed in to Engineering for engraving. This became a contest to see who could get the funniest names through the system. I could only see a couple of them now: IP Standing; Hugh G Rection; Mike Hock; Mel Noorisht; Hugh Jasse.

If Engineering got suspicious, they would check it out with HR, and the Banquet Supervisor in question got a slap on the wrist. My all-time favourite was 'Gloria Stits.' I had actually caught two of the more 'permanent' banquet girls fighting over it one day. The guests barely ever noticed the names. Even when they did notice, they would usually laugh. They were at the banquet for a good time after all!

Drew was already leaning on the bar as I tiptoed out of the ballroom and into the lounge. Inventory count. Nothing said 'I don't need this job' to me like getting down on my hands and knees to count pop cans and beer bottles after four hours sleep.

Fifteen minutes into the count, Diego called. "Mike, can you come down to the changing rooms please?" I didn't even ask. As I trudged past Wee Nags in Room Service again, I wondered who it was this time.

Diego stood on one side of the shower stall; his ninety pound security guard on the other. I held my breath as he dramatically threw the curtain across for me. Andrew!

Andrew had come from New Zealand for six months, and desperately wanted to experience the Edinburgh Hogmanay party.

He had begged on his knees for the night off; swearing on his life, when prompted, to make it in to work on time. I had to admit, he had been as good as his word. Instead of going home, he had slept in the hotel shower stall.

I stared down at the unconscious huddled mess of jeans, t-shirt and muddied boots. Conscious that the grin on Diego's chops was getting bigger by the second, I walked away.

"You can't just leave him here," he shouted after me.

I turned; brushed past Diego, and turned the shower on. Andrew didn't budge, but it wiped the smile off Diego's face as I squeezed past him again.

Food and Beverage Managers are used to staff getting too drunk to make it in for work. As long as they can get to work, open one eye and throw up only on their breaks; there is no problem.

The reason: staff shortage. Managers have a horrendous time finding staff. You have to be ruthless in this. After all, if you can't cover the shift, you're working it! I was actually banned from a nearby hotel one time for accidentally dropping a business card too many to their staff.

Luckily, the next one I was to steal actually found me. During a refurbishment, a delivery company was bringing in the furniture. I noticed one of the movers reading the 'vacancies' board outside HR on his break. I moved in.

"Hey, ever worked in a hotel?"

"No. I just started this last week. I was stuffing voodoo dolls in a warehouse down by the docks for a few months before this."

Australian accent; this would be easy. They were always broke when they were traveling. When I mentioned 'free meals' his eyes nearly popped out. Two days later, Daniel was Sofia's new shortbread slave in the lounge.

Although he had no experience, he had all the qualifications: two arms and two legs. I had long since removed 'speaks English' from my list of requirements after hiring Jozef.

When Poland was welcomed into the European Community, the UK was immediately inundated with Polish job seekers. In their first year of membership, ninety percent of the job applications the hotel received were from Poles.

A great many had professional qualifications, but the lure of the British currency was very strong. Many of them had left their partners and children behind to earn more money cleaning rooms and serving coffee than they could as Doctors back home. They would send the bulk of their paychecks back home to support their families.

Therefore most of them had two great qualities that the other ten percent, the local applicants, did not. First, their biggest concern at work was not: 'which pub will it be tonight?' Second, because of this, and because they were highly motivated to support their families, they were far more reliable.

There was only one drawback really: language. Jozef spoke very poor English. Luckily for Jozef however, we were very under-staffed when he was interviewed. The problem was going to be slipping him past HR.

"Sally, he's an incredible pointer and I think he can lip-read in English. It might just be a confidence thing!" She shot me a sideways glance as her eyes narrowed to slits. Sally wanted more.

"We'll use him only as a busboy. Very, very little guest contact." I felt like I was groveling to my parents to get a puppy. Sally finally caved in, just like my parents twenty years earlier. After twenty years of hearing about it from my parents, I knew I would have to do a better job of looking after Jozef than I did Spot.

This wasn't going to be easy for Jozef either. At six foot five inches, he closely resembled 'Jaws' from the James Bond films. The tables were around his knees, which would certainly make it hard on his back too. As it turned out, he was an exceptional pointer. He also understood what he needed to fetch when people pointed and mouthed things too.

In time, Jozef learned a few useful phrases from his Scottish co-workers in the staff room. However, when I overheard him reply to a couple of guest enquiries with phrases such as 'fucking right' and 'shit yes,' I decided to keep him on a shorter leash.

Six months later I shook my head in amazement as I watched how professional Jozef appeared, actually taking orders from guests. Not one grunt or 'useful Scottish phrase,' and only an occasional point of a finger.

My parents have never let me forget how I promised to teach Spot tricks if they let me keep her. Other than attacking the cat, Spot did not learn any tricks under my tutelage; mainly because I was too busy playing football and going out with the boys. Spot had been left with my parents more often than not. How I wished my parents were there to see Jozef now. I had certainly taught this one well.

Against such stiff competition, I was somehow able to progress to 'Bar and Room Service Supervisor' fairly rapidly. Now I quickly became aware that I had to beat out the competition of other Supervisors to become 'Bar and Room Service Manager.'

Gary Duncan was the biggest threat. To himself that is. He was a good Supervisor, but his big mouth was as big as his appetite for alcohol. I had kept him out of trouble a few times, but it was inevitable that he would crash spectacularly eventually.

"Mikey! Where's the party?" Gary shouted. I looked at my watch…11:00pm. Gary was plastered. Staff weren't allowed in the hotel sober unless they were working. This was suicidal.

"Gary, get the hell out of here. Diego's just starting and he'll be on his first walkround right now." I grabbed him by the collar and marched him through Room Service, leaving him at the staircase down to the staff exit.

After twenty minutes, I'd heard nothing and began to relax. That's when Diego was on the phone again. "Mike, can you come down to the changing rooms please?" Gary would have left long ago, surely.

I headed for the shower stalls: nobody there. "In here," Diego called. I opened the bathroom doors to see Diego and his sidekick security guard standing over a dead body. It was Gary.

"What the fuck?" was all I could find to say.

"Well, it looks like he was sitting on the toilet, passed out while he was going to the bathroom and fell forward. His head must have smashed against the cubicle door as he flew forward.

I took in the crime scene. Gary was lying face down on the cold, tiled floor. A trickle of blood had dried on his forehead. His arms were splayed down at his sides; pants around his ankles, bare ass staring skyward. It was not a pretty sight.

Amazingly this was only a final written warning. I suppose the real suffering was the embarrassment. It didn't take Gary long to finish himself off after this though.

It was a Friday; another going-away party. Gary was in full-party mode by 7:00pm. Obnoxious, drunk and harassing any female that passed him by. I had finished work at 6:00pm, and walked to the pub with Jane from HR, who had also just finished. By 8:00pm, Gary's excitement was reaching fever pitch. Jane approached him.

"Gary, you're opening at 6:30am tomorrow. Don't you think you should be calling it a night now?"

Perhaps the tone didn't register with him. He glared at her and slammed his pint down on the bar. "Hey, I can handle it," he shouted.

Jane let it go. Not for long though. When he was a complete no-show for work the next day, Gary was not so much reminded of his comments, as told what he had said for the first time. Gary was now out of the way for my next step up the ladder.

When you reach Manager, you don't really compare yourself to other managers, because everyone's role is so different. Your worry is now the Supervisors you just beat out, because every mistake they make reflects on you now.

The lesson is: once you have learned how to beat out the other staff; keep your house in order. Years later, at The Plaza, I learned this the hard way.

As Director of Food and Beverage, I was having problems with my General Manager. She had been on my back for months when we started the interviews for my assistant.

There are two types of Assistant F&B Manager. The first has no experience; just youthful exuberance. Staff don't really respect these managers because they are usually too busy brown-nosing to prove their own worth than helping the staff. Therefore, they aren't able to control the staff.

The second type has lots of experience; but lacks motivation. These people are usually climbing their way down the corporate ladder for one reason or another. It is essential to diagnose which problem you prefer to deal with at the interview stage.

We only had three applicants for the position. The first applicant was type one. The second applicant was doing not too bad until he was asked what he liked to do in his spare time.

"I like to drink," he replied. I don't think he could quite believe he had said it himself. In a pathetic attempt to recover, he stumbled on: "Yeah, I uh, like to have a few drinks." Type two I noted.

Isaac in HR ended the interview fairly abruptly after that.

I pondered which of the two nightmares I would rather deal with when the third applicant walked in and introduced us to an unheard of third type: 'The Dick.'

The Dick arrived for his interview in a spotless black suit. It was, incidentally, the last time anyone would see it clean. He seemed to have both experience and motivation, answering all the questions with a good deal of knowledge; and asking some pretty good questions about the role as well. HR needed to do an official reference check on him before we could offer, but my current assistant knew someone where The Dick had just finished working. When Aaron called his informer, he came back with a one-word reference; The Dick's nickname…Psycho.

This worried me a trifle, and I held my breath until the official reference came in. "He's clean," Isaac smiled. "Should I offer?"

I considered the options briefly before nodding.

During the first few weeks, The Dick was on his best behavior. He was also insincerity personified; referring to me as a 'genius' so many times that I nearly mis-diagnosed him as a serial brown-noser. Rather sadly, this era was altogether short-lived. It was replaced by the real Dick.

The real Dick was lazy and rather unhealthy: a nice sized pot belly hid the belt buckle that held his pants up. It was a shame the belly wasn't large enough to hide the stains on the crotch of his pants. It looked like toothpaste, but I wasn't about to ask. However, when it was still there three days later, I nearly cracked. "For Christ's sake, do you ever wash that bloody suit?"

His suit jacket set an office record of at least three weeks without being cleaned. It was difficult to track exactly how long it actually was because I only started counting when I spotted the stain on the back of the collar.

I thought this particular characteristic was most peculiar because The Dick had expensive tastes when it came to clothing. His suits and ties were all Armani and DKNY. He had champagne taste on a beer salary. Yet, more often than not, these expensive clothes were filthy and badly treated. I would often find crumpled ties and shirts on the floor behind the office door. After weeks of pleading for him to remove them one time, he just picked up the whole lot and threw them in the garbage bin. The dry cleaning was free. All he had to do was stick it in a bag!

The Dick was a chain smoker too, although he was in denial over this. One time he claimed to have stopped smoking completely. When I asked why the sudden change he came clean.

"Well, I was having sex a few weeks ago and I nearly died of a coughing fit right in the middle of it. I had to stop completely and she got pissed off and that was it over."

This wasn't to be Dick's last smoke-related sexual problem either. I knew he had a girlfriend on the horizon when he flat out defied me to schedule him for an evening shift on Valentine's Day. He then suddenly started to show up for work earlier and earlier. Despite his excuses I recognized instantly that it was all a ruse to get off work earlier so he could meet his new belle.

I didn't have a problem with this in principle, however we still needed supervision at night and I wasn't about to let him off the hook until he could admit he had a girlfriend. The Dick struggled with this.

Eventually he broke down though: "I've been seeing her for three weeks now and we still haven't had sex. I'm going crazy. She's the most beautiful girl I've ever met!"

I laughed loudly. 'Beautiful' to Dick meant large breasts. That was all he cared about. She could have two heads and a cleft palate; he wouldn't notice.

Dick's birthday was just after Valentine's Day. He had that night off too. I expected to see him roll in early the next day so he could rendezvous with his beloved again. Much to my surprise, he shot in like a cannon at 3:00pm. The Dick was not happy.

I knew he wasn't happy when I didn't get my handshake. World War Three could be going on around him but when he saw me, his hand would reach out to me with my standard: "Good day Mr. Kelly. How are you today sir?"

I knew he wasn't listening to my response, because he would ask me another three times in the next half hour, but I always liked this quality in The Dick. This had to be serious. "What's wrong Dick?" I asked cautiously.

"Fuck my life!" he exclaimed. This was going to be good. Whenever he started with these three words, it was always good. "Cappuccino sir?"

I nodded as Dick yelled into the corridor: "Two cappuccinos for the office." Two staff members fought over the right the make them. Dick's main duty every Thursday was the staff schedule for the following week. Staff would do anything for him to gain his favor and get the days off they wanted. Controlling the schedule was real power.

As the cappuccinos arrived and the office door closed, the story unfolded: The Dick was taking Belle out for dinner last night. She phoned him before he had left his house: "Pick me up half an hour earlier. I want to give you your birthday present first. Dick did not miss the signal.

He knocked on her door forty five minutes early. To quell his excitement however, he smoked two cigarettes on the way. This was a problem. Belle was very anti-smoking; and was completely unaware of two-pack's habit.

Normally Dick covered up the stench of smoke that surrounded him by showering himself in his cologne. It didn't so much get rid of the smell of smoke, as clear the area of people who were around to smell smoke.

On closer inspection, this 'covering up' technique was an excellent analogy for Dick's life. He would bugger things up spectacularly and then think about how to cover his tracks afterwards.

It was no exaggeration to say that people ran from the office gasping for breath when Dick arrived for work. I made the nearly fatal error of heading for the elevators after his arrival one day. As the doors closed and the odor intensified in the small space, I realized The Dick had just come up in the same elevator.

Belle didn't notice the perfume on this occasion however, because he had forgotten to load the ten-gallon tank of it in his car, no doubt in the excitement. He would have to try to cover it up until they got to dinner.

Belle was not going to make it easy. She opened the door wearing only a two-piece, black lace lingerie set. Dick could catch only a glimpse of the candles glowing like an airport runway along the hallway behind her, no doubt leading to the bedroom, before she threw two arms around him and tried to kiss him.

Panic set in. If she kissed him, he was bound to leave a bad taste in her mouth. He pushed her away instead. It was his only hope. "What's wrong?" she asked sharply.

The Dick was unable to answer without incriminating himself. For the first and certainly only time in his life, The Dick was speechless. How I wished I was there to witness it. Speechless is one thing, but silent he was not. The irony of his position was too much for him. The Dick laughed a nervous laugh.

In her exposed, self-conscious state however, one laugh seemed no different than any other kind of laugh. Belle assumed The Dick was laughing at her. Without warning, she pushed The Dick back with two hands. "You didn't have to go to all this trouble if you didn't like me!" she screamed as the door slammed closed, leaving The Dick exposed now, and alone on the doorstep.

Belle would not open the door for The Beast again. She ignored the doorbell and his phone calls, so he battered her with text messages next. After thirty or so, she responded with a simple and elegant: "I will never speak to you again."

Some may have tried flowers next; others might have waited until she'd calmed down and told her the truth. The Dick didn't. He hit the 'reply' button: "Fuck off you stupid bitch."

He broke from the story and, taking a sip from his cappuccino, looked at me sadly: "I think it's all over now."

I nodded my agreement.

Driving home at breakneck speed after the date, he poured himself a few martinis and stewed. As with any crime of the heart, blame must always be placed elsewhere in order to justify one's actions. The Dick blamed the cigarettes.

Seeing it clearly now, he picked up the two packs in front of him and headed out the door. Heads appeared at windows all along the street to watch the nutcase standing in the middle of their street screaming loudly: "Fucking cigarettes have ruined my life! I will never smoke another fucking cigarette again!" All the time, removing the dastardly cigarettes from their packets and throwing the missiles away in every direction.

The Dick awoke at the crack of ten the next morning. When the hangover had lifted enough, he sheepishly got down on his hands and knees on the grass outside. Not daring to look up at the windows around him, he scoured the area to retrieve as many of the missiles as he could find.

Two weeks after this, The Dick was again claiming to be going 'cold turkey.' I asked him for a ride to the liquor store to pick up some wine for a last-minute function. "Sure, just let me clean up the car a bit. I'll come back up for you in five minutes."

Thirty minutes later he returned. The car was absolutely filthy. I opened the door and reached for the shirt on the passenger's seat. "No," he insisted. "You'd better sit on that." What he'd been cleaning for thirty minutes was a complete mystery to me. Although, it smelled suspiciously of cigarettes, I couldn't see any evidence.

The following afternoon, I parked next to his car in the parkade. As I got out, I couldn't help but peer in the window. On the passenger seat I counted eleven cigarette packs.

This fine physical specimen nearly paid a heavy price for his two packs a day habit and his zero-tolerance attitude towards exercise. A teambuilding event had been scheduled for 5:00pm one Wednesday evening. Teambuilding events are scheduled precisely four weeks after HR tells the GM that team morale has hit rock bottom. The GM would never notice this on their own of course…their world of champagne receptions being just fine.

We had all been told to 'dress for the weather.' I, and everyone else, judging by their attire, assumed this was going to be an outdoor event. It wasn't just raining outside, it was bordering on a monsoon. Dick showed up, ten minutes late, in his suit…minus the tie.

He tried to slip into the room unnoticed. The scent of cigarette smoke filled the air as the organizer of the event announced: "This is a scavenger hunt. The first team to collect all the items and return to this room is the winner. All eyes turned to The Dick's paling face as yet another "fuck my life," whispered its way across the room.

It was a close race in the end. My team beat the runners-up by only minutes in the two and a half-hour, five-mile race around town. I was on my second barley beverage when The Dick's team pulled him out of the rain and into second-last place forty five minutes later. The last place team, hampered by a very overweight Director of Sales, no doubt had to stop at every Starbucks along the route for him.

Dick nearly coughed up a lung, trying desperately to catch his breath while his teammates recalled for everyone how Dick had tried in vain to convince them to take a taxi from one site to another, at his expense. Ten minutes later, nearly breathing normally again, he reached in his back pocket for his resuscitator: his ciggies. His face still burning red after a few smokes, Dick pulled a chair up to the nearest table and sat for an hour without flinching so much as a nerve in his entire body. For the next two days he was almost unable to walk.

Strangely, all these people laughing at The Dick was playing perfectly into The Dick's plan. Dicks like to give the impression they aren't capable of doing much. This, they assume, will deter others from asking them to do anything at all.

They will also tell others that they prefer not to be the F&B Manager because they 'don't want the hassle,' or 'don't want to play politics.' Ensure you are wearing your bullshit protectors when your Dick starts talking like this.

Don't be fooled into thinking Dicks aren't motivated though. They can be, but Dicks are only motivated to do what they want to do…not what anyone wants or asks them to do. This is partially because Dicks believe they are smarter and more competent than anyone else, including the F&B Manager. Do not hire a Dick if you are looking for someone to stroke your ego.

If you are considering hiring a Dick, the key is to find out exactly what motivates your Dick. Although I discovered it too late, what my Dick wanted was to stir up trouble. And he excelled at that.

My Dick was good at getting reactions from people. I would be wary of recommending this type of Dick if you have a rocky relationship with your General Manager. However The Dick was perfect for creating a distraction for me.

I began to realize that when she was angry with my Dick, I was in the clear. I gave my Dick free reign. He was unleashed on the Sales and Front Office teams, and took to the task with all the venom of a Black Mamba.

The Dick didn't even have to try doing anything. It all came so naturally for him. At Catering meetings he would point out how much the room hire revenue was down compared to last year. At Front Office meetings, he would complain that the Managers on Duty were giving away too many complimentary breakfasts; thereby putting Food and Beverage in trouble.

All of these things were true of course; and everyone in Food and Beverage knew it. But when the Sales and Front Office Managers are the GM's best friends, it comes down to whether you want to remain in employment or not: that simple.

From this point on, for just being himself, everyone in Front Office and Sales reported stories of The Dick's sarcasm, rudeness and general all around asshole-ishness to their managers. The Sales Team hated him; they never mentioned me any more. The Front Office Team hated him; they also no longer reported me.

My relationship with the GM was improving too. Now it was time to call The Dick off. Of course, calling off a rottweiler when its jaws are locked in the neck of a poodle is easier said than done. This was first highlighted when The Dick lost his Blackberry.

The Executive Committee had just been issued with new Blackberry's. Dick retained the old smaller flip-top phone he was issued with. Dismayed at this, he pleaded with the Financial Controller and IT Guy, to no avail. After two months of haggling, or 'pestering' according to Kent in Accounts, a compromise was reached: Dick could buy the new Blackberry himself and IT would add it to the hotel system...at no charge.

Dick was delighted with this result. He walked around the hotel for the next three days, showing off his baby. On the fourth day, The Dick returned to the office from the restaurant to collect his Blackberry from his desk. It was gone. The hotel was on full alert within seconds.

The Dick ran out of the office and nearly flattened Tony from Concierge on his way out to look for the thief. "Hey, I just kicked a bum out of your office," Tony informed him.

"He stole my fucking Blackberry! Why didn't you keep him here?"

Tony shuddered. "I dunno. I just thought he was wandering. I didn't know he took anything."

"What did he look like?"

"Long coat....beard....dirty...a bum," Tony stuttered.

Dick ran out of the hotel and down the street. Two hours later, it was a very angry, sullen and still Blackberry-less Dick that returned to the office. He plonked himself down on his seat and didn't even look at me or Chef. "I am going to kill the bastard that stole my fucking Blackberry!"

I didn't doubt it one bit. I looked at the grinning Chef and sincerely hoped he wasn't pulling a fast one and hiding it from Dick.

Of course, The Dick was not entirely blameless in this theft. A laptop had been stolen from the office, in a locked cupboard, a week prior to this crime of the century. Everyone was on high alert for any 'suspicious' characters in the area. 'Most important of all,' the memo stated, 'the office door must be kept locked at all times.' It would take a braver man than me to remind him of this now.

That very day, after his shift, Dick went out and purchased some insurance: a baseball bat. He spent all evening, from 9:00pm on, wandering around downtown with his bat, speaking to every down and out he could find. "Hey, someone stole my Blackberry from my office at the hotel down this street. Know anything about it?"

At first, they all knew nothing of course. Then The Dick tried to buy them. "I'll give you twenty dollars if you can point me in the right direction. I just want to buy my Blackberry back. Tell them I'll give them fifty bucks. No questions asked."

Now everyone knew something about it. For his twenty dollars, Dick got helpful tips such as: 'I think his name's Dave. He stays on the other end of town…by the park.'

Dick and his bat tried the park…no luck. It was after midnight now, so Dick decided to try again the next day.

The next day, the news got worse for Dick. He received several phone calls at work from friends and relatives to say that someone was calling them from Dick's Blackberry, demanding money from them in return for the phone.

I arrived at work to find an unusually high number of homeless at the entrance to the hotel. When I mentioned this to Dick, he was off like a bolt. This is what he wanted. Obviously hearing about some lunatic handing out twenty dollar notes for nothing, they were coming to him now.

One hundred dollars and five minutes later, Dick returned to the office full of information again. "His name's Jim. He hangs out a couple of blocks from that same park every night."

Dick was so close he could almost smell his Blackberry. He drove around the park area in a one-mile radius; baseball bat lying in the passenger seat. This was not a good area. Drug addicts and prostitutes were the only visitors here. Well, not quite the only visitors.

It was 2:00am when the flashing lights pulled The Dick over. It was obviously not for speeding; he was doing a steady five miles and hour. When the police flashlight caught the baseball bat on the seat, Dick was invited to keep warm for a little while in the back of the police car, while explaining the situation to them again.

"I think they thought I was a drug dealer," Dick told me later. Although what gave him this impression I couldn't fathom.

No doubt deciding that nobody could possibly believe them if they had to hand in a written report, the police let Dick go after forty five minutes; and sent him home.

Dick continued to buy info from his street friends for the next two days. On the third day, a triumphant Dick came bouncing in to work. Held aloft in his left hand was his Blackberry. "I paid the guy fifty bucks, no questions asked," he grinned.

For Dick, everything was about winning; in this case: getting the stolen one back. God knows, he had paid his street pals enough to buy himself six Blackberry's.

Because of this aggressive, competitive style, it would be fair to say that my Dick was not the most popular person in the hotel. He walked with his back tight to the wall to avoid the daggers with his name on it. However; in all my time with him, he was able to avoid a documented verbal or written warning. This was quite an achievement considering the number of people that wanted him written up. He managed this with two expertly conducted techniques.

First, my Dick turned his motto: 'the best defense is a good offence' into a lifestyle. He quickly and viciously turned any question into an all-out attack on the questioner.

This was astutely demonstrated when it came to his first, and only, performance review. When I informed The Dick that his review was coming up in two week's time he replied: "You better give me 'outstanding' in every area. I don't deal well with criticism."

As this was already painfully obvious to everyone in the hotel, I laughed, thinking he was having a crack at sarcasm. He was not.

When we sat down, the tension emitting from my radioactive opponent was intense. I tried in vain to lighten the mood. I then noticed he had no notes in front of him when I began.

"So Dick, 'relationships and employee satisfaction.' How would you rate yourself?"

"Outstanding." Was he even listening to the question? I think if I'd asked him: 'what time is it Mr. Wolf?' he would have replied the same.

I looked at my notes. The GM insisted that when a manager's review was approaching, you had to e-mail all the departments they worked with and ask for feedback. The GM didn't like Dick. Well, she hated everyone; but Sales, Front Office, Reservations, Kitchen; even Concierge; had all slaughtered Dick when the feedback piled up in my inbox. 'Selfish, aggressive, arrogant, bully.' These were only the ones I could write down. I certainly couldn't use their exact quotes.

"Well Dick, you seem to have had more than a few run-ins with other departments. How would you describe your relationship with Sam in Sales for example?"

"She's a stupid bitch! What did she say about me?"

"Dick, we need to work with Sales, not criticize their every move. What have you done to help them?"

"I always help them. I am ten times more popular in this hotel than you. The Sales Team hates you!"

After ten minutes we agreed to disagree, and I left my mark on 'needs improvement.'

Feeling a need to lighten the mood, I skipped the written order and jumped to the one area he did well. "Okay, technical skills and knowledge. How would you rate yourself?"

"Outstanding."

"Agreed. Section three: what time is it Mr. Wolf?"

"Outstan... What?"

"Just checking." I shuddered as I looked at the next one. "Okay, 'communica....'"

"Outstanding!" I couldn't even finish the sentence.

"Dick. You haven't brought any notes for this, you're not even arguing on facts. Does that not tell you there is a communication problem?"

"This is bullshit! This is the worst review I've ever had."

That I did not doubt. He had probably scared or bullied everyone else into getting it over with as quickly as possible. With every example or quote I used, the answer was the same, followed by a justification: "I think I know who said that. That was a one-off. I was just joking, but she walked away before I could explain."

Eventually, instead of arguing, he just got angry. In every ensuing section, he somehow managed to insert a few comments about how he was either more popular than me or better qualified than me.

When the battle was finally over, The Dick refused to sign the review and stormed off. Not for good unfortunately. He went to stir things up.

Concierge Kim was the first to fly up to the office. Something appeared to be bothering her. "I thought feedback for reviews was supposed to be confidential!"

"It is," I shrugged.

"Dick just came to me and told me: 'I just had my review. Thanks a lot for your comments. Why would you say that about me?'"

"What did you say?" I asked her.

"I told him if he thought speaking to people like he does is acceptable, then he's in the wrong place. Then he said 'aha!' and walked away."

"Kim, I didn't tell Dick anything. He just tricked you into telling him what you told me!"

She stood with her mouth wide open for ten seconds until the penny dropped. Kim was first in line at HR when a proud Dick returned to the office.

"Dick, what the fuck do you think you're doing?"

"You see sir, I'm going to find out who said all these things about me and prove to you what they said isn't true."

Two or three others also fell into The Dick's trap until he was brought in for a chat with the GM. That was the end of the entrapment, but he never let me forget how it was the worst review he had ever had.

The Dick's second technique was more of an acute case of paranoia. It served him well for a long time though.

Dick was accused of many unethical practices, perhaps looking ahead to the GM curriculum. I knew most of these accusations were true, but they went unpunished mainly due to a distinct lack of evidence. But because he was always brought in for questioning, his paranoia grew. That's when The Dick tried to catch people off guard. He would accuse you of betraying him to the General Manager or HR and stare intensely at you to watch your reaction. "Why did you tell someone you want to get rid of me?"

"What are you talking about? Who?"

"I can't tell you."

"Dick, I don't know what the hell you're talking about!"

Then came his catch phrase: "Okay I'll tell you, but you have to swear you won't say anything to them."

"Okay, I promise." This was the crucial mistake.

"Isaac in HR told me today: 'Dick, I want you to know that whatever happens, I wanted you to stay.'"

I went to see Isaac. "Dick said what? He's full of shit. Why would I say that? Bring him in here, I'm going to ask him to repeat it in front of us."

"I can't. I had to promise I wouldn't say anything!" I replied.

It was a pretty good technique The Dick had developed. As it stood, neither Isaac nor I could question him further on it. The Dick managed to test his security in this manner many times, until The Chef, HR and I decided that we had to have our own little 'Dick Policy.' We agreed that when confronted with the catch phrase, we would always respond with: 'No. I'm a manager and if you tell me something I may have to act appropriately on it.'

It was very ironic that his 'paranoia technique' was brought to an end mainly because of his own paranoia. When he could no longer raise suspicion between the three of us, he knew that we had figured him out.

Still, in all my time with The Dick, the only person that ever gave him a serious dressing down was Former President Bill Clinton. After being briefed by Homeland Security, it was decided that only two of our staff would be allowed to service the banquet room while President Clinton was present. Since I had already been vetted, I had to find one other. The Dick clung to my leg like a horny Jack Russell.

Once he had gained entry, you could not wipe the smile from his face...or so I thought.

Since President Clinton had flown in on an early flight, one of the Homeland Security Officers asked The Dick to order an omelet for him. The Dick returned ten minutes later with the omelet and was clearly at a loss as to what to do with it.

Mr. Clinton was standing in a circle of ten men, clearly leading a serious discussion. Even The Dick knew better than to just tap the Former US President on the shoulder to warn him that his omelet might go cold.

The Officer that ordered the omelet, seeing the problem, whispered advice in The Dick's ear: "Stand behind him on his right side; and hold the plate out in front of you for him to see."

For only the second time ever, The Dick did as he was told. As he waited, and waited, his arm went numb with pain as Mr. Clinton refused to acknowledge The Dick or his omelet.

After five minutes, Mr. C finally cracked. Turning furiously towards The Dick, he unleashed his rage. His long finger an inch from The Dick's nose; he gritted his teeth and spoke slowly in his southern accent: "I do not eat when my company is not eating. Do you see anyone else eating? Put it down over there!"

With this he threw The Dick's shoulder towards a table in the corner. As The Dick cowered from the room, the Security Officer that had ordered the omelet came over and apologized to Dick: "Wow! I've never seen him do that before!" It was the closest to tears I ever saw Dick. I almost felt sorry for him.

After he'd recovered from the trauma with the help of a few cigarettes, The Dick soon bounced back of course. Unfortunately, within ten minutes The Dick was back to his old self again; bragging to everyone: "You should have seen President Clinton giving me shit."

Perhaps the only redeeming quality with The Dick was his timekeeping. He was willing to work any hours. Normally this would be a dream come true for any F&B Manager. The problem with my Dick was trying to keep him away from work for any amount of time so everyone got a break from him. And everyone needed a break from The Dick.

The staff knew The Dick was a bit different from other Assistant F&B Managers they had worked with too. The '666' tattoo on the back of his neck and the two-inch pinky nail on his left hand certainly struck the fear of the devil himself into several of the staff. So he had no problem getting their respect; or attention at least.

Dick's management style could best be described as: 'in your face.' Dick simply did not know 'subtle.' I would often overhear his motivational speeches when he didn't know I was around: "Hey, just shut up and do what you're fucking told. I don't care what you think sweetie." Dick by name; dick by nature.

However quick he was to overheat; The Dick was equally quick to cool down. Chef found this out when he had to intervene one afternoon. Dick and a similarly hot-headed demi-chef almost came to blows while exchanging insults. Chef dragged his demi, who had already handed in her notice, into his office to separate them and find out what happened. This was more discreet than The Dick cared for.

Following closely behind them, The Dick was banging on the closed door: "Fucking bitch!" Then, when Chef opened the door to shoo him away, he mustered up all the sarcasm he could, shouting: "Thanks a lot for sticking up for me Chef! Asshole!"

Ten minutes later, when the demi had been dismissed from Chef's office, The Dick reappeared to throw an arm around him. "Don't worry about her Chef. She'll be gone in a week."

It was for incidents such as these that Chef often referred to The Dick as 'Bi-Polar Dick.' Unfortunately, The Dick was only slightly more subtle when it came to guests. Tri-Polar would have been a better fit.

A multi Grammy award-winning recording artist was having lunch in the restaurant one afternoon when The Dick passed by his table. "Excuse me," he called to Dick. "Is Sting staying in the hotel?"

It was a reasonable question. The Police had been in town for weeks, preparing for their world tour. Sting had even been spotted in the Starbucks across the street from the hotel.

After that sighting, we had many people sniffing about the hotel believing he was staying with us.

The Dick was not a big music fan. I doubt he would have recognized Sting himself, so he certainly had no idea who John Legend was. Regardless, The Dick answered politely: "No sir. The Police are not staying with us."

Not fully trusting The Dick, he continued: "Well, if Sting is staying with you, tell him John Legend says 'hi.'"

The Dick bit. "Absolutely sir. No problem sir. And when I see Tom Cruise…I'm going to tell him as well." His work done at this table, Dick left Mr. Legend to ponder that insult.

Before he had walked far however, The Dick noticed the stunned looks on Mr. Legend and his two guests. The Dick walked quickly to the office and typed 'John Legend' into Google.

"Fuck my life!" was the cry once again as a picture of the guest sitting in the restaurant appeared on his screen. Wasting no time now, a limp Dick positively dribbled apologies all over Mr. Legend's table. Free drinks here, free food there; he even managed to drag the girl in Reservations out to meet him. 'Drag' perhaps not the right word.

Emily was the only girl in the hotel who was familiar with his music; and she was a massive fan. She brought out one of the many John Legend pictures that she kept on the wall at her workstation. She was reduced to tears by the mere sight of him. The Dick almost had to carry her back to her office.

Mr. Legend's ego suitably recovered, The Dick was off the hook. This was truly the stuff Legends are made of.

In the end however, I was unable to keep my Dick under control. He was on 'full-attack mode,' with no 'off' switch. I knew that if I didn't keep my Dick busy with something positive soon, he would get me into trouble.

And that's exactly what happened. The GM decided that if I couldn't control my Dick, she would. I could hear the Orchestra warming up as she prepared for her operetta: 'The Symphony of a Sacking.'

Chapter nine – A Distinct Society

Paper again! I always lost at rock / paper / scissors when I went with rock. I cursed my luck as I buttoned up my shirt again. With a deep breath I took the slip of paper from Matt's hand, put my tie back on and started off on my short trip to the kitchen.

Simple Davie, without turning his head, eyed me suspiciously as he chopped his onions. Catching a glimpse of my slip of paper, he put the knife down. So far so good. This reduced my odds of an airborne assault dramatically.

"Sorry Davie…"

"Oh no, no! Fuck this! I'm already behind on my breakfast prep. Every bloody night man!"

I tried again. "Sorry Davie. I'm trying to get out of here too you know. It's not my fault these drunks stagger back here at this time." I checked my watch: not even two in the morning yet; time for another couple of beer anyway.

"Right, leave the order there," he sighed. "I'll get it in a minute."

As I retraced my steps down the kitchen corridor, I could hear the giggles coming from around the corner. Matt and Mo were crouched down low, listening. Stretching over them, I too turned an ear towards the kitchen as we did our best to keep silent now, and waited.

"Fucking salmon and prawn toastie! Two fucking ham and cheese toasties! Fucking French fries! That's it! I'm speaking to Chef tomorrow. I can't get any bloody work done in this place!"

Simple Davie's elocution was not to be missed. It wasn't just the quality of his limited Chef's vocabulary that we enjoyed. It was more about his enunciation. Each small sentence started in a low pitch and ran through the entire vocal range, finishing off in the highest-pitched squeal imaginable. It was truly the most enjoyable part of his nightly performance.

As a show of appreciation, Matt let out a clear and distinct, yet ill-advised, yelp of laughter. We ran for the safety of the banquet room; tonight's performance basically over anyway. Mo cracked open three beers and passed them round. Tears were still streaming from Matt's eyes.

"You idiots!" I half-laughed, half-berated my accomplices. "He'll go mental if he…"

Just then the door opened. In our rush to get back in, we'd forgotten to lock the door again. Simple Davie stood motionless, taking in the scene. The gig was up for sure this time.

This had been a post-closing shift routine for the three years I'd been at the hotel. So who knows how long it had been going on before that! When the bar staff finished, they'd sneak a few beer into an empty banquet room, lock the door and relax for an hour or two.

The Bar Manager at the time, Peter, knew all about it too. "Just make sure it gets accounted for," he winked at me one night. We'd fill in a transfer sheet and charge the restaurant for the beer, or put it on the wastage sheet. Why should Peter mind? It kept the staff happy. Of course, that wouldn't save us if Diego, the Night Manager caught us.

Once the bar had closed, Diego could run the night audit. This meant he'd be occupied with a massive bowl of ice cream, as well as the audit, for several hours. It also meant that all the computers were 'down' in the hotel. So any food orders coming in at this time had to be hand written for the night chef. When the computers came back up at 6:00 am, these food orders were supposed to be rung in, to charge to the guest's room.

Since the night chef finished at 6:00am, they didn't bother to check if everything was rung in. Simple Davie had been getting pulled away from his work to make the bar staff sandwiches every night for years. This was clearly hitting home now.

"Fucking arseholes!" he screamed, his large knife glimmering in the dim light. With that, he turned and walked out. Surely he was going straight to Diego. We quickly finished the beer, got rid of the empties and awaited Diego's imminent arrival.

Yet twenty minutes passed and still no shadow darkened the door. "Maybe he didn't turn us in." Mo's remark seemed more like a question.

Matt turned his mind to more practical questions. "I'm starving. How are we going to get something to eat now?"

The eerie silence was worrying me a little. "I think we should get out of here before he comes back."

Right on queue, Simple Davie opened the door again, and he didn't come empty handed either. To our great astonishment, he came in with a large tray of toasted sandwiches and french fries. With a humble grin on his face, he addressed us again: "You guys are fucking arseholes! All of you. The next time you want something to eat, you can make it yourselves."

Matt ran and grabbed another round of beer, and one for Simple Davie as we all burst out laughing. From that night on, bar staff had to wait until Simple Davie told us he was going for a break; and the pantry was open season.

The late-night snack was appreciated, but it wasn't quite the same. The comedy of Simple Davie's tantrums was appreciated far more than the quality of his toasties. To be perfectly honest, Simple Davie probably should have been making McMinimum Wage somewhere, but as HR would tell you, trying to find someone who is willing to work from 11:00pm to 6:00am; and who can be trusted with a sharp object, is not easy.

Case in point: Simple Davie's relief night Chef, Crazy Davie. Crazy Davie covered Simple Davie's three nights off each week. Only Mo, who was a few apples short of a picnic himself, dared to utter the term 'Crazy Davie' in the hotel. Everyone else referred to him as 'Davie Two,' for fear of retribution. But even Mo didn't mess with Davie Two.

Davie Two wandered the kitchen all night muttering to himself. Throughout the night random shouts of things like 'Bloody spuds;' 'fucking bitch' and 'God-damn Mushrooms' could be heard. It occurred to me years later that this could have been a cunning tactic to prevent these 'staff orders' on his shift. Either way, it was no surprise to anyone when he eventually went MIA one evening.

A few hand written room service orders (real ones) were brought down to him one busy night. It was a sandwich too far. Davie Two was last seen walking out the fire exit doors a few minutes later, at roughly 3:00am. The cops, spotting the large knife in his hand, picked him up rather quickly.

Davie Two is 'taking some time off for a rest' Jane's memo said. We all knew what that meant: nervous breakdown.

Originally I had put the personalities of the two Davie's down to the fact that they worked only at night. It was bound to have an affect on their bodies and what was left of their minds. As I worked with these two for so many years, they were fundamental in my analysis of a chef's behavior. You could say they put the 'fun' and 'mental' in my analysis.

I don't remember much about Davie Two's replacement. I do recall he suffered from Tourettes Syndrome. Jane asked me to 'keep an ear out for it' as he admitted to her that he occasionally forgot to take his medication. I thought she was joking. Someone with Tourettes was hardly going to stand out in the kitchen! Actually I was wrong though. He did stand out, in that he swore much less than anyone else in the department.

Swearing is usually considered part of a chef's identity. They are distinct in this from the rest of the hotel. It is a very rare occasion indeed when a chef is reprimanded for coarse language; and entirely unheard of for a group of them to get into serious trouble for it. Such was the case though, when Sebastien took his team on a teambuilding retreat. Alcohol was, needless to say, a contributing factor in the case.

Ten of the chefs had gathered for a mid-day drinking session in one of their hotel bedrooms. A couple of hours later, three hotel managers and a police officer opened the door to find nine beer-swilling guys yelling excitedly at another male who was drawing dirty pictures on a flipchart.

"I don't know what the hell's going on here?" the hotel manager screamed, "but you're all leaving this hotel immediately!"

It seems the Manager had received a dozen or so complaints to the effect that there was an orgy going on in the room. When the Manager came up to investigate, numerous explicit shouts of 'suck my this' and 'lick my that' greeted his ears. He called the police to eject the group of orgy-seekers.

The astonished chefs gathered up their flipchart paper and left, their game of Porn Pictionary over.

I had been in Food and Beverage for a few years now and it struck me that the general conduct of chefs had not evolved much in that time, unlike all the other departments. My further consideration of this took me back in time to a pub in North Vancouver: my first job. Rockin' Rick was hardly a 'Chef' by trade. Due to the world wide Chef shortage, Rockin' Rick was pushed up the ladder out of necessity.

On a positive, Rockin' Rick was reliable. He claimed to have an apartment about twenty minutes away from the pub. However, rather than spend money on a bus to and from the alleged apartment, Rockin' Rick chose to spend each night sleeping in the park a few blocks away. He arrived on time for work every morning, fresh as mold.

It was a nice park; and it was close. None of us ever asked to see the apartment, to be fair; and since he showed up every morning, there was no problem really.

Like any lab rat, Rockin' Rick learned by rote. Simple things at first: how to turn the dishwasher on and off. Then, slowly but surely, he learned how to deep fry a chicken wing without burning his entire arm. Presto: a Chef was born.

Rockin' Rick was not permitted in any public part of the pub; and with good reason. Even the worst-dressed in the crowd would have frowned in the general direction of the plethora of filthy afro-like locks that jutted out at a ninety degree angle from under his ever-present baseball cap. Throw in either of his two t-shirts: Metallica or Motley Crue, and the whole package just screamed 'unsuitable for public viewing.'

At exactly ten minutes before closing time every night, Rick placed his beverage order with the bar staff. Twenty minutes later, Rockin' Rick could be seen heading up the road to the park; five-pack in one hand, an open can in the other…headphones blaring.

Nowadays anyone with a few weeks of dishwashing experience can put 'prep-cook' on their resume. Many Head Chefs in lower quality hotels were probably the dishwasher six months previous to attaining this position. The biggest task allotted to these pseudo-chefs is finding the cheapest frozen chicken parts. Do not be fooled though. There is an almost discernable gulf between the quality of a Chef in a four or five-star hotel and the average dishwasher.

Due to the worldwide shortage, the Chef is one of the few professions in the world that laughs in the face of job security. Forget about unions; Chefs have no need for these. What Hotel Chefs desire above all is for chefs in hotel kitchens to be declared 'a distinct society.'

The Chefs movement initially started as a symbolic revolt in honor of the plight of French Canadians to split politically from the rest of mainland Canada. Chefs, like French Canadians, have a very unique view of themselves. This view is, needless to say, not shared by the majority.

Similar to the French Canadians, Chefs would dictate the terms on which they would split; thereby keeping the benefits they would no doubt lose under self-government.

The Head Chef is the master politician when it comes to absolving himself of blame in the revolt that he himself has created in his kitchen. In the Executive circle, he must be seen to agree with the policies of the hotel. In the kitchen therefore, he cannot be seen to be the root of the kitchen uprising, ignoring these policies. It is a carefully calculated move, and it is not without risk.

The Sous Chef then becomes the executor of the Head Chef's orders; ignoring hotel policies in the kitchen. 'Sous Chef Syndrome' occurs when the authority of the Head Chef appears to be compromised. The Sous can become more respected with the chefs in the trenches than the Head Chef. This is natural in a sense, since the Sous is more of a 'working' Chef than the Head Chef. It becomes dangerous though, when the Sous believes he is more powerful.

For the beleaguered F&B Manager, this becomes a political game of high stakes. The F&B Manager's credibility is compromised if he ignores the numerous indiscrepancies of the Sous. However, he also knows that constantly drawing the Head Chef's attention to these breaches of policy may make him a target.

I had a particularly fine line to walk at The Park. I knew the Head Chef would not appreciate having to send his Sous Chef to HR because I had found him wolfing down champagne in the Chef's office during a busy lunch rush. Since they kept a full fridge of alcohol in the Chef's Office anyway, it was highly likely the Head Chef was at it as well. I chose to ignore that one.

I chose only go to the Head Chef for 'small' breaches of policy. This Head Chef had no problem sacrificing a trench chef now and again, in a bid to make HR believe he was making an effort. For me, it was a chance to show some authority over the kitchen staff.

For his part, the trench chef believes their job is unique and that nobody else can do their job. Foolishly, they believe they are untouchable.

Chris was one such fool. I caught him in the restaurant one day struggling to make an espresso for himself. None of the serving staff were brave enough to remind him this was a policy violation.

"Chris, what are you doing?" I asked casually.

"I need a double espresso for the crème brulee recipe," he replied boldly.

I paused only briefly. "Oh! Here, let me help you with that."

"Thanks!" was all he said as he returned to the kitchen, with a smug grin on his face.

I gave Chris a full five minutes before I made my way through the kitchen again. The trench chefs were obviously enjoying a laugh at someone's expense. Their laughter died significantly when I knocked on the Chef's office door.

"Chef, I just gave Chris a double espresso to make the crème brulee."

"There's no espresso in crème brulee!"

"I know that. It was for him obviously."

Chef jumped up from his seat and made for the pantry. All the trench chefs were silent now. "Chris, what the fuck are you doing asking the F&B Manager to make you an espresso?"

Chris opened his mouth, presumably to change feet; but had no answer. "Let's go and see HR," was all Chef said as he marched off. Chris, tail between his legs, dragged after him to the raucous applause of those still in the trenches.

Had I simply told Chris that I knew there was no espresso in the crème brulee, he would have returned to the kitchen, only to try again later. He certainly wouldn't have received another written warning either. By making him the espresso, allowing him to gloat about it, and then turning him in, I had sent a message to all the trench chefs. I smiled as I went back to the restaurant for a celebratory cappuccino.

I had an intuition that Chris's attitude may have been inspired by Jean-Paul. I thought back to my first, and unfortunately not my last, social outing with our Executive Sous Chef. Our hotel was up for two awards at a black tie affair.

The first award we were up for was 'Hotel Bar of the Year.' I was disappointed to finish runner-up. Most of the table looked my way and offered their condolences. Jean-Paul did not.

Obviously not partial to the dessert placed in front of him, he waved a waiter over instead. Jean-Paul pointed at the offending plate and told everyone at the table, not just the waiter: "I want a cheese plate. I am French."

What everyone heard was: "I want a cheese plate. I am an asshole." In all likelihood, he knew it too. He just didn't care.

Moments after gorging himself on his cheese, Jean-Paul leaped out of his chair as the winner of the 'Hotel Restaurant of the Year' was announced. I felt obligated to applaud as I looked around our table. Sebastien, our Head Chef, was still sitting at the table while his Sous Chef collected the silver platter and took the applause. Sebastien, catching my glance, smiled and shrugged back at me.

Sebastien was definitely suffering from Sous Chef Syndrome.

Jean-Paul was also an elitist. He hired French chefs exclusively, believing them to be genetically superior in the kitchen. Of course, this could have been a natural reaction to his introduction to Scottish chefs. Tim and Tam were hard work. They were from Glasgow and their accent was difficult for Edinburgh Scots to understand at times. It must have been horrendous for a Frenchman.

You could also say the quality of their work was questionable. Frankly, I could never tell if they were sober or just between hangovers; the two of them always smelled of alcohol. They were hard not to like though; and I always laughed when I saw Tim. He wore thick spectacles, which made his eyes look extremely large; and when he talked to you, he always seemed to be facing the wrong way.

Intoxicated or not, at least these brothers got along with each other. Damien and Laurent did not. Jean-Paul's theory of superior genes took a serious blow with these two. Damien hailed from Bordeaux, Laurent from Paris; and this seemed to be the foundation of their mutual hatred.

Damien would sing little ditties for Laurent while he was working: 'Parisienne, tete de chien' ('head of a dog' translated literally). In return, Laurent would complain about Damien to anyone who had an ear. "Look at that stupid French bastard!" Laurent remarked to me once.

I looked at him incredulously. "But Laurent, you are French!"

"I know. But even the French hate the French," he returned quite seriously.

The only thing these two agreed upon was the need for the kitchen hierarchy system. For trench-chefs, the hierarchy system gives them a sense of belonging; outcasts clinging to each other. As they move up the ranks, it allows them the opportunity to verbally abuse those below them. All chefs believe whole heartedly in this system.

HR in contrast, believes in exactly the opposite. They envision an environment where everyone gets along. A place where staff smile at each other as they pass and think to themselves: 'what a wonderful place to work.' They dream of a lunch room where chefs and other staff sit together on their breaks. HR tries to break down the system that the Kitchen tries doggedly to maintain.

In an attempt to prevent HR's utopia, and achieve their 'distinct society' status, the chefs unite in a campaign of harassment. It is a systematic approach designed to maintain a high level of disrespect between all departments and the kitchen.

Females are targeted first. Sexual innuendo is a must and any female passing through the kitchen area, must receive at least one outrageous remark. Homosexuals, female or male, are targeted next. This is more dangerous because they can bite back with sexual innuendo of their own, which can cause embarrassment to the more junior chefs. Harassment of homosexuals is therefore generally not attempted by a junior chef. However, it is a rite of passage in the kitchen and must be attempted if the junior chef wants to move up the ranks.

Managers are next in the firing line. This is always played as a duet, with the first chef making a comment just as the manager passes out of earshot. The accomplice sniggers loudly to ensure the manager knows they are talking about him. This is all an attempt to get the manager to react. It is usually unsuccessful, but if the manager is under pressure for some reason, it can have spectacular results.

Ingo had certainly fallen for it a few times, resulting in a few plates being thrown in the general direction of a chef. This is like winning the lottery for a trench chef. For years he will gloat to others: "Remember the day when…" F&B Managers are targeted more frequently than other managers with this technique, mostly due to their close working proximity to the kitchen. The general rule of thumb is, the bigger your ego, the more likely you are to fall for it. In a classic example, The Dick fell for it every time: hook, line and sinker.

No matter who got the brunt of it, the harassment was a great source of entertainment for the chefs. They needed it too! Chefs do not have the easiest life in the hotel. They work long hours; often with split shifts.

To fill in the two hour gap between their lunch and dinner shifts, the chefs at The Park usually held a daily meeting. I discovered where these meetings were held one unusually hot and sunny afternoon, when their pub put tables and chairs outside. I could see them from the restaurant windows. It must have been a good meeting; they were all quite animated.

At five o'clock, I watched as Barry was the first to limp across the street. Barry, our Scottish Sous Chef, not only suffered from gout, he was a carrier. He moaned about it from morning 'til night so everyone else could suffer too. Barry's head start was a signal for the other meeting delegates to quaff down their refreshments and return to work. I cringed at the thought of this half-baked group of lobsters working with sharp knives.

Over the years, I became aware that gout was a common work related hazard in hotel kitchens. I always made sure to include it on the kitchen's risk assessment. This came to mind during a Human Resources meeting one day. The topic on the table was how to attract more chefs to the hotel. I suggested advertising at alcohol abuse clinics and in pubs. Sebastien nodded approvingly at the idea, which seemed to annoy Jane more than my suggestion.

Alcohol and the chef are well-acquainted, despite what Jane liked to admit. At The Grosvenor, Andy used to keep a rum and coke on line with him at all times when I started. Sara, the GM of sorts, turned a blind eye to it. Eventually, my pleading with her for action led her to issue a written warning for using glassware in the kitchen, where it could chip and fall into the food. When Andy switched to a plastic mug, I knew he and Sara would both have to go.

Andy was clearly a Head Chef who had benefitted from the worldwide chef crisis and come up quickly through the ranks. By my estimation he was washing dishes no less than one week before my arrival.

My first argument with Andy was over a fruit basket. I had asked him to prepare one for a VIP arriving. When I went to double check that it was in the room, my jaw dropped. In the wicker basket was: one brownish banana, one apple, one orange and three tomatoes. I returned it to the kitchen immediately.

Andy put his mug down as I approached. "What's this?" I asked.

"You asked for a fruit basket?" He sounded surprised. I'd have to spell it out.

"The banana's brown. All the fruit have stickers on them and there are three tomatoes in here!"

"So what?"

It was his trainee prep cook / dishwasher who backed him up, clearly thinking I was an idiot. "Tomatoes are fruits, not vegetables."

Knowing he wasn't bright enough to be baiting me, I bit. "Hey, I know it's a fucking fruit okay? But have you ever picked one up from a table and taken a bloody bite out of it?"

Despite Sara's help, it was not difficult to get Andy sacked. Surprisingly, at his termination dispute hearing, he admitted to drinking on his split shift before returning to work.

Michelle, the Sous Chef, was asked to run the kitchen until a new Head Chef could be found. I liked Michelle. She had a great attitude and put up with my bad jokes. Like the runaway majority of women I have worked with in the kitchen, Michelle was openly gay.

Adam, the new Restaurant Manager, and I were having a discussion late one evening when we stopped suddenly to watch Michelle. She had stopped her prep work to don a large set of blue gloves.

Adam had to ask. "Michelle, baby, what's with the gloves?"

She looked up, quite in surprise. "Oh, I'm allergic to fish."

I don't know if she ever recovered psychologically from the sight of the two of us bursting into a hysterical fit of laughter. Adam managed to stagger out the back door for fresh air. I fell in the opposite direction and collapsed into a chair in the empty restaurant. It took days for the two of us to get over the childish joke. Every time Adam saw me, his eyes would well up and he'd stutter: "A lesbian…allergic…to fish!" before he'd stumble out of the room again. Adam was nearly hospitalized a few weeks later when Jamie, a gay chef, was waxing lyrical about how much he loved the beef dip!

A woman's life in a hotel kitchen is tough. I don't know how Michelle stuck it out at times: the Ramsey-inspired language; the long hours and poor pay, not to mention the music you had to endure. Only a chef could crank up Metallica to full volume at 6:00 am every morning to cure their blinding hangover. Call me chauvinistic, but the kitchen always seemed like a 'man's' area to me.

Coincidence or not, all but two of the women working in my hotel kitchens were either gay or going through a sex change. The Lesbian in the kitchen is no big deal. They are usually the 'butch' type and fit in perfectly with the other testosterone-inspired chefs. Pat was the first trans-sexual I'd worked with, knowingly at least. Pat was in the hormone replacement therapy stage, before the operation, when she joined us at The Plaza. By the end of the year he would be a card-carrying member of the male chefs, or a member-carrying male chef at the very least.

In the present however, the trench chefs were very wary about the newcomer. There were the predictable jokes about which bathroom Pat should use. He could have used either really. By looking and speaking to him, it was impossible to tell if he was male or female. This caused serious problems for many people, but mainly for Chef himself. Pat insisted on being referred to as a male. However, it seemed impossible to get through an entire conversation in his presence without referring to him as 'her.' The conversation always ended in a sudden and awkward silence when the speaker realized their faux pas.

Not everyone realized their faux pas until it was too late of course. I was sitting in on a kitchen meeting one day, keeping a running total on the number of times Chef had referred to Pat as 'she.' By my tally, it was eight. There were a few giggles each time and I could feel tension mounting as others grew embarrassed for Chef and Pat.

As I contemplated how to alert Chef to the issue without making it glaringly obvious to everyone else, Jason hit the 'she' button a ninth time. Pat rose from his chair and calmly walked out of the room, tears running down his or her face.

Jason looked around the room in astonishment. "What the fuck's her problem?"

Apart from this issue, Jason was easily the most HR-friendly Head Chef I had come across. In hotels, the Head Chef has risen out of the kitchen ranks and spends most of his time in meetings, creating menus and scheduling. For this he is rewarded with the title of 'Chef.' Do not call him anything else.

If you happen to make the mistake, expect a tongue lashing along the lines of: "I have worked all my life to achieve the role of Head Chef. I have earned this title and everyone will address me as The Chef." Jason was the only Head Chef I have ever met who did not insist on this with any regularity.

Despite a few incidents where I was implicated as an accomplice, Jason was a relatively small drinker compared to most other Chefs I'd worked with. With all this extra time on his hands, my biggest job here was to keep him away from guests, normally a given.

The kitchen is a secure area in hotels. Guests don't get in, and chefs don't often get out to see the guests either. This is by design. The guest believes firmly in the 'guest is always right' theory. HR's entire training program is also built on this theory. The problem is that because they don't see the guests, chefs extrapolate that this theory does not pertain to them. The kitchen is always full of bravado when guests complain.

Again, it is the F&B Manager who must provide the voice of reason in these situations: the liaison between the unreasonable guest and the diminutive Chef. In many cases, literally running between chef and guest, translating for each other:

Guest says: "This is the worst steak I have ever tasted. It is fatty, underweight and completely over cooked."

This should be translated to the chef as: "I'm sorry Chef, the guest thinks his steak may be ever so slightly over-cooked. He sends his apologizes for being fussy, but he would like another one. Perhaps we could give him a bigger cut for the inconvenience?"

Chef says: "There's nothing wrong with it. And I weighed it myself! Fucking idiot."

This should be translated back to the guest as: "Chef sends his sincerest apologies and is cooking a new one for you immediately sir."

One evening, while jogging between the chef and a guest, my eyes caught the coat check disclaimer sign. It occurred to me that my life would be much easier if I could hang another sign at the entrance: 'The Chef cannot accept responsibility for absolutely anything.'

Steaks are the most common problem for F&B Managers. The chef will tell you what the problem is every time: the cut, the grill, the refrigerator, the guest: everything except the person cooking it. When this conversation starts, it can go on all night. The F&B Manager must have his 'steak speech' prepared, and cut to the chase.

"Medium; medium-well…what's the fucking difference? Just cook the fucking steak. She wants it cooked for another five minutes!"

"That's not Medium!"

"Just fucking do it!"

With the advent of the internet, keeping the chef and the guest apart has become more difficult than ever. Jason used to consult me before replying to most of his guest request e-mails, but a couple slipped through the net now and again. Sometimes it's good for the Chef too: to know how far out of their depth they are when dealing with guests.

One particular snob pestered Jason repeatedly, annoying him immensely. He knew it was all a pretentious act for the lady to impress her friends every time she came in.

"Oh just tell Chef Jason I'll leave it up to him to surprise me," she'd say to the waiter.

Jason's reply of: "Who the fuck is this bitch?" was again translated for the guest. "I reply to one fucking e-mail and now she's stalking me! How the fuck am I supposed to know what she likes?"

It all ended in tears one evening, when the guest did not like the meal sent out to her. Jason refused to go out and see her. Just as well really; he was livid! She called him the next day to complain about it, at which point I was handed a phone number to call her back.

Direct phone lines are also a no-no for the Head Chef. I had to admit The Dick and I found great amusement with one persistent female who called Jason to request a deep fried fish and chips dinner. She called a week in advance, so he could find her 'a nice piece of halibut.' He agreed to it, reluctantly of course, since he had to buy it in specially, and that was extra work.

Jason was extremely disappointed when the day of the big fish and chips dinner was upon us, only for the lady to call the restaurant, not his direct line, to say she'd have to cancel her reservation.

Jason walked around the kitchen for ten minutes, waving a piece of halibut in the air. "I can't fucking believe it! What the hell am I supposed to do with one piece of halibut?" As he was quite tall, it reminded me of John Cleese in Monty Python's fish-slapping skit. I ran for cover.

Unfortunately for Jason, he kept biting at this bait. She called him back a few weeks later; to apologize and again ask for her special fish and chips. Once again, she called the restaurant to cancel her reservation on the night. She did this four times in total. On the fifth occasion, her request was denied and she was never heard from again.

In a one-restaurant hotel, the menu is designed to have something for everyone and the menu is usually changed three times a year. One item that never changed was Jason's popular signature appetizer: the Ahi tuna and prawn tower. But even the most popular dishes are subject to change; prices for ingredients can go up and availability can go down.

As it happened, the cost of the prawns and the tuna did go up significantly. We decided that, at thirteen dollars, we could not raise the price enough to reach our budgeted profitability with the dish. The other problem with this dish was labor. It took ninety minutes to prepare all the ingredients for each service. Bitch-Nicole was all about labor control; and she rubber-stamped the decision to take the tuna and prawn tower off the menu.

It did not go over well with the Sales team. They loved to show this dish off when entertaining clients in the restaurant. Every time a menu changes, there are complaints about some dish being removed. However the barrage of complaints over this one was nothing short of incredible.

The Dick and I were publicly dressed down several times by diners. Some even walked out when they saw it wasn't on the menu. Others chose to voice their displeasure over the phone, others via e-mail. Whatever their vehicle, I could not believe the number of them. I was glad my office didn't have a window. I was sure the hotel was surrounded by sign-carrying picketers. It led me to wonder where all these guests were coming from. Had they been dining regularly with us, we wouldn't have had to take it off the menu.

That was the other thing that annoyed me: they all claimed to be regular guests. If by regular, they meant annually, it was a possibility I suppose. Whatever their definition of regular was, the complaints went on forever. Through practice, I had become quite proficient at dealing with these 'tower' complaints.

A tuxedo was standing over his table of four friends one evening as he lambasted me for the amusement of his party.

"I have been a regular here for years. I come here three times a month and every time we order the tuna and prawn tower. The only reason I brought these gentlemen here tonight was for that dish. I want to know who made the decision to take it off the menu!"

"Sir, it's been off for the menu for ten months. I'm afraid I cannot remember who made the decision that long ago."

Real regulars will always give you their impression of the menu too. In hotels, the regulars are all food critics of course. I was sure one of them was going to give me an earful about The Tower one afternoon as I approached his table. I was much relieved to find it was the grilled tuna sandwich Mr. Brown was whining about instead.

Clearly feeling his verbal complaint did not carry enough weight, he asked for a pen and paper. I thought he was writing to the General Manager to take his complaint to the Supreme Court.

Jesse, the server, brought the handiwork through to the office when he had gone. Mr. Brown spent thirty minutes drawing a cartoon. It was a picture of him sitting at a table, with huge tears flying out in all directions. The caption above read: 'Stanley was not happy about the tuna sandwich being removed from the menu, but eventually got over the shock and continued to return, if less frequently.'

Stanley definitely had a talent. That was one of my top three favorite complaints ever: subtle and unique. After I showed it all around the hotel, it stayed on my office wall for over a year.

The 'tower' complaints had been going on for eight months when the second menu change of the year came about. The Sales Team press-ganged Chef, begging him to bring back The Tower. He wavered. They press-ganged the GM next. She didn't waver so much as do a complete U-turn.

For my part, I tried to remind them all why we had gotten rid of it in the first place. At the next menu meeting, I reviewed the kitchen's labor since the removal of The Tower. Bitch-Nicole, with renewed faith, agreed once again that The Tower was banished. The Sales Team would have to find something else in the kitchen to complain about.

It didn't take them long. With the taste of defeat still on their greedy little palates, they went for the throat.

Bitch-Nicole conspiring as ever with the Sales Team, and no doubt feeling she had let them down in the battle for The Tower, announced the next move in this chess match. "Chef, I want you to revamp the staff meal program."

My heart sank as Chef's face quickly paled to a stunning white. If you ever want to cut the heart out of a chef and serve it to him on a platter, or simply keep him frustrated and busy for six months, ask him to revamp the staff meal program.

Staff meals are given verbal abuse at every monthly staff consultation meeting. This is always fobbed off by the HR Manager with the 'I'm sure Chef would love to hear your suggestions' response. Nobody ever suggested anything, so it was easily swept under the table…until someone wants to deliberately ambush the Chef.

Hotels allocate a paltry amount to feed the masses, in this case $2.65 per person. With this ration, the Chef is to provide one hundred and fifty staff with a three-course meal every day that is fresh and healthy; with cold and hot options for vegetarians and carnivores. Chef and I knew it was impossible to please even a small minority, never mind the majority. I was sure Bitch-Nicole knew it too.

Now Chef would have to do the countless hours of meaningless work to prove it. I knew it was meaningless; the food and the program would never change at the end of it. After seeing this technique used in other hotels, I was sure of it. Sadly, Chef was not.

Until tasked with this chore, the most attention a Head Chef pays to the staff meal program is drawing lots to see which newly promoted dishwasher is assigned to the job. All the Chefs hate the meal program. And why not! They all eat whatever they want, whenever they want. Why should they have to cook for the peasants when they are the chosen few?

Anatomy of a white elephant:

With HR's help, Jason chairs two meetings with departmental representatives, or 'the chronic complainers' as Chef refers to them. These meetings go nowhere as the suggestions of prime rib and lobster are not viable options at $2.65. Loaves and fishes might have been easier for Chef to produce.

Next up is the survey. After every member of staff voted, the results spoke volumes as to the degree of difficulty in getting something to work with. Healthier food v more desserts; more vegetarian options v more meat options; more salads v more hot food. Each choice was split virtually fifty-fifty.

Step three is the 'false hope' phase. "Well, if they can't agree on anything, I'm just going to scrap the whole program!" Bitch-Nicole told Chef. Until this point, every recent conversation I'd had with Chef had been 'fucking staff meals this' and 'bastard staff meals that.' Now he had hope. It cheered him up immensely; too much actually. I knew he was headed for a big fall and tried to calm him down, but he wouldn't listen.

"Chef, I want to see some viable menu options for the next staff consultation meeting!" Bitch-Nicole insisted.

For the next four weeks, Chef sweated blood putting menus together and costing them out. He hadn't put this much effort into the new restaurant menus!

As the most appealing proposals were slightly over budget, Bitch-Nicole suggested a final meeting for staff to vote on the menus. There was also an additional option for staff to contribute one dollar a day and go with a higher quality menu Chef had put together.

The staff contribution menu was an overwhelming 'no,' with only nine of the one hundred and forty-eight votes willing to contribute anything. Chef was nearing fever pitch as the votes on the other menus were a stalemate. "She has to scrap the whole program now, surely!" he whispered excitedly.

It was a much-deflated Chef that I escorted out of Bitch-Nicole's office than had strutted in thirty minutes earlier. "Well, we'll just have to keep it 'as is' and if they don't like it: too bad. They had their chance. Thank you for all your effort Chef."

"But...but..." his voice trailed off without conviction as I tapped his shoulder and walked him out: a broken chef. It took several beers to cure this nasty case of shock. As he recuperated, random shouts of 'fucking bitch!' filled the pub in the midst of our conversation.

It took me back to Crazy Davie immediately; and Ingo's advice about Chefs in general: you can always tell a chef...but you can't tell him much!

Chapter ten - The Royal Family

"Four bottles of Moet for the Executive Office," Babs called from Room Service. "Ingo asked for it ASAP."

Billy wiped the cappuccino foam from his moustache and mouthed at me: "For who?"

"Sales no doubt," I mouthed back, trying to avoid Babs' radar ears.

"Bloody ridiculous!" Billy piled the last of the foam onto his moustache. "They're treated like the Royal bloody Family around here!"

"And Ingo knows it too!" I reminded him. Billy shook his head a few times before nodding in agreement. "Coming down?" I asked.

"Humph! They can go fuck themselves." Billy's fart put the exclamation point where it wasn't really needed.

The relationship between Sales and Food and Beverage was always strained, but Ingo was doing his best to reach out here. I took his lead and brought the bubbly down myself.

As I approached, Ingo ran excitedly to the GM's Office and pulled a very unenthusiastic-looking James out. He then danced over to Cynthia's door and knocked. The Sales and Reservations area was usually quiet between 9:00am and 5:00pm, when the phones were busy. Ingo broke that silence a few minutes early: "If I could have everyone's attention please. I just wanted to congratulate the Sales Team on a wonderful job, getting the contract for the new American Investment Company. A three thousand room-night deal! Well done everyone!"

I had timed the 'pop' of the first champagne bottle to coincide perfectly with Ingo's final word. Sadly, it was drowned out by Cynthia's reply: "Actually I'm right in the middle of a conference call, working on another deal, if you don't…"

I presumed the last word was 'mind,' however as her final word coincided with the slamming of her door, a guess it would remain.

Ingo's red face gave his feelings away, but he maintained the semblance of a smile as he stood there holding the two glasses of champagne. I feverishly popped and poured the Moet, passing it around the rest of the Sales Team before the red mist could envelope him.

Between gritted teeth, he somehow choked out a few final words: "Congratulations ladies, keep up the good work." He held one of the glasses high for the toast. Then, quickly, and without a single sip, he placed the glasses down carefully. It was the concentrated effort of a man who doesn't fully trust himself with what he's holding.

He slipped unnoticed into his office again. Just in time too.

"Moet is so passé! None of my friends would be caught dead drinking this stuff."

"They could have brought strawberries with it!"

"It's not even all that cold!"

The comments were flying in from everyone now. Not one 'thank you' was forthcoming, but I knew that would be the case. The Sales Office is a snake pit. They will find someone or something to complain about in any and every situation.

Ingo probably knew it wasn't worth the effort too. I put an ear to his door: silence. No doubt he was about to fly into a rage in there. I waited for the door to open; to see Ingo drag the Director of Sales out of her office. To watch him pour the warmish Moet down her ungrateful throat until slightest moan of a seemingly impossible 'thank you' could be discerned. Alas, his door remained closed.

"You know, I really prefer Bollinger."

This last one was too much for me. Alana: the biggest lush in the hotel. She would happily drink fluid from a cigarette lighter after a few gin and tonics. Less than three weeks earlier I was in the party charged with removing her from the pub and stuffing her into a taxi after a few too many.

She also had a verified reputation for sleeping around a lot too. She wasn't choosy about her drinks or her men; so how she became a connoisseur of champagne all of a sudden was certainly a surprise to me. Of course, it was all part of the job description for Sales.

The DOS' door suddenly opened and a vividly red-lipped Cynthia stepped out to a loud cheer from her half-pissed ensemble. She looked like she had been in a makeover salon, rather than her office. I brought forth a glass of champagne. Without even glancing at me, she snatched it and held it high to her girls: "Cheers!"

As the girls wasted no time polishing off the four bottles of 'rat piss,' Cynthia stuck her tongue out in disgust. "Ughh. Moet?" They all nodded back sourly, equally disgusted.

Food and Beverage and Sales have a tempestuous relationship by the sheer nature of their roles. The Banquet department is completely dependent on the Sales team bringing in the business. Sales does not rely on F&B for anything.

F&B are therefore always on the back foot when they need anything from Sales. A victim of circumstance, who could blame the poor the F&B Manager for feeling like the ugly duckling?

The Sales Team on the other hand, are the glamour girls of the hotel. To outsiders, it's the dream job: jetting off to exotic destinations, staying in luxury hotels. A life of champagne, company credit cards and expense reports. The Sales job is a life of leisure.

The Sales Team for their part, constantly bemoan how difficult their life is: they never get to see the cities they travel to because of presentation deadlines and tight travel schedules. They miss their own beds; the barista that knows just how they like their lattes, and their boyfriends. All bullshit of course. This is 'lying 101:' Basic Training for the Sales Team.

As I collected the lipstick-plastered glasses, I snuck a quick look in Cynthia's office. There wasn't even a conference phone in there! I glanced up at the sign on her door again as I left the area: DOS.

The Director of Sales. I always thought this was a typo. A dyslexic had obviously been commissioned for the signage and nobody had noticed. It should have read SOD.

The SOD is ruthless. Only four days prior to this treat, the whole Sales Team were invited to the race track on the outskirts of town. The hotel sponsored a horse race every summer for a charity event. It was advertising for the hotel, and more importantly for the Sales lushes, complimentary beverages. Cynthia had charged the Reservations Manager, Michael, with bringing the quite large trophy.

As the race began, Michael was asked to bring the trophy down to the front of the race track. He turned white, but said nothing as he sprinted to his car. Had his last name been Schumacher, he would not have stood a chance of driving to the hotel (where he had left it on his desk) and back in time for the end of the race. His valiant effort had robbed Cynthia of a valuable photo opportunity. The next morning, he was exploring new opportunities for employment.

The SOD's secondary role is to oversee the Sales Department; which is divided into Catering Sales and Room Sales. Room Sales account for the majority of the hotel's revenue. Catering Sales book the banquet rooms and therefore account for the majority of the Food and Beverage revenue.

However, the primary role of the SOD is to ensure the F&B Manager's life is as miserable an existence as possible. This is achieved in part by carefully withholding information that could help the F&B department to service the events that are booked; and by conspiring and coordinating with the General Manager, passing on information that the GM may use against the poor F&B Manager.

The GM adores the Sales Team; showering them with gifts every time a contract is signed: champagne, extra time off and, most sickeningly of all, undeserved praise. Billy was right: the GM ensured they were treated like the Royal Family. The F&B Manager, far removed from this kind of treatment, must take the oath of allegiance also however…at pain of death by ridicule.

The careful F&B Manager must therefore only communicate with the SOD if and when absolutely necessary. Every word must be carefully chosen, for the SOD will repeat each word of every discussion back to the GM, verbatim.

Unfortunately, there is no 'good' time to communicate with Sales. No matter what the business level is, it can only detract from the situation. When there is an unexpected surge in business, Banquets are scrambling to find enough staff on short notice. In this case, one might think the Banquet Manager would be justified in asking why there was no notice given, when the initial enquiry was two months previous. After all, nobody books an event for four hundred people only seven days in advance.

As tempting a question as it seems to be, F&B Managers must not ask this. Any enquiries will be met with a disgusted glance and the standard reply: "We need the revenue. Should we have turned it down?" Your life will not be worth living if you get to this stage. Any reports of someone suggesting that revenue should be turned down will have them signing a pre-prepared resignation letter quickly.

Very occasionally, if Sales have booked the event so last minute that they know it is near impossible to set it on time, Catering may offer to help with the set up.

F&B Managers must not be tempted to allow this. Ninety percent of the time they will not show up anyway; nine percent of the time they will show up just after all the work has been done. But that one percent of the time when they do show up, under the pretense of help, they are actually there to criticize how the work is carried out. Not to the F&B Manager of course.

The next time the General Manager sees the F&B Manager, they will tell him what 'they' think is wrong with the banquet service. It will be obvious where their information has been weaned from when specifics are given.

Of course the larger the banquet is, the greater the stress; and the greater the strain on the fragile Sales / F&B relationship. I first noticed the strain on Cynthia and Ingo's relationship leading up to the Commonwealth Heads of Government Meeting, or CHOGM as it was referred to around the hotel. We were the closest hotel to the Conference Centre, where the meeting was to be held.

Several delegations were staying with us. Pakistan and India, two of the largest, had to be kept on separate wings of the hotel. Keeping the delegates apart was easy. Keeping their chefs apart was much harder.

One of the arrangements Sales had made when the contract was signed, was that the delegates could place their own chefs in our kitchen to cook for their own delegations. At the pre-conference meeting, Chef did not really seem put out by this news. In fact, he assumed it would be less work for his kitchen staff. "Eet's okay Eengo. Eet weel be easy for us, non?"

Ingo disagreed. He had been pushing Sales to find out what the requirements would be. They obliged with this news one week before the event. Very helpful! "Chef, I have dealt with this kind of thing before. Believe me, this is not good! Billy, make sure you're here until at least nine o'clock every night. I want full staffing in all departments for this."

"What the hell am I going to be needed for at eight o'clock?" Billy asked me an hour later, when Ingo was well out of earshot. I didn't have high expectations of Billy sticking to Ingo's advice as he'd already knocked an hour off. Ingo turned out to be right though.

It started out well enough for me. "Mike, someone asked to see the Room Service Manager down at Reception," Fast Eddie announced. Whenever someone asks to see a Manager in a hotel, it's not usually to tell him what a wonderful job he's doing. Eddie knew it was probably a complaint, and let his enjoyment show in the form of a large grin.

I was almost stunned as the massive hand shook mine. "The Sultan of Brunei wants to ensure that he is a priority when he requires any of your services sir."

"Absolutely sir, I will ensure he is looked after appropriately." As he had a relatively small entourage, I had almost forgotten The Sultan was attending this meeting as well.

Slipping his glasses back on, the hand shook me again: "Here is a list of The Sultan's immediate requirements for his room. The Sultan thanks you in advance sir!"

I looked down at the list that had been slipped into my palm as we shook hands: glasses, plates, cutlery, linen, coffee cups. Easy! Underneath the list, two $100 US bank notes poked out. I raced upstairs.

"Eddie, I need this list to be up in room 459 in ten minutes, no later!"

After all the intensive security checks were done and the delegates checked in, the hotel was virtually sealed off from the outside world. The restaurants and banquet rooms were pretty quiet over the five days. Room Service and Minibars however, were doing a brisk trade.

The Sultan was what we call a 'high user' in Room Service. He wanted only two people to deliver to his room over his stay. Fast Eddie and Wee Babs were given the assignment. These two normally stopped just shy of announcing over the PA System anytime they got a good tip. Now, however, they kept silent.

They stuck to their task with rigorous vim. They wouldn't even tell me when I asked how much they were getting at each delivery, but every now and again, Eddie's guilt got the better of him and he would slip me $50 US as a 'thank you' for the assignment. Babs of course, would never have entertained such a thought.

The Sultan seemed to like the Scottish shortbread. Every day he would order a box of it. We had no idea what to charge. It wasn't usually sold as a 'bulk' item. I called Drew.

"Charge him seventy pounds," Drew said, half in jest. He was joking, but as we discussed it, we decided The Sultan probably had no idea what anything cost anyway. We charged seventy pounds for each box: a profit of sixty pounds per box! The Sultan, or his money men who signed for everything at least, didn't blink an eye.

The other delegations did not go so smoothly. A brigade of chefs would just appear en masse and take over areas of the kitchen. They not only commandeered the cooking areas, but when one delegation's chefs spotted another delegation's chefs, a war broke out. There was not only a push for space, but a war over cooking essentials: pots, pans, and utensils were hot items.

The groups sent scouts out all over the kitchen area and took whatever they could find. Whoever got a hand to it first got to keep it for the week. Even as it was being washed, they would stand over it and wait for it to come out the other side of the dishwasher.

Quickly, Chef and Billy were starting to understand why Ingo was unhappy with Sales' arrangement. Orders would come in for the kitchen, and they had nothing to cook with. The groups of foreign chefs spoke very little or no English, but they made it pretty clear they were not going to share anything they had claimed. They wheeled it all lock, stock and barrel, up to their rooms each night, and back down again for breakfast.

As the two group's chefs appeared to be cooking for their own large groups, Chef wasn't too stretched at breakfast. Lunch time was a little different once the conference began though.

"Mike, what the fuck ees thees?" Chef didn't appear at my office very often.

"Chef, they just phoned the order in. They want the food in their room with two bed sheets in fifteen minutes."

Chef read the order out in front of me as in disbelief: "Twenty five chicken deeshes, twenty five fish deeshes, twenty five beef deeshes, twenty five orders of rice? Are you crayzee?"

I hated this. Every time you put an order in that the kitchen didn't like, it was your fault. Presumably for allowing the guest to order! "I just got a call from their guy. The conference has broken for lunch. They'll be in their room in fifteen minutes."

"Seventy five people in one room?"

"No. The guy doesn't have time to take an order from them all, so he ordered one dish of each to cover all bases."

Just as he was about to lambaste me again, the phone rang. Chef was about to walk away but I quickly waved him back as I repeated the order back over the phone: "Twenty chicken dishes, twenty fish dishes, twenty beef dishes."

Chef breathed a small sigh of relief. "They cut back ze order down to twenty?"

"No. That's the other group. They want the same thing for twenty people, without all the extra rice."

"Oh la la!" As he stumbled away, mumbling and no doubt swearing at me in French, I ran down to housekeeping for the bed sheets.

"What do you need those for?" Lorraine, the Head Housekeeper asked.

"I'm not sure actually. They asked for them with their lunch." Reluctantly, she handed them over.

With a couple of restaurant staff to assist, Eddie delivered to one group while Babs delivered to the other.

Billy, shaking his head and muttering to himself, came out of the elevator with his trolley of kitchen supplies as the food finally went on its way up. The groups were calling every sixty seconds to check on its progress. I didn't dare ask Chef to 'put a rush on it' as they'd requested.

By this time, Billy had forgotten all about paperwork completely. He almost emptied his storage area trying to get enough equipment up to Chef, who in turn started locking it in his office when it wasn't on a stove. Security was tighter around the kitchen than around the Sultan of Brunei!

Barbara was back first. "What's the sheets for?" I asked.

"It's disgusting! They just put the sheets on the floor and emptied the whole trolley of food in the middle and sat down and ate from it." She certainly looked disgusted.

"Babs," I tried to enlighten her, "that's their culture."

She wasn't finished though. "And then one of them pulled me into the bathroom. He just stood and pointed at the toilet and kept saying 'clean' to me."

I, and the crowd that had gathered, all laughed heartily. "It's not funny," she persisted. "There were two other males with me, but he kept telling me only. I tried to tell him I'd call housekeeping, but he cut me off every time."

This went on for a couple of days and the more she told everyone about it, the more upset she got. "I'll come up with you next time," I giggled, trying to calm her down.

Shortly thereafter, we went up to clear the food as the group returned to the conference. One of them opened the door and let us file in. Eddie and I got through the doorway and into the converted meeting room (the bed was mysteriously missing) without incident.

We turned to see the gentleman standing in front of Wee Babs, pointing at the toilet. He had obviously learned her name from the name badge as the instructions changed slightly. "Bar-ba-ra clean," he announced in broken syllables. Eddie and I managed to maintain a straight face until we looked at each other, and then blew raspberries. Babs stormed off down the corridor as Eddie and I quickly tied the corners of the sheets together, thereby removing the dining room table, and followed after her.

At the nine o' clock F&B briefing the next morning Cynthia was a surprise, and rather unwelcome guest. "One of the groups doesn't like the room service menu. They would like more 'Indian' style food. Tandoori chicken, you know…that kind of thing."

Chef's red face indicated he would have liked to answer first, but Ingo cut him off sharply. "Thank you Cynthia. Can we get back to you in an hour or two with some options?" Sensing her presence was not welcome, she left with a quick about-turn and a slight incline of the head.

"Eengo, I am not cooking fucking Indian food…this is a five-star hotel!"

"Chef, can we just do a couple of dishes? Please!"

"We are not a fast-food take-out joint! We cannot do this!" Chef was putting his clogs down firmly on this one, but he had inspired Ingo.

"That's it!" he rang out as we all looked at each other. "We'll order from a take-out and serve it on our plates!" He looked thoroughly pleased with himself. There was silence for a moment, and then a few sniggers, which ended in great bellowing laughs.

"This has to remain top secret," Ingo added gratuitously.

Chef himself was dispatched to the nearest Indian take-out restaurant. Ingo typed the menu onto hotel letterhead paper and £5 added to each dish. An hour later, Cynthia was clearly impressed as she perused our new 'Indian-inspired Room Service menu.'

The menu was a hit. The secret orders were taken directly to Concierge, who phoned in the order and made the short journey to collect it. Concierge returned the food to Chef, who removed the tin foil containers and plated the food on hotel crockery.

For three nights it worked like a dream. On the fourth night, the order was taking longer than usual. Chef called Concierge to ask why it was taking so long. "We forgot to phone it in!" he was told.

"Merde! Tell them to rush it. Vite! Vite!"

Chef picked up the phone when it rang only seconds later. Concierge: "They closed fifteen minutes ago."

There was no time to waste now. Ingo, Chef and three other chefs jumped into taxis and set off in opposite directions looking for Indian restaurants. Within twenty five minutes they were all back in the kitchen, emptying tin foil boxes onto plates. In a panic, Ingo had just bought ten of everything at his take-away restaurant, hoping it would cover what the others couldn't find.

"Take it all up!" he shouted as he wiped the sweat from his nose with his rolled up sleeve. I didn't even know what was on the plates as they were rushed up to the room. Luckily, this was their last night.

Cynthia was an unwelcome sight again at the F&B briefing the next morning: hands on hips and cheeks sucked in; she meant business. "What is this?" she spat as she waved a glossy brochure in the air.

There was silence for a moment as she threw it down on Ingo's desk.

Steve White certainly didn't care what Cynthia thought of him, so he grinned like the Cheshire cat, trying to wind her up. "Looks like a take-out menu from across the road. I hear they're very good. Anybody want to order some lunch from them today?"

Ingo shot him the death stare as Cynthia continued on her mission. "It was found on one of the room service trolleys last night; when it was delivered with their order." Her work done here, she picked up the menu and left. She left the door open though, so Ingo could watch her march straight into the GM's office. Lorraine was only seconds behind her, carrying some of her food-stained bed sheets.

After the take-away fiasco, nobody was sorry to see the large groups leave. Everyone was sorry to see The Sultan leave though. None more so than Fast Eddie and Wee Babs.

They were called down to Reception on his last day. The money men were waiting for them. "The Sultan thanks you for your service," they received with their respective handshakes. Unlike the Room Service Manager, they did not receive a couple of US bank notes. They received an envelope.

I never did find out exactly how much was in them. Much to Eddie's annoyance, Wee Babs could not keep her mouth shut for long though. Although she wasn't exact, it being higher than she could count to, she gave everyone the impression it was several thousand pounds.

Drew was happy too. The Sultan asked to purchase every box of shortbread we had in the hotel, at seventy pounds a box. He flew home with over one hundred and fifty boxes of it, at the bargain price of ten thousand pounds! A pretty good bit of business that had everyone smiling. Well, almost everyone. Sofia was not impressed when she was told there would be no shortbread for three days...the light or the dark stuff!

When there is no banquet business, the strain between F&B and Sales is at its peak. Banquet Managers sweat blood to find their staff shifts in other departments, knowing they may lose them completely if they get no hours at all. They lose sleep trying to dream up excuses and promises they can make to those they couldn't find hours for. And as they watch their bonus go down the toilet, the F&B Departmental Managers watch the Sales Team wander in with their Starbucks cups, giggling with glee, in the anticipation of another quiet day on the phones.

When communicating with the SOD, there is no point trying to be positive with them; they will still tell everyone that F&B are negative. Do not use comedy as an opener in an attempt to put them in a positive frame of mind either; they have no sense of humor. And whatever you do, do not buy them their usual Starbucks fare in an attempt to sweeten them up; it will not be as hot or as tasty as it is when their own barista makes it personally for them.

There is only one rule for communicating with these SOD's: avoid it at all costs. If you somehow get caught out and accidentally communicate with them, place some cotton in your ears, a pillow down your pants, bend over, and enjoy the short wait for the GM to rush in and test how many feathers are in the pillow.

The F&B Manager must also never, no matter how obvious, point a finger of blame in the direction of the SOD. They are governed by none, above the laws of the rest of the peasants. In reality, their mistakes are usually so glaring that this is not required anyway. The F&B Manager will become all too familiar with the signs of a SOD cock-up.

Always, there is the sullen look on their wounded chops. Then, the sneers, sniggers and whisperings from the rest of the Sales Team are directed at the SOD. Finally, there is the sickening pity the General Manager asks of everyone.

I have seen it several times over the years, but my favorites were at The Grosvenor. The SOD arrived at the hotel one morning without a Starbucks cup in his hand, and a very glum look on his face. This turned out to be an unrelated coincidence. Ten minutes later, the General Manager walked into my office and closed the door, to explain the real reason he wasn't his usual sickening self.

"Listen, don't go up to Sales today. They are all in a terrible mood up there. Alex sent an e-mail out to the whole Sales Team and he forgot the attachment had all their salaries on it. Now they're all asking for a raise and they're not speaking to each other. I don't know what I'm going to do. Poor Alex."

'Poor Alex!' I couldn't believe my ears. Had anyone else in the hotel been this stupid, they would have been frog-marched into HR (not passing Starbucks, not collecting a non-fat mocha with extra whip) for at least a final written warning. Now we were all supposed to feel sorry for him?

'Poor Alex' was the cry again when he, as part of a promotion, handed out over a hundred tickets to a theatre show to the hotel's best clients and some they were trying to woo over from competing hotels. Normally the clients will send a thank you card or letter afterwards. Worry began to grow when none of the clients had responded after a few days.

The Marketing girl, Natalie, had been given a couple of extra tickets for herself. The next morning she informed a howling crowd at the 9:00am meeting that she and her mother had walked out after twenty minutes. Apparently the very frank lesbian theme was not to their particular taste, although 'the very rowdy gay crowd appeared to have no problem with it.'

Alex, obviously tipped off, did not attend that meeting. Perhaps he was working out how much business this promotion had brought the hotel.

This particular SOD spent virtually no time with his Catering Sales Team. This was partially because of the smaller revenue they generated, but mostly because he did not have a clue about anything to do with Catering. This leaderless lot was therefore left to do as they please, but being part of the Sales Team, they were still protected.

A hush settled quickly over the peasants inside the arena as the doors were slowly opened and held. On the left: Rachel, Marquess of Level Three. On the right: Lisa, Baroness of Starbucks. This was a sight for lowly eyes already, but today was truly a special day. The Prince himself was attending court. Nobody had expected this.

Prince Alex stood proudly in the doorway for several seconds, allowing everyone to drink in his Royal Greatness. All stood as the doors swung closed in slow motion; the sun catching his rainbow cufflinks and sending a shimmer across the eyes of everyone in his audience.

The Marquess settled herself in and, reaching for her proclamation, officially opened the proceedings: "Friday. ECL in Meeting Room C."

Thus began the weekly catering meeting.

Every Thursday the Food and Beverage Manager, Chef, the Catering Sales team and our Meeting Specialist, Julia, would meet to review the remainder of this week's and all of the following week's events. The Director of Sales was supposed to attend these as well, but rarely lowered himself to it.

For Food and Beverage, this gathering was an opportunity to point out all the obvious errors on the Event Orders. The less obvious ones would be pointed out by the organizer of the event, when they arrived on their scheduled date: "No, no, no! This is not how the room was supposed to be set up!"

"Wrong," Chef objected. "I have Strategic Intelligence in Room B." The events were supposed to be run through in time order, starting with the earliest event. This seemed to be a struggle for the Royal Family, most likely because their day was not dictated by any time. They dictated when things happened.

Rachel flipped rapidly through her binder. "Yes, I see. The food is served earlier with ECL, but the other meeting actually starts first." A justification! That was as close to an admission of error as I had ever heard from a Royal.

Rachel cleared her throat. "Nine o'clock boofette," she continued. "Consisting…"

"What?" It was Julia's turn to interrupt the proceedings now.

"Nine o'clock boofette," Rachel repeated; looking up in surprise.

"What's a boofette?" Julia was new at this time and hadn't acclimatized herself to Rachel's classics yet. Then again, Chef and I had been here two years and hadn't warmed to her patronizing ways. Julia was still getting used to the pronunciation of Rachel's name. According to Rachel, it was pronounced 'Raquel.' Much to her frustration, everyone therefore pronounced it 'Raychelle.'

Rachel had been a Sous Chef of sorts, navigating her way through countless disciplinaries, before coming to the realization that she was very close to being sacked. Most of these disciplinaries had concerned her attitude.

Chef couldn't stand her. Apart from the attitude, she was a hopeless chef and an even worse leader. Panic didn't set in amongst the other chefs until she stepped in to help them. Fortunately that didn't happen often; but when it did, Rachel was the first to point the finger of blame. This, despite the fact that she was supposed to be supervising, and had stepped in far too late to help the situation.

The only thing she excelled at was the one thing Chef hated more than anything else: the use of the condescending tone. She must certainly have known she had struck a chord with Chef in particular too…in the form of the pet name she had devised for him.

Seeking her way out of a dismissal, the most natural place on earth for her to transfer to was the Sales Team. Here her attitude could seethe and flourish relatively unnoticed, amongst the other snakes at least. Although customers would certainly feel her tongue lashing at them down the phone line.

I could understand perfectly why Chef wanted her gone; but why Sales could want to take her, and how HR could allow such a problem to move, was beyond me. "Chef," I had pleaded. "You're not getting rid of the problem; it's going to be worse! Imagine trying to get information out of her? Now we won't be able to do anything about it. Her attitude towards us is going to be worse!"

Nobody listened to the Food and Beverage Manager on this occasion; and now we were paying a heavy price.

It being clearly below Rachel to answer Julia, Chef stepped in. "Buffet. She means a buffet."

Rachel sucked in her cheeks, glared at Julia and stared straight through her: "May I continue?"

As we continued, Julia and Chef highlighted items from the smorgasbord of 'cut and paste' errors on the Event Orders. Dates, event numbers, number of attendees, prices; not one event order was free from error. During rebuttal, The Marquess crossed the excuses off the checklist that lay between her and the Baroness, as they were used up.

I dared to sneak a peak at Prince Alex. He twirled his pen almost thoughtfully, not even feigning interest. To be fair, he knew absolutely nothing about anything these peasants were discussing with his entourage. Nor did he want to know.

The tension in the room was indirectly proportionate to the number of excuses on the checklist. As the excuses ran out, the tension soared. "The organizer hasn't gotten back to me," Rachel sneered at Chef.

"Well it's less than eighteen hours until the event. Perhaps you could phone them and ask how many people are coming and what the hell they think they might like to eat!"

'Sirrah,' I thought to myself. He'll be hung for such talk to Royalty. Carefully, I stole another glance at Prince Alex, still admiring his cufflinks; before searching for the Marquess' checklist. All her excuses had been scored out now. Rachel stole a quick glance at Lisa. With the slightest hint of a nod from The Baroness, Rachel played her last card.

She dug up her softest, most condescending voice and let loose: "Cheffie, it's a last-minute pick-up. I have left a message for her."

'Cheffie.' Nothing made his blood boil like this. "Try the fucking phone!" he belted out, his face reddening. "I don't think she's going to find you in Starbucks you useless cow!"

I stared in horror at the three Starbucks cups in front of the Royal Family. One of the main reasons we never got all the information, or got the wrong information, on our event orders was that The Royal Family spent too much time at Starbucks. At least four times a day we would see them scurrying across the street. When spotted with the evidence upon their return, they usually felt the need to justify the field trip. 'The phones are really quiet today,' was the standard defense.

The Sales Office was on Level Three. It consisted of two bedrooms that had been converted into office space. On the left: the Room Sales office; on the right: the Catering Sales office. In between, the SOD's office, which no doubt was previously the toilet.

As you entered, you were immediately aware of two things. First, it was spacious. Prince Alex's office alone was larger than the F&B Office (shared by three of us) and the Chef's Office (also shared by three) combined. Prince Alex would never be accused of being anorexic, but even with the addition of his own private buffet in the office he would have had room to spare.

When Rachel had moved from Sous Chef to Sales, she had also upgraded her 'box' office for shoe space. She was definitely a shopper. On any given day there were at least twelve pairs of high-heeled shoes lined symmetrically under her desk.

In any other department, this would have been surplus to requirements. For the Sales Team however, dress codes were a thing of the past. Even the General Manager was powerless to do anything about it.

While staff in F&B were being pulled into HR for such unprofessional conduct as a missing name badge or unpolished shoes, Christina was setting new trends. One day she appeared dressed in a full nurse's outfit, missing only the white hat. She was garnering a fair bit of attention from the businessmen as they checked out. For quite some time she stood beside reception, seemingly oblivious, waiting for some clients who had arranged a site inspection. Perhaps they did show up, and failing to recognize her in the new hotel uniform, took their business elsewhere.

Christina's 'piece de resistance' (and my personal favorite) was without question her zebra outfit. A tight, short-sleeved white t-shirt was loosely covered with a black and white striped open vest, which stopped just short of the hips. Her plain white pants only served to accentuate the zebra-skin, high-heeled shoes.

Nicole was not best pleased when she saw the zebra standing in the lobby. "Is she wearing those things again? I can't believe it! That is not suitable attire for a hotel of this stature."

On the other hand, Christina was a member of the Sales Team, so Nicole did nothing; apart from bitch about it to everyone but Christina. Because of this, the lobby soon developed into a fashionista's catwalk. Not to be outdone, Rachel started wearing her knee-high black boots with four inch heels. This, with a mini-skirt, really put the 'F' in five-star for me.

"She looks like a hooker!" Nicole commented to anyone stopping to stare. So it came as a surprise, albeit a gentle one, when Nicole donned an eerily similar pair of knee-highs on the day Former President Clinton visited our hotel. As a former SOD herself, I decided not to joke about the dress code at the daily meeting that morning.

Apart from the obvious fashion faux-pas, the lobby floor was marble. Something had to give. I suggested to Nicole that she could put a stop to the boots, on grounds of Health and Safety, thereby eliminating any slight the Sales Team may feel.

The second thing you noticed when entering the Sales office was the light. Natural daylight! In the coffin-sized offices of F&B, I could easily go twelve hours without seeing daylight. The only time I noticed the weather was when a server passed by the office with wet hair.

Overlooking the pool below, the Catering office had views to the busy plaza across the street and, at kitty corner, gleaming like a beacon: Starbucks. It was easy to see why no work ever got finished up here.

I had briefly considered suggesting that Sales work from the Starbucks across the street. We were short on storage space for F&B and I thought they could use their laptops and cell phones just as easily over there. In the end I did not put the suggestion forward. The notion was so obvious that Sales must surely have done so already, and the move was probably imminent.

The Catering office was also home to the 'Fuck-Up Fairy.' Every Sales Team has one. This is the Catering girl that causes chaos every time her 'magic wand' touches something. The most interesting thing about the Fuck-Up Fairy is that no matter how many times they wave their magic wand, they seem completely and utterly oblivious to the magnitude of the problems they cause.

They are the only ones that can maintain a seemingly genuine smile in all the confusion. At first I mistook this for the kind of cool, calm grace that all service staff strive for when under pressure. It isn't. It is the irritating, foolish smile that does not belie the height of ignorance within. At The Park, I was to see it on the face of Katrina many times.

Katrina was the master of double-booking banquet rooms. She had done it so many times that I expected to find her dangling from a chandelier in a banquet room one day. Of course, at other times she didn't book the room at all.

It was 8:30am on a Saturday morning when I discovered the Fairy had waved her wand again. Some of the meeting rooms in this hotel were actually in the guest rooms. There was a long boardroom table in the room next to the sleeping quarters.

'Boardroom' set-ups required only minimal attention: pens, paper, water and maybe a couple of flipcharts. However this particular meeting required a TV and video player and two boxes of presentation handouts the organizer had sent ahead of time. The room had been set the night before, so all I had left to do was deliver the water and coffee when the meeting began.

As the door was locked when I tried to open it, I knocked. No answer. I knocked again, louder. Finally a bleary-eyed, robed gentleman opened the door. He did not look like he was about to give a presentation in less than thirty minutes.

"Good morning sir. I'm terribly sorry to have woken you. I didn't realize you were staying in the room as well. I have the tea, coffee and water for your meeting. Would you like me to set it out now, or come back in thirty minutes?"

"I think you have the wrong room. I don't have a meeting." He was pleasant enough, but as he was obviously just up, I tried again.

"We have a meeting here at 9:00am for the 'Critical Thinking Group.' Are you with this group sir?"

As he shook his head and closed the door I started a little critical thinking myself. Jill was Duty Manager this morning. What luck!

Jill was the current Catering Manager, but had one eye firmly set on the SOD position. She certainly had the personality disorders it. Jill was short for her weight; but she was certainly not short. What little personality she did have was overbearing, but control was her key attribute.

However, when she had no control over a situation, she crashed, spectacularly. Of particular annoyance to Jill, as with everyone else, was Katrina.

I phoned Jill from the lobby to explain the situation. "I'll take down all the signage; they'll be arriving any second. I'll wait up here 'til you can get up here and tell me where we can move it to. I don't want anyone else knocking on this guy's door."

Jill was a mess by the time she flew out of the elevator minutes later. When she reached me she bent over and covered her face with her hands. "I don't believe it," she shrieked. "I honestly don't believe it! I told her three times: 'make sure you block off the bedroom in the system.' I could kill her!"

'This is no laughing matter,' I thought to myself; however as she straightened up I realized she was really crying. Great! The organizer would be here any second and now I had two traumas to deal with.

As a man with a briefcase headed down the corridor toward us, I had to get her refocused: "Go and find us a room on lobby level while I try to explain this. I'll keep him here to re-direct people to the lobby. That'll give me time to set the room."

Jill was milling about outside the new meeting room, too scared to come in and help as I feverishly set it up. "Here comes the organizer with the last of his attendees," she whispered at me.

"All set?" he stated more than asked me. He was clearly unhappy, but just wanted to get on with his meeting.

"Absolutely sir. Jill here is just going to retrieve your two boxes from the other room and you are all set to go. Once again, please accept my apologies."

Inevitably, the Fuck-Up Fairy is never around when the shit actually hits the fan. I really expected to see Katrina with a black eye on Monday afternoon after this weekend debrief. It was not be.

A new rule was put in place for this special Fairy though. From that day on, she had to be present to 'meet and greet' the organizer from all her events. It didn't stop her from waving her wand around, but at least Banquets could get on with the business of correcting her mistakes while she was left to do all the apologizing.

If you hadn't already guessed, Rachel was the 'Fairy' at The Grosvenor.

You could be forgiven for thinking that if the phones really were as quiet as Rachel would have you believe, the few events she did manage to book, she would get right. You would be wrong though. But even this was not the biggest issue for F&B. It was the Fairy's outright refusal to take responsibility anytime she waved her wand. Unfortunately, her cock-ups were generally overshadowed (as far as the Royals were concerned) by a snide retort from F&B. It was a daily challenge, coming to a head at the weekly catering meeting.

In this case, Chef was right of course. Nobody can run a kitchen when you have a Sales Team depriving you of information. We knew that she would run upstairs after the meeting and find the scrap of paper she had taken the notes on probably two or three days ago. Ten minutes after this, a 'revised' event order would be e-mailed out, with a note: "I just got hold of the client and demanded the details from her right away."

Ironically, Chef could be equally culpable when it came to the issue of responsibility. It was only hours before this meeting that we had a complaint in the restaurant. A burger was taking too long. Jesse, the server, did his best to keep the lady calm. "I'm so sorry madam, we do make our burgers from scratch and they are all cooked to a minimum of medium-well for food safety. Because of the size of the burger, it does take a little bit longer."

Jesse's calm, reassuring demeanor worked. It was thirty minutes on the clock when he finally delivered it to her. One minute later, it was back in the kitchen. "Chef, she's been waiting thirty minutes, the burger is almost raw!"

Chef took a quick look and blew out a large sigh. "I've got to change these fucking burgers. They're shit!" Obviously it could not have been a cooking error.

The problem was that Chef's reaction would outweigh the real issue every time. Once again, 'Cheffie' had been outwitted.

The Marquess now shot her best disgusted glance along the table, closed her folder and pushed it forward. That was enough for Prince Alex. He squeezed out of his throne and shot through the doors, not even waiting for his ladies-in-waiting to open them for him.

I looked at Chef. Like a deer in the headlights, he returned my stare. We both knew Prince Alex was off to seek counsel with the Higher Power.

I had tried, obviously in vain, to work with Chef on the rules of engagement with The Royal Family. They had clearly been breached here.

"Communication with the Royal Family must be avoided wherever possible," I had told him. We collapsed back to the F&B Office for a recap of the rules.

"Chef, what the hell are you thinking? You fall for this every time!"

"Fucking bitch! I'll 'Cheffie' her if she ever calls me that again."

Chef knew all too well that the rules were simple in theory, but difficult to execute because of the emotion involved.

When communicating with Sales via e-mail, always have someone review your message before sending it. Remember that this is a written statement that can and is absolutely guaranteed to be used against you in the Kangaroo Court that is the GM's Office. If

Sales sends you an e-mail asking for something; reply and copy the DOS and GM on your response…it will save everyone time and let Sales know you are on to them.

If you e-mail Sales a question, ensure 'please' and 'thank you' appear a minimum of three times per paragraph. This will certainly not guarantee a response, but may save you an added comment that you were being 'negative' as well. Wherever possible, the best practice is to avoid contact by e-mail.

When communicating with Sales by phone, never leave a message. This can be tempting because they never answer their phones. However messages, if not forwarded to the SOD directly, will be played back in his presence at the very least. In some extreme cases, a phone message must be left, or else you will be charged with failing to return a Sales call. There is no defense when charged with this crime. In this event, leave a 'positive' message that you are returning their call and that they can call you back at their earliest convenience. Do not leave details of the answer they seek. Also ensure you have a witness for this 'call back' as it could also 'disappear' from the Sales phone and you will be duly charged.

The best time to call Sales is when a couple of them are on a Starbucks run; when you know the one you need to speak to is alone in the office. However; the best advice here is to try to avoid contact with Sales by phone altogether.

If communicating with a Sales member in person, try to catch them when they are alone, and make sure you have a witness. This will ensure the lies they make up about your reply cannot be substantiated. Bear in mind that it is difficult to catch them alone; their Starbucks orders generally requiring at least two sets of hands to carry. Even this communication method holds danger though: approaching a member of the Sales Team before they approach you will be construed as 'aggressive.'

Being physically confronted by a member of the Sales Team can be quite an ordeal for the F&B Manager too. When this happens, they are generally trying to catch you off guard and want you to agree to something you will instantly regret. In reality, whether you agree to it or not, unless your witnesses outnumber theirs…they'll say you did agree. The rule is obvious here: avoid verbal communication with the Sales Team at all costs.

If you are in your office when they approach, pick up the phone and mouth to the press gang that you will call them back when you get off the phone. Eventually, even the Sales Team will catch onto this ruse though; and wait at your door until you hang up. In this case, you have no option but to speak to them in person.

Remember: don't panic. Keep it short and sweet; and agree to nothing. A simple 'I'll get back to you on that' will do nicely. Keep all responses to a maximum of two sentences and nothing over two syllables to prevent your tone from being construed as aggressive. If you absolutely cannot avoid verbal communication, the Golden Rule is: no name-calling, shouting or sarcasm.

Cheffie had broken all the verbal rules here. He was in deep and he knew it. Chef needed help.

"What we need here is a distraction Chef," I offered. "You can't be taking the bait every time."

He hung his head and nodded. As he opened his mouth to speak, The Dick passed by. "Hey Chef, Nicole's looking for you. She wants to see you in her office right away."

When Chef returned thirty minutes later, he looked rather pale, but said nothing. We went out for a beer to continue our earlier conversation.

It took a few beers to see the answer clearly, but when it came it was a revelation. "The Dick!" Chef yelled out for everyone in the bar to ponder. "That's it! We'll bring The Dick to the catering meeting."

"Why?" I asked before the light bulb instantly lit up above my head. "Of course! He'll drive them nuts and we'll be in the clear."

"Two more beer!" Chef shouted triumphantly at the bartender. His excitement was palpable.

The truth was that Sales had scored The Dick off their Christmas card list a long time before this. I had a feeling it wouldn't take long for him to create a distraction in a meeting. But five minutes into his first catering meeting, he was surpassing even our high expectations of his annoyingness.

The Starbucks cups had barely hit the table when Rachel started us off again. "Okay, Monday in Meeting Room D."

The Dick cut in: "Why is there no room rental here? Is that a typo?"

"No," Rachel sighed. "I chose to reduce the room rental in order to secure the business." This was a constant war cry from Sales that was untouchable for Chef and me.

"You didn't reduce it, it's vanished completely," The Dick corrected her.

The Fairy rolled her eyes to the ceiling as she slowly swung her head around towards me. Although she remained wordless, she seemed to say: "May I move on now?"

The Dick wasn't done though. "Room rental is down three thousand dollars against budget in the first four days of the month. This is crazy!" he laughed, holding the evidence up to the courtroom.

Chef and I stole a careful grin across the table. This was fantastic! It wasn't just room rental either. The Dick didn't miss any of the Fairy's errors; and he pointed out every one of them, laughing incredulously at the sheer number of them. He was clearly enjoying himself.

The Fairy quietly took a sip of coffee to regain her composure every time The Dick opened his mouth. Prince Alex however, silently picked up his notebook and cup only halfway through the meeting and disappeared. Chef and I stole another glance, a more worried one this time. 'Too much, too soon?' we both wondered.

The Dick swung by the office shortly after the meeting again. Only this time it was to inform me that it was my presence that was requested in the GM's Office. As I neared the office, the SOD slithered out from under the GM's door and slipped away. Rumor had it this snake could sink low enough to slither under her door with a top hat on.

The relationship between the F&B Manager and the GM is totally dependant on the relationship between the SOD and the GM. This current GM was promoted from SOD to GM. That meant trouble for me.

When a SOD is promoted to GM, they have two choices: promote another sales person from within or hire a new SOD from outside the hotel.

Promoting a sales person from within will inevitably end in a road rage incident, because the GM still likes to have control of Sales. In this scenario, the GM promotes their former direct report in the arrogant belief that they will maintain the status quo (initiatives the new GM had put in place). A power struggle then ensues as the new SOD changes the SOD Classics' initiatives…perhaps highlighting their errors along the way. This is the preferred option for the F&B Manager as their frustration for each other will overshadow their hatred for the F&B Manager.

Hiring a SOD from outside is fraught with peril for the F&B Manager. At the interviewing stage, the GM can highlight the initiatives they put in place as SOD and assert their authority at this point. Very few 'new hires' will challenge the GM at this point, especially while on probation.

Of course, an even better solution for the GM is to hire a friend they used to work with (when they still had a friend) who they know cannot do the job. This sends a message to everyone else that the SOD is untouchable. This SOD is basically an ill-disguised informant; a rat in rat's clothing. Theirs is an incestuous relationship. The GM retains control of the Sales Department. In return for information, the new SOD has the GM's two hundred percent very vocal backing on every issue. This worst-case scenario for the F&B Manager, was the situation I found myself in.

By the time they have reached GM, a SOD has perfected their techniques for showing their disdain and jealousy-inspired hatred of the F&B Manager. However, it is important for the F&B Manager to remember that, as a SOD, they are still learning their craft.

I pondered this as I diligently took a seat in the principal's office, staring at the rat's notes in front of my GM.

"What is going on at the Catering Meeting? I heard that poor Rachel was almost in tears because Dick was badgering her every step of the way about room rental. Does he have any idea how hard it is in Sales?"

This was perfect! No mention of me or Chef. Our plan had worked. "Yes, I know he was out of line. I couldn't just pull him out of the meeting. I was just about to speak to him about his attitude when I got pulled through here. It certainly won't happen again."

I wasn't so confident about that last line, especially after having a chat with him. "Dick, just tone it down a little. Ease off to a tornado next week."

The Dick didn't ease off though. For the next four weeks, I didn't even wait for the call. I just headed straight to the GM's Office after the Catering Meeting for my weekly beating.

Pretty soon, the problem wasn't Dick any more; everyone knew he was an asshole. But he was consistently an asshole, and they had gotten used to The Dick's twisted and unethical ways. "Oh that's just The Dick," they would say when he had pissed someone off. The GM and SOD didn't see it that way though.

As far as they were concerned, the problem now was the poor F&B Manager because I didn't control my Dick. In my defense, Hercules would have struggled with this task. Contrary to their belief though, it wasn't from a lack of effort. The Dick simply paid no heed to my threats, or anyone else's for that matter. I banned him from attending the meeting. He still showed up. I moved the meeting from a Thursday to a Friday. He found out, and again showed up.

In the end, I stopped going to the meeting. Prince Alex stopped going too. Shortly thereafter, my weekly dose of verbal abuse came to an abrupt end also. I held a glimmer of hope that F&B had won the war of attrition.

If you are ever foolish enough to believe you have won a small battle with the SOD: beware. They are actually sucking you in deeper; drafting in reinforcements for a bigger battle. This aid comes from the other Royal Arm: The Front Office Manager. The F&B Manager must tread very carefully around this dangerous animal.

The threat posed by this manager can be diminished greatly by identification. The F&B Manager can work for years in the same hotel as the Front Officer Manager without ever meeting them, or knowing what they look like. You may receive e-mails with their name and title on it from time to time, but even this is rare.

At The Park, I had to be taken aside after a meeting in the GM's Office. "Mike, I needed your support in there. You never opened your mouth once!"

"Ingo, I didn't feel it was appropriate to talk hotel politics in front of our most frequent guest!" I replied.

"What? That's fucking Donna!" he shouted at me. I shrugged, still none the wiser. "Our Front Office Manager."

I had seen her around the public areas every once in a while. As she clearly found it beneath her to speak to me, I just assumed she was a guest. Ever since that time, I have made it a priority to ask to see a picture of the Front Office Manager when I start in a new hotel.

Sightings of snow leopards are reported more frequently than the FO Manager. They are similar creatures though; and you can bet they can see you coming before you see them. Over the years, I became a great tracker of the elusive Front Office Manager.

On one occasion, I had been charged with the task of tracking the beast to drop off a gift from Accounts. As I approached reception, the stench of lavender hung heavily in the air. I followed the beast's scent. I knew I was close.

As I entered the back office, I spotted a hole in the full length mirrored wall at the far end. As I neared the beast's cave, I realized it was a door…slightly ajar. I inched closer, holding my breath. Had it heard me? I couldn't resist a look behind me. Nothing. I didn't want to startle it and precipitate any sudden movements. I inched closer still and knocked bravely on the door. Silence.

The scent was overwhelming now. But the scent had changed: it now smelled like marshmallow. Was the beast was trying to throw me off the trail? In a daze of excitement I pushed the door open to find the lair empty. Well, not quite empty.

All the tell tale signs of the beast were apparent. Light background muzak hummed sweetly in my ears. On the desk, the zen garden sat front and centre. The trail of smoke from the lavender candles surrounding it indicated that I had narrowly missed my target. One was still lit on the window sill.

As I turned to leave I noted how the beast had remained at large so long: camouflage. I could see the entire back office from this cave, but nobody could see in. Here, the beast could sit in her cave acutely aware of her predators. It even had a trap door that led directly to the Reception area, should she need a quick getaway.

Fearing I had taken too long, I retraced my steps and went to leave when I noticed something else. Two rakes sat in the zen garden where there was usually only one. Had I discovered a nest? The sand looked like it had recently been disturbed too. As I leaned closer, the normally brass-colored rakes appeared to have a sticky white residue on them. Risking certain death, I carefully slid open the desk drawer.

There, on top of two Mars bars, sat an open bag of marshmallows. It seems the beast had been roasting them over lavender candles with the rake from her zen garden. All the talk of yoga and a 'new exercise regime' had been a red herring, as I'd suspected. I raced up to the SOD's office to confirm the identity of her accomplice. Sure enough, there was Prince Alex's zen garden, front and centre on his desk…minus the rake!

I have worked with many Front Office Managers over the years. A few had been accused, privately, of having a cocaine habit. I knew the truth. The little white powder specks between their nose and their upper lip was really nothing more than a marshmallow habit. I judged at her current weekly weight gain, The Mute was roasting two packs a day.

The Front Office Manager at The Grosvenor was known in F&B as The Mute. Marshmallows apart, she was secrecy personified. The only quality of The Mute that I liked was that you didn't need to worry about 'rules of communication' with her. In fact, you didn't need them at all. She just didn't communicate with F&B…directly.

In her communicational absence, I tried to communicate with The Mute via her staff. Unfortunately, most of her staff were also her equal in communication skills. As luck would have it, it was always Stefan Petrov on the desk when I needed to ask a question or give instructions. Whatever it was, it had to be hand written for this special employee. He would still screw things up, but at least I had a hard copy for back-up.

Mr. Petrov was definitely not playing with a full deck. Perhaps he was a 'Fuck-Up Fairy' in a former life; but whatever the reason, absolutely nothing I asked him to do ever got done. I mentioned this to Carol in HR over lunch one day, as she dissected the restaurant service.

"What's the deal with Stefan? Did he transfer down from Sales?" I enquired.

She nearly choked on her lobster thermidor. Taking a quick look over her shoulder, she shook her head. "He is insane," she laughed. "Pop by my office after lunch."

When she had wiped the lobster sauce from her chin and finished her critique of the restaurant service for the day, Carol enlightened me a little further. Mr. Petrov happened to be walking a tightrope of written warnings. His latest transgression involved writing his local Member of Parliament. The language in the letter was abrasive and the central theme could certainly not be missed, even by a MP.

"Brother…I encourage you to stand up and be counted in this fight… We must fight the power…to keep these refugees out of our country. Stop immigration now!
Your faithful servant,
Stefan Petrov."

Freedom of thought is generally allowed in most hotels. Freedom of speech is also occasionally permitted, even encouraged in the Front Office and Sales departments.

Freedom of the press on the other hand, can be different. Mr. Petrov had typed his abbreviated version of Mein Kampf on hotel letterhead paper. He may have gotten away with this, had he not left the original copy in the photocopier. What he needed a second copy for I could not hazard a guess. As luck would have it, HR was next in line for the photocopier. To top it all off, Mr. P had immigrated to Canada himself only three years prior to this!

I kept a closer eye on Mr. P from this point on. I was always happy to see him on the front desk. It meant he wasn't fucking up room service orders on the phone in the back office. He was the best I've ever seen at this. No order was too simple for him. On the odd occasion when he did get an order right, he would get the room number wrong (if he remembered to get a room number at all) or forget to send the order to the kitchen. But what really set Mr. P apart from the others was his originality and sheer defiance in trying to cover it all up.

Where others were satisfied with a bemused look and an elegant 'how did that happen?' Mr. P would try to hide the evidence. As with every error, I tried to find out where it had all gone pear-shaped; to ensure that the same mistake wasn't replicated for other guests. Mr. P had his own agenda though: avoiding yet another written warning.

I'd dig the scrunched up order (with his handwriting) out of the garbage or recycling bin and ask him what had gone wrong with the order. "It wasn't me," he'd say in a panic. "I was on a break." Then he'd pick up the phone and point at the switchboard: "I'm too busy to talk about it." As the phone never rang, he obviously presumed I was deaf as well as dumb.

In spite of this, Mr. P managed to survive in front office for quite a while. He had to be bribing someone. I had a suspicion he was bringing in a bag of marshmallows for that special someone every day, because everything he touched turned to shit. I must have sent The Mute a dozen e-mails chronicling his ridiculous errors before I realized I was wasting my time.

Mr. P was even kicked off the hotel's 'beer league' volleyball team for being 'over-competitive.' Several complaints had rained in. Not just from other hotels and referees, but from his colleagues as well. I only found out by accident when I asked him how the team was doing.

"Who needs those fucking whiners? Anyway, I coach a twelve year-old girls soccer team, so I could use the time off." A comforting thought.

Unfortunately, The Mute trusted only herself with the Top Secret task of programming passwords for the computer systems. So I had to persevere with e-mails to her for this. Predictably, they were never returned. In F&B, only The Dick and I had been issued computer passwords, because we were on the books before she arrived. The rest of F&B had to use our passwords for access to everything. Of course, this was a problem from a security point of view, but there was little I could do about it. So it came as a gentle surprise when The Mute went to the GM about this 'serious breach of security' herself. Looking back, a much bigger set up was in store for me, so this was obviously a trial run.

From the witness stand, I presented my evidence to the judge in hope of clearing my tarnished name. "Your Majesty, I can produce over a dozen e-mails pleading for passwords for nine members of the F&B department."

In a surprise tactic, the judge retired to consult with the prosecution. The prosecution was unable to produce, as evidence, a single response to any of the humble requests. Incredulously this led only to a hung jury, instead of an acquittal. "Send her another e-mail with a list of all the staff that still require a password," was the verdict handed down. "And copy me in on it."

Eight packets of marshmallows and four days later, I still had no reply from The Mute. I forwarded the same e-mail to both judge and prosecutor again, as a gentle reminder. Still, there was no reply. I changed tack; walking past the beast's lair several times that day, hoping to jog its memory.

At each passing, her eyes barely surfaced above the rim of her computer to see who dared trigger the silent alarm set at three paces from her door. Her computer screen faced her and she faced the door so that nobody could see what was on her screen. This would allow her to close down the Top Secret files she had open on her computer, should someone get too close. Had I known what she was working on, I would have known why she needed the extra security.

Near the end of the day, I was dragged into the GM's Office one more time to be accused of 'badgering' the poor Front Office Manager. Never again did I trip the alarm outside The Mute's door. Nor did I ever receive the passwords. I decided a 'zero contact' policy was the best way to communicate with the Royal Family. They, however, had other plans.

Like a character in a Kafka novel, each dawn brought a new trial for some mysterious crime. Each day I would grow more desperate to clear my name. Each day I awaited my trial to find out what heinous crime my jailors had accused me of now.

Chapter eleven – Inhumane Resources

"That Isaac is sooo nice!"

As I gave the new F&B employee a tour of the hotel, I thought back to my earlier years; to a time when I had shared the same innocent thoughts. Years of hard labor in the Gulag had changed that of course. My alarm bells were blaring. I thought about giving her some hard facts on Isaac, the friendly Human Resources Manager.

"Yes, isn't he just?" She'd find out soon enough no doubt. Everyone does; one way or the other.

Jane seemed like my best friend when I arrived at The Park. Perhaps ten years my senior, I was flattered by the amount of personal attention the Director of HR paid me. I'd often see Jane in the cafeteria and she'd invite me to sit with her for lunch.

I noticed it made Peter, my direct boss, a little uneasy whenever she'd float up beside me and ask how things were going. When I became a manager, I realized why Peter was sweating. The truth is that when HR asks the new employee how things are going every few hours throughout their first week, what they are really doing is checking to see how thorough the training is going. Any negative comments or questions from the oblivious newbie will be added to the dossier to use against the aspiring F&B Manager.

Pretty soon, it wasn't just Peter who was looking uneasy about my friendliness with HR. I knew that a lot of staff disliked Jane. It wasn't hard to hear them snarling and sneering about HR in general. I never took any notice of this. I had always put it down to the fact that HR people were always so happy and exuberant. Of course, it's HR's job to be the happy, smiley public face of the hotel, and this was guaranteed to annoy a lot of people. Anyway, the unhappy staff were not exactly the Glitterati of the hotel. They more like the Shiterati: in and out of HR only to collect their written warnings.

The Shiterati are also, inevitably, the mouthpieces of the hotel. Mutely picking up their warnings, only to defend themselves in the public forum of the local pub. I still had to be careful though. On one hand, this was an opportunity to get my nose in with the career-makers. On the other hand, I couldn't isolate myself from the staff I secretly hoped to manage one day; and my current boss, who I would need to learn from.

Leaving nothing to chance, I decided to get some outside help with my development. Mary McDonald was the Training Manager at the hotel, and Jane's best friend. She was even more upbeat and bubbly than Jane; and with good reason. Mary was commanding a large salary. She had made this known to everyone in the form of her brand new BMW convertible. It was her pride and joy.

Mary and Jane taught me many management skills. Despite their best efforts however; I was never been able to master the art of brown-nosing with the General Manager, much to my financial misfortune. They went to great lengths to show me the importance of this skill though. The most shamefully obvious time being a 'Manager's retreat / planning meeting.'

It wasn't much of a retreat in truth. All the departmental managers got to spend eight hours cooped up in a meeting room at the hotel on the next block, with the Executive Committee…quite a thrill.

The idea was that we would discuss all the possible 'opportunities to improve' in the hotel. These would be narrowed down during the day, and we would all vote on what two issues were to be the Hotel Focus Issues for the next year. This was, from HR's perspective, a chance for the GM to show that he trusted the managers and their decision-making.

All was going fine until the votes were cast. No secret ballots on this occasion. Everyone went up in a scramble, to cast their seven check-mark votes beside the issues they felt most strongly about. Mary, presiding over the occasion, counted and then read out the votes. "So our focus issues for next year will be 'maintaining staffing levels' and 'revamping the staff recognition program!'" A small applause was quickly drowned out by the GM, casting his veto.

"Can I just say that I'm disappointed with this. If I'd known how this was going to turn out, I wouldn't have done it this way. I think we should focus on the two issues over here," he pointed at the flip chart next to the exit. The handwriting looked suspiciously like his own. All heads now rolled over to read it: 'more accountability for departmental payrolls,' and 'revamping the guest recognition program.'

My lightning-quick assessment that these seemed the very opposite of the popular vote was interrupted. "Let's vote again then!" Mary told her stunned audience as they observed a moment of silence.

It was blank looks all around the room as Mary, now joined by Jane, shocked everyone into action further. They quickly and dutifully placed all seven of their votes on the two issues their GM had suggested. The gauntlet had been thrown down. The rest of the Executive Committee followed suit. Enough of the other manager's felt obligated to vote accordingly too, as James reclined on his chair, hands folded behind his head: the 'power position.'

Champagne and strawberries were delivered into the room as Jane announced the new Hotel Focus Issues. Once again there was silence. What was there to celebrate? What had been achieved? Glasses were passed around for a toast to celebrate the coming together of managers from all departments to decide how to resolve the hotel's most worthwhile issues. You could have heard a pin drop.

In one sense, nobody could disagree with James when it actually came down to it. How could employee satisfaction come before guest satisfaction? It was all in the way it had been handled. What was the point of orchestrating an all-day meeting when he could have just e-mailed out his focus issues to everyone? Maybe he should have gone with the popular vote and lived with it for a year; putting it down as a lesson learned.

In any event, he didn't. He showed everyone what he thought of their opinions, lest there was any doubt in some of the more junior managers present.

He also ensured it didn't happen again as well. For her part in 'the Issuegate Scandal;' not being able to direct the group to the GM's issues in seven hours, Mary was relieved of her duties as Training Manager. Well, technically it was due to what the hotel called 'necessary restructuring.' Apparently the hotel no longer needed a Training Manager.

Jane was almost as angry about the situation as Mary. After all, it couldn't be easy firing your best friend. Jane was also no doubt aware that since restructuring is basically reallocating someone's duties, most of Mary's duties were going to fall on her desk. Mary's BMW convertible barely had time to collect her personal plates before both car and plates had to be returned as she 'restructured' her finances.

Most hotels don't have a Training Manager anymore. Most of their paperwork now falls on HR's desk, while department heads carry out the training duties, ironically with little or no training in how to do most of these tasks themselves. This is most glaringly obvious when it comes to the art of interviewing.

I had spent many hours training in this art with Mary and Jane. Unfortunately, a lot of managers feel they are able interviewers simply because they have the 'manager' title.

It all starts with the application form. Call me a snob, but I always like to see nice, legible handwriting and correct spelling. After all, if they can't get it right on their resume, how were co-workers going to read their handovers in a logbook, or written orders at the bar?

Many applicants never even get to the interview stage though. A resume can speak volumes about a person's personality and therefore, suitability. I can recall several resumes that went around entire hotels, just so the department heads could have a laugh.

Such was the case of the young man who applied to our five-star hotel when his only food and beverage experience was highlighted by HR at the bottom of his resume: 'once dressed as a Christmas Elf and handed out mince pies.' HR was not happy with the reason I gave for not granting an interview: 'Perhaps when the Christmas season is upon us, Santa will bring us a gnome for the lounge.'

Related experience and flexibility in availability is what the F&B Manager looks for in a resume. When interviewing applicants, you are looking to double check their experience and seek their personality to ensure they are a good match for the environment and the staff they will be working with.

Some people put a lot of time and effort into their resume. I remember one that caught my eye. It was written like a restaurant menu. Under the 'starters' title were her contact details; under the 'Main Courses' banner, she had listed her work experience; and under 'desserts' were her references. It was thoughtfully laid out, and her attention to detail was excellent.

Others seem to write their resume while heavily medicated. Such was the case of the self-proclaimed 'Jedi-Dish Master.' This single-page resume started off well, with his name appearing to be spelled correctly. Under his name was a brief synopsis of the person: 'singer / songwriter, dishwasher extraordinaire, and really nice guy.' A sense of humor is a must in F&B. I continued reading.

In the 'about me' section he penned classics such as: "I do not get squeamish at the sight of clogged toilets...and actually find tasks such as peeling potatoes somewhat meditative. Really!" Under 'interests' appeared the gem: "I...foster delusions of future stardom."

But Dish Master saved his best for last. There was apparently no need for us to do a reference check because: "My employers write things like 'Silverware Saviour' and 'Jedi Dish-Master' on my tip envelopes. It's true! They love me there! They call me reliable, hardworking, personable and fiendishly attractive. And I'm a dishwasher! Can you believe it? I'm a rare thing, like unicorn sightings, or Elizabethans with teeth. I know you want to hire me, thus enabling me to maintain the sort of lifestyle to which I would like to become accustomed."

Of course, even a great resume like this one does not guarantee a good interview. Bronagh looked good on paper. With years of experience in The Park's sister hotel in Australia, I thought this interview was going to be a formality. So much so that I let Barbara sit in on the interview as part of her development.

The interview started innocently enough. When I enquired why she wanted to work in a hotel, I got the standard response: "I love meeting new people." I always laughed when I heard this. You knew someone hadn't been working in hotels long when they said this. I wondered how she would cope with Angus Reid, Sofia and some of our other nightmares.

However, the interview took a dramatic downturn when I asked Bronagh how long she planned on being with us. "Probably not very long," she cheered, stretching both arms up above her head and giving a smile she had obviously been saving up for a long time. "You see, I'm going to be a superstar."

As I was really looking for team players and not individual stars with their heads in the clouds, I quickly scribbled 'NFC' on her resume. HR phoned Bronagh the next day to give her the bad news; but she wasn't taking 'no' for an answer. I was enjoying the next day off when Bronagh appeared in the lounge. She asked for Barbara in my absence.

Wee Babs went out to find Bronagh crying up a storm. "Why didn't you hire me? I have lots of experience. I should be working here!"

Wee Babs, never one to take responsibility, replied in a panic: "It was Mike. I was just watching the interview. You'll have to ask Mike." The stress being too much for both of them, they ran off bawling in opposite directions.

On a positive note, this saved me a lot of valuable time since Babs was no longer interested in learning how to interview. Now I wouldn't have to teach her the 'interview over' signals for writing on a resume during the interview.

This is an essential communication tool between interviewers when you are interviewing someone together. It's customary to take notes during an interview, so you can review and compare the interviewees later. The problem is that the person being interviewed inevitably tries to read your notes while you are writing them. Therefore the notes must be written in code.

If the interview is not going well, there is no point dragging it out to thirty or forty-five minutes. So you want to communicate to your co-interviewer that you're going to cut it short and they should stop asking questions. HR always preferred interviewers to write '110' on the top of the resume. This means 'NO' (add a diagonal line between the 1's).

HR were responsible for all communication with applicants after the interview. Sometimes they called to offer the interviewee a job, but the vast majority of applicants were informed that they were unsuccessful. So the 110 was not only a note to the co-interviewer to cut it short, it also told HR (if they weren't at the interview) that they should send out a 'regret to inform' letter.

I didn't like the 110 rule. I went with 2FC (two fucking chances), and NFC (no fucking chance), much to Jane's disapproval.

Of course, there is also the possibility that the interviewee may send a regret to inform letter themselves. This happened to me at The Plaza when our HR Manager, Isaac, and I interviewed a young lady for a minibar attendant position.

Minibars is the Mother Of All Nightmares as far as hotel recruitment goes. Referred to in F&B circles as MOAN, due to the reaction from HR when they discover the impending vacancy. No wonder though! What kind of person wants to push a trolley around, by themselves, all day long and refill tiny fridges (at knee height) and coffee packets. A criminal record check is essential for these applicants.

Isaac was obviously excited when he threw her resume on my desk. He folded his arms and watched me as I read it. "She has lots of similar experience." I smiled at him. "Well done Mr. Isaac!"

"She's coming in today at noon!" he went on. "And she can start right away!" I hadn't seen him this happy since the last 'staff representative meeting' was cancelled.

The interview didn't last long. Isaac cut it short; no doubt scared she might say something he didn't want to hear. His only concern was that the minibar trolley might be too heavy for such a petite girl. "I think it will be alright Isaac. It's really not going far; just in and out of the elevator."

"No," he replied. "I think you should take her down and get her to try moving the trolley. Make sure she's comfortable with it." My F&B Manager instincts told me this was a bad idea.

I led her into the 'receiving' area where the trolley was stored. "Okay, there it is. Just push it back and forth along the ramp here," I said.

I stood back and watched in disbelief and horror as my suspicions were realized right in front of me. A scream emanated from her mouth as she jumped back. The color drained from her face as she covered her mouth and stared down at the ground where her feet had been only seconds before. A mouse, hiding inside, had jumped out to escape the moving trolley, only to be run over and splattered by one of the wheels.

One of the Concierge boys, hearing the scream, popped his head in the door. "Everything okay here?" He looked down at the dead mouse. "Oh! Another one! Wow there must be loads of 'em in here," he laughed.

I tried to soothe her as she covered her mouth to keep herself from vomiting. "Oh, it's a recent thing because of the construction across the street," I stammered. "We have pest controllers coming in today to put traps everywhere. They'll be gone in a week!" It was no use. As she turned to leave, I recognized the slow, confused walk of someone in shock.

I experienced a feeling of déjà-vu as I relayed the events to Isaac. The same shocked stare faced me as he slumped into his chair and covered his face with his hands. After a few seconds, he looked up again. "Any chance she'll still take the job?"

We didn't have long to find out. On Isaac's desk the next morning was a letter from our minibar hopeful. "Dear Isaac, thank you for taking the time to meet with me yesterday. I enjoyed learning about your wonderful hotel and I would like to be considered for any position in the hotel, except minibars."

Whether Human Resources like it or not, interviewing comes under their jurisdiction. Some HR Managers take the responsibility to train Department Heads in the art of interviewing. This frees up time for the HR Manager. Others feel it is their responsibility to interview every hotel candidate. If your HR Manager is in the latter category, you may have a Control Freak on your hands. Here's how to find out for certain:

Make it difficult for the HR Manager to attend the interviews. This can be done in three ways. First, schedule as many interviews as you possibly can. Second, bring in candidates whose resumes wouldn't normally make it to the interview stage. Finally, schedule interviews for times that are early morning or late evenings so they have to work long hours. Additionally, you may want to try scheduling interviews for times when the HR Manager will be in other meetings. They have the option of rescheduling their meeting in this scenario, but it is still an inconvenience.

If they still insist upon attending all the interviews, you have a Control Freak in HR. The option now is still good for the F&B Manager. This is when you must hand over all the resumes to HR, for them to interview. The Control Freak will prefer this option anyway. Now the sly F&B Manager can relax and wait for HR to come back with the list of candidates narrowed down from fifty, to three or four. Let HR do all the work for you!

Everyone in hotels thinks HR is the best job in the world. Part of this is because they always seem unreasonably happy. They do get some good assignments, but they also have to do a lot of other people's dirty work. HR is really the KGB of the hotel world. They are the General Manager's eyes, nose and ears. Theirs is a mysterious and dirty world that secretly plots the fate of hundreds behind closed doors; albeit with an alleged open-door policy.

For example: handling promotions. It is usually HR's job to announce anyone being promoted in the hotel. However, HR cannot win on this one because every decision will be frowned upon as 'unfair.' For every one person promoted, there are at least a dozen others who are disappointed with the decision: the people who didn't get the job or the co-workers in the unsuccessful (or successful) candidates department. The irony is that it is the Department Head that made the decision. HR just put the memo out!

By far the worst job HR has to do is letting people go. The Department Head is always there when it happens, but it is HR's job to lead the sacking; just to ensure it doesn't end up in a tribunal for unfair dismissal. No matter how much you may dislike the person getting sacked, this is never easy.

Every hotel has a different protocol for the firing of an employee. For Sally, Director of HR at The Grosvenor, it wasn't too bad. She covered HR for the three hotels in the local area. She could sack two chefs in one afternoon and still remain remarkably upbeat. Of course, she didn't have to work the extra sixty hours to keep the kitchen running. She also had the option of just picking up her briefcase and working at one of the other hotels for a few days, until the Head Chef had cooled down.

Isaac didn't have that luxury. He did have his own little preparedness routine for getting rid of people though. All he needed was a couple of 'heavies.'

Isaac winked at Chef and me as we chatted next to the HR Office. "Hey, can you guys hang around here at two-thirty sharp today?"

We grinned at each other. "Sure."

When Isaac had closed his door I asked first. "Any ideas?"

Chef shook his head. "Let's see…who's on this morning?"

They always did it at the end of your shift. That way they weren't caught short for scheduling and they still got eight hours out of the poor bastard. "The new Manager On Duty!" we whispered at each other. She had been high on my Death Wish List since she had arrived eight weeks ago.

The e-mail came out first. Unusual, and risky, but Engineering had the right day at least…an improvement! The new five digit code for the staff entrance let the entire hotel know at once someone had been sacked.

The HR office door opened at 2:45pm sharp. Pretty quick! Evidence of a few tears, but no kicking or screaming this time. Isaac shook his head almost invisibly. We were free to leave; our restrain and escort from the premises services not required on this occasion.

This tactic had obviously been borne out of necessity. You never knew how people were going to react. My first job had been in a pub. I was only nineteen, but I can vividly remember watching the General Manager getting a lesson in how quickly things could turn for the worse.

Dan was one of the pub's managers. He had handed in his notice, of his own accord by all accounts. Word was that he was going for a little holiday to a rehab clinic. On his last day, he was officially unemployed at 3pm. He shook hands with Milan, the GM, and they exchanged pleasantries. Milan even bought him a beer. Many of the regulars did too. By the time Dan's wife arrived at 6pm, Dan was being loaded into the back of a police car, kicking and screaming.

Four staff and the bouncer had tried to contain Dan as he suddenly snapped and started verbally jabbing at Milan, for no apparent reason. "Fuck you cockbreath! I'm going to kill you!" Dan was certainly no heavyweight, but Milan couldn't have weighed eighty pounds, even with the six-pack he left with in his backpack every night.

Dan, no doubt spurred on by Milan's refusal to be drawn into the ring, lunged at Milan. He caught Milan with at least one good shot, before Dan was pinned down long enough for Milan to escape with his life, and six-pack, out the back door.

It was with this thought in mind that I made my way to HR for another disciplinary. David, one of my Room Service staff, was suffering form chronic tardiness, and was on a final written warning when it happened again. As the three of us sat in the cramped office, I wriggled in my seat.

"David, how can we help you arrive on time? What can we do to make sure that you get here on time?" For twenty minutes, Isaac asked these two questions only, over and over and over; emphasizing different words on each occasion. His questioning technique was surely in contravention of the Geneva Convention. It was so ridiculously rhetorical that it was cruel and unusual; inhumane.

At first, the culprit failed to answer the questions. After a couple of minutes, David's head swayed from side to side in a 'no' gesture. Finally, as Isaac repeated the question for the hundredth time, tears began to flow freely. Isaac's handiwork finally completed, he handed over a tissue box, with his parting comment. "If you'd like to resign before we convene in private about what decision to make here, I would accept it."

That was one I would have rather missed. It's never fun to watch a grown man reduced to tears through interrogation. One I was sad to miss out on however; was Lucia's. She was hardly the quiet, introverted type. By all accounts, she had staggered into the lounge one evening with a rather unsavory group. She washed back several martinis before marching into the kitchen and stripping off her top to give all the chefs something to talk about.

And talk they did! Apart from the immediate rowdy disturbance it created, it also started a great debate as to whether the breasts in question were authentic. Unfortunately we never did find out for certain. Lucia and her alleged fake breasts had breached a couple of hotel policies here. I tried to imagine Isaac's face as he sat through the disciplinary, soon to be dismissal, hearing; the breasts in question pointed straight at him.

After Lucia had been dismissed, Chef went straight to Isaac and pleaded with him to give her another chance. Chef had twenty bucks riding on 'fake.' It wasn't the strangest request Isaac had ever seen though. HR get a lot of strange requests from staff.

Another of my special F&B employees had been harassing him for months over her benefits package. Karen argued and argued with Isaac for months that since her dog was technically dependant on her, her dog should be on her benefits program as a dependant.

"What's wrong with that?" I replied when he told me, looking for sympathy. "Give her the forms and tell her: 'when the dog can print and sign his name on them, you can take him to any Doctor you want!'"

This dog was no laughing matter though. It was the bane of my, Isaac's and her co-workers' existence. It had more lives than a cat, but it lived on death's door for years. At least once a week, Karen was late or sick because the dog had some sort of ailment. I tried to be partially sympathetic at first, but it was hard. We had a hotel to run! If she did come in when the dog was sick, she was the picture of misery; dabbing at her eyes and showing staff and guests pictures of the soon to be departed dog.

Alas it was not to be. She would take the dog to a naturopathic healer; burn incense for it and finally, complain about the cost of the vet when the first two efforts didn't work. Unfortunately, the dog always made a recovery of biblical proportions as I secretly wished for the bloody thing to keel over. Karen would need several months off to recover from the ordeal of course, but after a reasonable mourning period normality could resume.

Karen and her dog were a common mention at the monthly 'staff representative meeting.' HR is obligated by Law to carry these out; to ensure staff have a voice in the hotel. If you were to go by the minutes from these meetings, you could be forgiven for assuming it was a meeting of mutes. The minutes were usually half a page long, with half of this being accounted for by the names of reps in the 'apologies' list, for failing to attend.

Ideally, this meeting serves several purposes. It is supposed to promote communication between departments, since staff are always accusing management of not telling them anything. Reps are supposed to give a brief synopsis of what is happening in their department including anyone leaving or any new staff arriving. They should also nominate someone in their department for the coveted Employee of the Month award. This should be based on performance, so reasons for the nomination are to be provided also. The group would then, in their undoubted wisdom, vote for the hotel Employee of the Month.

Not being an ideal world, the meeting usually fell a fraction short of HR's expectations. Nobody ever came prepared for the meeting. In fact, most of the reps didn't even know why they were there; they had been told to attend by someone more senior than themselves. So, with nothing else to say, they simply repeated what they had been told to say by their nominator.

I was also forced to attend these meetings as the hotel's Health and Safety Committee Chairman. Jonny was the first to speak somebody's mind on one particular day: "We are really understaffed. Everyone is working so hard, it's really hot."

Jonny must have been a renowned negotiator back in the Philippines. He had only been here three weeks and already he had been appointed the Housekeeping Rep.

Isaac interrupted him and reiterated what the point of the meeting was for Jonny, and every one else I'm sure. "This is not an opportunity to tell everyone every week that you are short-staffed. You are here to share information about your departments, and relate information about other departments back to the staff in your own departments." This speech was to become the first point of duty for Isaac at every meeting thereafter.

Isaac also decided to solve the preparedness problem by issuing the reps with a 'meeting prep sheet.' The sheet asked the reps to prepare by getting consensus with their departmental co-workers on the following three questions: 1.What's new in your department? 2. Who is leaving / who is arriving? 3. Who does the department nominate for Employee of the Month and why?

Apart from the Night staff, who were outcasts anyway, nobody really wanted to win this nightmare award. The lucky winner could always expect such congratulations notes as: 'brown-noser,' 'ass-licker' or 'slut' adorning their photo on the corridor within a week. A heavy emotional price to pay for the fifty dollar Wal-Mart voucher.

When the Reps still didn't take responsibility for getting this information, Isaac changed his tactics again. He issued a new memo stating: 'While it is the responsibility of the staff to pick their rep; it is the department manager's responsibility to ensure they attend.' Isaac didn't notice he had left 'prepared' off the end of his sentence. The Dick noted it well.

F&B had chosen Cheryl. She could talk for Canada, but like most people who have too much to say, she was not very bright. In fact, in the unlikely event her IQ ever reached fifty, I would have advised her to sell. I quickly delegated the responsibility for Cheryl's attendance to The Dick. While other reps were only distinguishable to their departments five minutes prior to these meetings, when they rushed about trying to ask everyone the three questions, Cheryl walked in fully confident and prepared on this occasion. Prepared by The Dick that is.

I overheard him as he walked Cheryl towards the meeting room one afternoon. His arm draped around her shoulders; he almost had her in a headlock as he muttered, not quite softly enough for my liking: "Listen sweetie, everybody's happy here. Just shut up and smile. Don't say anything."

Sound advice for Cheryl. For once The Dick sounded reasonable. I made a mental note to increase my medication. I could have melted from the glare the GM shot me at the previous month's meeting when Cheryl informed the group that F&B's Employee of the Month nominee was Chris. When pressed for a reason she replied: "We all felt sorry for him. He's never been nominated before."

I waited patiently as Isaac skillfully conducted his way around the band of department stars, only to find none of them had shown up with his prep sheet. There were only two staff left to grill and we still didn't have a single nominee for Employee of the Month. Isaac turned a not overly hopeful glance toward Jonny.

"The staff don't like the cafeteria food."

"Thank you Jonny," Isaac interrupted before he could update us on the Housekeeping staffing levels. Isaac tapped his pencil violently on the table now. "Do you have a nominee for employee of the month Jonny?"

Even before Jonny could shake his head, Isaac's blank stare was fixed on Cheryl. Here it was: my moment of glory. I was sure she would pull out the prep sheet that I given her five days prior, and stun the crowd with how prepared she was. I had even filled in the dates of leavers and new arrivals for her, and suggested several candidates for nomination. Confidence flowed through me as I waited.

We all waited. I tried to cover my face as I mouthed the words to her: "Your sheet."

It woke her up. "Oh I forgot my notes at home." She looked nervously around the room as both Isaac and I slumped back in our chairs simultaneously. I had hoped she would take The Dick's advice, but not quite so literally.

Nicole wasn't letting me off the hook either. As Isaac pondered his next move, she smiled at me. "Mike, you're a F&B rep as well as Health and Safety. Who would you nominate from F&B?"

I wasn't sure what her plan was here, but I knew it wouldn't be anything good. I thought for a moment. We had no other candidates in the hotel. I quickly surmised that she would be hard pressed to veto the only person nominated. Was that it? Was I to get the backlash for choosing the dreaded Employee of the Month? This was dirty!

I could play dirty too though. It wasn't an easy choice. My bunch of ingrates wouldn't pull me (or anyone else for that matter) out of a burning car unless they were guaranteed a fifteen percent gratuity in advance. All eyes burned on me as I nodded my head slowly. "Karen," I replied.

The look of horror on Nicole's face slowly turned to a smile. Not a pretty one either: she had a nose only a Roman could love. She lowered it now and pointed it straight, as straight as was possible anyway, at me. "Okay, all hands up if you're voting for Karen," she stated, her bent beak never wavering from me.

'Only the dismal effort to pick a winner eclipses the performance of the lucky winner herself,' I thought to myself.

Another battle was in the offing now. Karen didn't care too much for any of the management team. However the entire hotel knew there was no love lost between Karen and 'Bitch-Nicole' as Karen affectionately called her. It would be a battle of wills.

Would Karen put aside her pride for the fifty bucks? It would kill her to have to accept it from Bitch-Nicole. Would Nicole break with tradition and forego the ritual of the cuddly photo shoot of the GM and the happy Employee of the Month?

I was glad I was not a betting man. I was pretty sure any of the servers would club their Granny for fifty bucks, but I was just as sure Karen would not pose with the Devil.

All bets were off when Karen cleverly managed to get one over on Bitch-Nicole. It appeared she was going to show up for the money-grab and the photo shoot, when Isaac received a phone call. It was Karen. Her dog had just been diagnosed with arthritis so she would not be able to attend the photo shoot after all. Needless to say, the photo opportunity was never rescheduled. Karen collected the prize money from HR three days later, when the dog had recovered sufficiently to allow Karen to return to light duties.

The information about Karen trying to get the dog covered on her benefits was supposed to be confidential of course. F&B Managers in Training take note: there is no such thing as confidentiality in a hotel. You may not be privy to all the goings-on, but you can be. All you need to do is stay on the good side of HR.

Jane had taught me this first. I knew who was going to be promoted to positions that hadn't even been vacated yet. And there was no stopping the flow of information once I arranged for one of my F&B Supervisors to do some cross-training in HR, because he was taking some HR courses. Within two days Matt 'the mole' Closs, under the pretext of carrying out admin duties, had informed me of the salaries of everyone in the entire hotel.

As far as HR goes, confidentiality is defined as 'not telling anyone who blabs.' You have to earn their trust first. Ironically enough, the best way to do this is to tell them something that is 'confidential.'

It was this discovery that led me to my initial theory that there is essentially only one species of HR Mgr: The Rat. I persevered with the scientific method, and through my series of trials and errors, discovered my theory was correct; but also that there were two sub-species of rat. One is governed by self-preservation; the other by self-promotion.

Rats governed by self-preservation are the Control Freaks. The Control Freak is good for staff, but very bad for managers. This species is readily differentiated from the self-promoter species by the type of information they hand over. The Control Freak personally benefits from the information they hand over, and show absolutely no signs of remorse.

In the Control Freak's effort to avoid doing any real work themselves, they go to great lengths to ensure that other managers carry out their work for them; like training.

I had come to the conclusion that Carol only attended the Executive Committee Meeting each month to ridicule Department Heads for their failure to document any training in their outlets. She had completely distanced herself from taking action on the topic though, lest action on her part be demanded.

Carol was an unwitting control freak; good at giving at advice, not so good at taking it. Her critique of the restaurant food and service was like a daily enema for me; without any of the alleged benefits of such a program.

The butter was salty. There was too much ice in the water. The fondue was bitter. The server couldn't recite all the ingredients of the lemon aioli. The busboy's name badge was askew. She managed to find a minimum of five complaints every day.

This wasn't hard for her. On the contrary, she obviously felt it was her duty to provide this service to the F&B Manager, perhaps in lieu of training. So much so that she spent ninety minutes over lunch in the fine dining restaurant every afternoon. She was certainly well-quantified, if not well-qualified, to provide a critique.

Bitch-Nicole picked up on it eventually. I had known for a while that Carol's dislike of Nicole was growing to Karen-like proportions. Carol often sounded off at me. "Can you believe that bitch is questioning my work ethic?"

Technically, I neither agreed nor disagreed. A shake of the head can mean many things.

Carol's dislike of Nicole was also becoming more and more public however; as she wanted people to make a stand for decency and denounce the GM. Nicole was soon in my office, testing the water and writing down the responses to my interrogation.

"How much time does Carol spend in the restaurant? Are you getting what you need from HR? Do you need more training in your department?" To avoid being sucked into this hate triangle, I distanced myself from both of them. There would only be one winner when the GM was involved.

Or so I thought. A week later, I noticed Carol was spending an obscene amount of time (and hotel money) in the restaurant. It was four courses and wine now, when it had been three courses and sparkling water before. Had Nicole backed down? Noticing my stare of disbelief, Carol waved me over. "Come and see me in my office after lunch."

An hour and a half later, I followed Carol into her office. Before I could take my seat the assault on my fragile ears had begun. "The fucking bitch! She's got statements from her buddies in Sales and Front Office. They all say I spend more time in the restaurant than in my office. She's forced me to resign."

My mouth hung open for quite some time before the words came to me. "She can't do that!"

"Well, she did. Fucking bitch!"

It wasn't quite what I had meant. Sure, Carol was losing her job, and that was unfortunate. But I was not only losing my HR Manager; I was losing my best customer!

Carol's departure spelled bad news from another perspective as well. Carol had hired me. Obviously with Nicole's approval, but Carol was also my biggest fan and promoter. I had been privy to everything going on in the hotel via Carol. Now I would need to start all over again with a new HR Manager.

Learning to work with a new HR Manager is like learning a new language. HR and the GM have codes for everything. You could be standing between them at times and be completely oblivious to the conversation.

Bitch-Nicole took the secret codes to a new level. So much so that she'd forget she was even doing it.

When I arrived at The Plaza, the Assistant F&B Manager, Aaron, had been trying to keep F&B afloat by himself for two months. Without the management skills of the F&B Manager, he had ended up working over seventy hours a week. He hadn't had a day off in two months.

The day of the annual staff barbecue landed in my first week of employment. Aaron approached me the day before the event. "Listen, it's my parents' anniversary tomorrow. They're going out for lunch and asked if I could go with them. I was hoping I could have the day off and miss the barbecue too?"

It seemed an easy decision to me. "Of course! Don't worry about it. You deserve it!" And he did deserve it, as far as I was concerned.

I was enjoying the beautiful sunny day at the barbecue immensely when Bitch-Nicole sidled up next to me. "Where's Aaron?"

"It's his parents' anniversary today. He's going out for lunch with them," I replied rather nonchalantly.

The shock was evident in her reply. "And you're okay with that?" she gasped.

"He hasn't had a day off in two months," I stuttered, trying to remain calm.

"Well that's a definite 'C L M,'" she spelled out.

I stared at her in wonderment until she realized her faux-pas. "Career-limiting move," she enlightened me before storming off.

I sucked my breath in sharply, wondering if I'd joined a hotel or the mafia. Abandoning my thoughts of leaving early, I ordered another veggie dog immediately.

Rats who are governed by self-promotion call themselves 'Developers.' Isaac considered himself a Developer. As far as the Developer is concerned, their primary job in the hotel is to ensure they are the first to congratulate someone anytime positive feedback comes in. More often than not, the 'positive feedback' was usually a staff member giving away something for free...almost always food or beverage.

The Executive Assistant's main role in a hotel is to ensure the GM's coffee hasn't been tampered with each morning. This is why they always order an extra pot: the first one is a tester. Licking stamps and filing may begin when this chore is successfully completed. But all admin duties come to a sharp halt when the mail is delivered.

The Executive Ass then tears open the mail in search of any positive feedback letters from guests. The letters are sorted into two piles: one for positive feedback, the other for complaints. The latter are passed directly to the KGB Director to schedule disciplinary hearings.

The Executive Ass then busies herself with the congratulatory e-mails. Each e-mail begins with a header along the lines of: "WOW I just received an incredible letter from Mr. X about the service provided by (enter moron's name here who gave away a free dinner for two because he sent them to a dirty room)."

The e-mail will conclude with something like: "It is because of staff like 'moron' who take personal responsibility for guest satisfaction, that we have the best hotel in the city. Keep up the great work team!"

I suppose the e-mail is supposed to provide a feel-good factor for the peasants in the Gulag. Presumably that's why these had to be e-mailed to the entire hotel. It usually had the opposite effect though. Chef would come running through to my office moments after the e-mails were sent. "Did you see how much they gave away last week? This is madness. And it's always food and beverage they give away!"

I had to agree. I was surprised we weren't bankrupt because of decision-making like this. No wonder guests kept returning! Didn't like the carpet in your room sir? No problem, I'll send up a bottle of Moet to compensate sir. My pleasure. Forgot to set your alarm clock madam? My apologies. Have dinner on us.

As Chef read off the list of freebies again for me, adding up the cost, the second set of e-mails started to 'ping' up in my Inbox. Chef put his calculator away. These were always a good laugh.

"Well done Maria. Keep up the great work."

"Congratulations Ali. What a great team player!"

This was definitely below his usual standard. It was Isaac's job to keep the good-feeling vibe alive via e-mail. He used to send out his follow-up congratulations within seconds of the first one appearing on our screens. And they were full-blooded affairs! "Wow, this is incredible feedback! Keep up the fantastic teamwork. This is what makes this hotel special for all our guests and staff!"

Absolutely sickening to be sure; but this is the handiwork of a Developer. What puzzled Chef and I was the sheer number of congratulatory e-mails coming in after his. Over the next twenty-four hours, brown-nosers from every department weren't happy unless they were filling up your inbox. It was a full-time job just deleting them all. I could never understand the need for these ass-lickers (one better than the brown-noser) to copy everybody in on it. You want to impress HR? Fine...send it to them!

Lately Isaac seemed to be going through the motions on these e-mails though. They lacked the usual gusto, which made it look half-hearted. Perhaps Chef and I had played a part in this. In an effort to show Isaac how ridiculous his e-mails looked, we would try to beat him to it.

As soon as the Executive Ass sent her e-mail out, we would e-mail Isaac immediately. "Isaac please send your follow-up e-mail out now. It's almost two minutes since the first one went out. Be sure to add: 'WOW what a great team' at the end." I didn't think it had worked at first. Isaac seemed to have absolutely no qualms with it. After all, Isaac knew he was a brown-noser. At least he was in on the joke this time. What he didn't enjoy was being left out of it.

The Executive Committee Meetings were becoming almost pointless. With all the nods, winks, funny looks and code language that was going on between Bitch-Nicole, Isaac and Prince Alex, it was like there were two separate meetings going on. The Snow Leopard was too busy stuffing her face throughout the meeting to notice this split. She would have joined any camp that threw her a marshmallow. Chef and I decided upon appropriate action immediately.

We decided to count how many times they 'excluded' us during the meeting. Every time one of us noticed them nodding or winking at each other, we would blatantly wink at each other. At this point, we would mark a consonant on our notepads. We used letters of the alphabet to count, as hash marks may have been too easy a code for them to crack. Their record for a two-hour meeting was thirty-six.

Prince Alex spotted us first. As he sat next to Chef, he was in prime position to copy Chef's notes. Prince Alex's eyes lit up like he'd spotted a free buffet when he thought he was on to something. Even from across the boardroom table I could see the large letters Chef had written for his benefit: 'NFB.' I got it right away: Nosey Fat Bastard.

Such was our confidence that they would never crack our code, I wrote back immediately: 'WFD' (Well Fucking Done). We tried to keep our three-letter codes to positive language like this, knowing they would be looking for more negative language in our codes.

I could hardly contain my laughter as I watched first Prince Alex, then Isaac, trying to discreetly copy the codes as they appeared on our notepads. As the meeting fizzled out, I wrote down 'TDB' (That Deserves a Beer) before both groups convened privately to discuss the events...and try to crack the codes. One group headed to Bitch-Nicole's office, while Chef and I raced to the pub two blocks away.

"That was brilliant!" Chef beamed.

"You should have seen that fat sneaky bastard's face when he saw half the alphabet on your paper," I laughed.

"How do we top that?"

I felt the color drain from my face. "Whoa! Chef, calm down. That was hilarious, but we've got some back-tracking to do here." He looked surprised, so I continued. "Look, Prince Alex and the Snow Leopard would love to get rid of us. I've already got a problem with The Dick pissing them off. We need to keep Isaac on our side! We can't keep doing this."

Over the years I'd had very few visits to HR for my own indiscretions. I'd definitely dodged a couple of bullets, but I wasn't about to hand them a loaded gun here.

My first close call was at Turnberry Golf and Spa Resort. Food and Beverage had had a wonderful year. Ingo was taking all the managers within F&B for a teambuilding weekend. Although there were a few fences needing mending within the group, we all knew this was Ingo's way of saying 'thank you.'

The scavenger hunt on the two hour drive from Edinburgh was interrupted only for a liquid lunch at the mid-point of the journey. Upon arrival at the hotel, we headed straight for the lounge where Ingo had champagne waiting for us as he handed out the scavenger hunt awards. I wasn't too bothered that I didn't win anything; my pal Drew had won a bottle of scotch.

As we finished our drinks, I noticed that the hotel seemed very quiet. 'Unusual for a world-renowned resort,' I thought.

"We meet back in the lounge at five o'clock for pre-dinner drinks," Ingo called out as we made our way to the check-in desk.

"Which way is the Spa?" Janet enquired.

"I'm afraid the Spa is closed for refurbishment this weekend," was the reply. The swimming pool was also closed for cleaning. "I thought you would have known," the girl continued. "To be honest, every other guest cancelled their stay when we told them."

We all looked at each other as Ingo's face reddened. It was noon. It was mid-winter and none of us were golfers anyway, so the option of a few holes wasn't even mentioned.

Drew spoke first: "Got a snooker table mate?"

There were ten of us in total. Ingo had included everyone possible for this trip, from the Purchaser to his Admin Assistant, Janet. It made for some tight shots as we all crammed into the small snooker room.

Drew quickly discovered that beverage service was available from the phone at the entrance to the snooker room. He ordered up a round, and then another. I suppose I never really noticed the others leaving one by one. What I can recall is that Drew kept ordering the beer and signing it to Ingo's room for quite some time.

I also clearly recall Janet's surprised face in the snooker room window a little while later. Seeing us, she opened the door. "You two are still here? It's five o'clock!"

We looked at each other, equally surprised, and burst out laughing. We hadn't even been to our rooms yet!

Staggering as quickly as we could to our rooms for a shower, we joined the others as they took their seats in the dining room. The room was eerie; surreal. I guessed it could seat at least five hundred people. My footsteps echoed loudly as I crossed the massive room's wooden floor toward our table. It was easy to spot. It was the only occupied table.

An alcohol-induced self-consciousness enveloped me as I took my seat next to Jean-Phillipe. I liked JP. Despite our age difference (he was fifteen years my senior) we worked together magnificently. And for a Frenchman, he had a great sense of humor.

Five-star hotels often means stuffy service. Ingo started counting the staff. "Jesus Christ! There's eight of them in here and we're the only table…and the only one's staying in the hotel!" Unlike JP, Ingo never relaxed.

Following protocol, Ingo deferred the wine order to JP. I giggled expectantly, knowing what was sure to follow. The sommelier returned to JP to present the white wine he had ordered. JP nodded slightly before the bottle was promptly opened and poured for him to taste.

You could literally have heard a pin drop on the far side of the room as JP swished it around his mouth, and swallowed. As the sommelier was about to move on to the next glass to begin pouring, JP's hand flicked out at the sommelier behind him. "Eet's off."

"Off sir?"

"Eet's off," JP repeated.

The sommelier was soon back at JP's shoulder with another bottle.

After a quick nose, JP threw his hand up in air. "Eet's off too," he stated very matter of fact.

The sommelier was rattled. "Perhaps I could recommend a bottle for sir, since I cannot guarantee the quality of this wine then?" At over two hundred dollars a bottle, the sommelier and Ingo had no doubt figured they weren't going to make much profit in this restaurant tonight.

JP took immediate offence however. Without even looking at his opponent, he sighed and snapped his fingers. "Bring me ze list."

When his dog had gone to fetch again, JP stuffed a piece of bread in his mouth and turned to show the semblance of a smirk. He leaned over and whispered in my ear: "Fuck him! Nobody tells me what wine to order. Today, I am ze guest!"

We both laughed aloud, but Ingo's cold, worried stare brought us down to size just before the sommelier's return with a new wine. I felt a kick on the shin moments before JP swallowed again. "I am sorry, but zees wine ees not right."

I recall Ingo's finger pointing at JP and wagging for several seconds before a new sommelier appeared. JP, obviously pleased that he had won the battle, allowed everyone else to finally enjoy a glass after the thirty minute ordeal.

After a relatively incident-free dinner, there was time for a nightcap in the lounge. "Teambuilding starts at nine o'clock," Ingo stated as he retired to his room. "And there'll be no more drinks signed to my room." He seemed to be speaking in the general direction of Drew and me.

Looking back, it was with good reason I suppose. However, we weren't quite ready for bed. Ingo may have cut off the hotel supply, but Drew had a bottle of scotch in his room. We decided to relax in front of the TV and enjoy one last drink.

I put my keys down on his coffee table, took off my tie and loosened my collar. I was about to recline on a chair when it occurred to me: 'I have to wear this suit tomorrow! I can't be lounging about in the pants and ruin the crease in them. It wouldn't look good.'

Instead, I took my trousers off and carefully folded them over another chair. Drew handed over what seemed like a pint of scotch as we sat down and turned on the TV. And that was that.

I don't think either of us took as much as one sip. By the time I woke up, God knows how long later, Drew was already passed out on top of his bed, fully clothed. I woke up on the chair with only one goal in mind: must get to my bed.

I stumbled out the door, got to the end of the corridor and halfway down the next one when I realized I hadn't a clue what my room number was. I had also left my room key on Drew's coffee table. Even worse, I'd left my pants on Drew's chair…and had no idea what his room number was either!

There was nothing left for it. I summoned up all the bravado I could and staggered down to the Front Desk in my boxer shorts and shirt, where a shocked Concierge and Front Desk Agent did not see the funny side of things. Not immediately anyway.

The two of them led me up to my room where I collapsed on the bed after somehow remembering to ask for a wake up call.

Never mind sober up, I still hadn't even woken up as I passed the Concierge on the way into the dining room to join the others for breakfast. The Concierge looked shocked to see me alive. He attempted to say 'Good morning sir,' but burst into a fit of hysterics and had to stagger away himself.

With or without Wee Babs, nothing on earth travels as fast as gossip in a hotel. A round of applause lit up the breakfast room as I walked in. The story had already made its way around not only the staff, but the guests as well.

Unfortunately, it had also reached my GM, Dorta, by the time we returned. I would have said she was cold-hearted if I thought there was the slightest chance of a heart being present at all. I dreaded what was coming.

Somehow, Ingo managed to intervene and bypass HR and Dorta. When he called me into his office, I still expected some sort of warning. However, as the door swung closed, he took his seat and smiled. "That was a good weekend huh?"

"Yeah," was the best I could do. 'Here it comes,' I thought. They always tried to make you feel good before hammering you. Ingo leaned forward now.

"Listen, Dorta's really pissed off. She wanted you disciplined."

"For what? Forgetting my key!"

"I know, but Mike, their GM called Dorta because it made their Duty Manager's Logbook." I cursed my luck. On any other weekend when real guests were staying there, this would hardly have been worthy of a mention.

We sat in silence for a moment until Ingo leaned back again. "Look, this is completely political, but this is what's going to happen. You're going to walk out this door and into Dorta's office and you're going to apologize to her. Okay?"

"But Ingo…"

"Mike, this is me giving you shit! Do you understand? This is political! Just apologize and it is over."

After a few deep breaths, I swallowed hard and did as I was told. Ingo had kept me out of HR, but I was still unsure which option I preferred.

It was with a heavy heart that I also had to remind Ingo I was due to return to Turnberry the very next week for my own team's teambuilding weekend!

He really didn't need to remind me to keep a low profile. In any event, the weekend passed without incident. The only noteworthy point being my return from a bathroom break during dinner. Much to everyone's delight, the band broke into an inspired rendition of 'Donald Where's Yer Troosers' as I re-entered the near-empty room and crossed the great hall again.

Strangely enough, it was while I was recounting this tale to the Head Chef at The Plaza, that I had another close encounter.

We had had a particularly tough week, and there was no break in sight. Chef and I finished our thirteen-hour day and had no choice but to visit our 'staff' pub nearby. After a few beer, Chef asked my opinion on some of the whisky he could see behind the bar.

Needless to say, we sampled a few, followed by a few more. When the bar had closed I rather sensibly remarked: "There's no way I could drive home!"

"I don't think I could walk to the bus stop," Chef hiccupped. "Fuck it, we'll get a room."

Thinking back to my previous tale, I hesitated. "I don't think that's a good idea Chef."

"Fuck off. I'll go and get the room. You take the stairs to the third floor, and I'll call you to tell you the room number."

Chef was on the phone to his wife as I opened the door: "Yeah, sorry honey. We just finished now and I need to start again at 6:00am. I just want to get as much sleep as I can."

I headed straight to the minibar. "Beer Chef?" I called when he had hung up.

"Fuck yeah!"

This was like a holiday. After we'd showered, we called room service. The bill was almost three hundred dollars for the food. I signed it to my account.

In the morning, Chef managed to get out of his bed and down to the kitchen for duty by eight o'clock. I was not quite as chipper that particular morning. As I struggled towards the shower at nine o'clock, I wondered how I was going to explain the room service bill to Bitch-Nicole at the end of the month.

By nine thirty, I managed to make it to the elevator. I got off on the third floor and took the fire exit stairs down to Lobby Level. There was no risk of seeing any other managers that way as most of them were far too lazy to take the stairs, and it brought me out two steps from my office.

I left the office door open briefly and told any staff walking past the truth: "I'm really not feeling well today and have a lot of paperwork to do, but I'm here if you need me." As soon as enough of them had spotted me, the door was closed. Three hours later, I went home sick, but not before my very last important duty.

I paged the minibar attendant. "Please re-stock room 609 free of charge. They were a previous complaint, so Front Desk told them to help themselves to it. I repeat, no charge for 609's minibar. Do you copy?"

The reply came over the mike: "No charge for minibar in 609. Copy that."

The truth came out eventually. Inevitably, all the staff found out at least. The Front Desk Agent who gave Chef a room and the Room Service Server who brought our mega-meal up had no doubt passed it on.

There was one major difference from my previous indiscretion this time though. Senior Management never found out. Chef was still terrified though. He was sure we would get caught when the room service bill had to be explained. I don't know why he was so worried; it was on my account!

There were perhaps two or three reasons we didn't get caught. First, we were Senior Management. No doubt some staff simply didn't feel they were allowed to complain about it.

Secondly, Chef and I treated our staff with respect. Most of the time anyway, but always to their faces. They could have dropped us in it if they had really wanted to. But the worst we heard about it was from Pseudo-Chef Davie: "What the fuck were you guys drinking?"

That was a statement coming from Davie. Although perhaps he really was just interested in what type of alcohol could get him so drunk.

Each month, Accounts would forward my account for me to sign and return to the GM. Where it went from there I had no idea, but I never paid for anything; that was all that mattered to me! This month the amount was certainly higher than my average. Of course, it wasn't in the same galaxy as Carol's weekly total. In any event, Bitch-Nicole barely glanced at it. "What's this one for three hundred?" she asked.

"A previous complaint with room service. They're happy now." General Manager's are terrified of complaints.

Fifteen minutes later, when I had recounted this to Chef, I could almost see the weight lifted from his shoulders.

The Dick looked at the whole thing differently of course. "Come on, what's the big deal? You should be allowed to do it. You're Executive Committee! Consider it a perk of the job!"

There was an element of truth to it being a perk I suppose. Although the free food and complimentary suites were what The Dick focused on; I was more appreciative of the fact that I was able to go home sick, well in this case hung-over, without any questions being asked. I wasn't even noticed.

However this 'perk' was also an Achilles Heel for the F&B Manager as I, and a few others, saw it. It said: 'expendable.'

Chef and I were now clearly on the outskirts of the Executive Circle, with an increasingly insecure and alienated HR Manager. F&B Manager's must be aware that when the General Manager doesn't trust you, and Human Resources don't return your phone calls; the game is no longer afoot…it's over!

Chapter twelve: The GM part II: The Fall and Rise of a General Manager

As Adam packed his dirty restaurant tablecloths and napkins into a laundry bag, I set the tables for breakfast. It was Adam's first week at The Grosvenor and Sara had stayed through the dinner shift to see how he was getting on. I checked my watch: 10:55pm. Our night would be done in five minutes when the Night team took over.

Helpful as ever, Sara leaned against the door at the restaurant entrance. She was watching us work when the phone rang on the podium beside her. Sara stared down at the phone. The shock of the loud ring must have caught her off guard, causing her to freeze into inaction. Slowly, she looked from the phone to her watch and back again.

Adam and I looked at each other. Was she going to answer it or not? She must have known that the 'standard' was to answer every call within three rings. After four rings, Adam decided she was not going to answer. With a furious purpose, he strode down the aisle and made straight for the phone.

As he put a hand out to brush her aside, she finally jumped into action. Blocking his route, she yelled out: "Don't answer it! It's a guest!"

It was Adam's turn to be stunned. The room service order duly lost, he returned to stuffing his laundry bag. When Dougie the Night Watchman showed up a few minutes later, the phone rang again. Dougie, unaware of Sara's ignorance of the standard, picked up the phone on the first ring; probably the first time he'd ever nabbed one before the eighth ring.

As Dougie wrote down the room service order, Sara strolled past Adam with a proud smile on her face. "See, you'd have been doing that order if you'd answered it."

Adam shook his head as he looked at me. It wasn't exactly the kind of leadership we had been used to. It shouldn't have been a shock to him now though. She had opened his eyes a few times in his first week.

He had had to ask his General Manager to stop serving tables in the restaurant because she was stealing the staff's tips. The staff claimed she was subsidizing her poor General Manager's salary by stopping at tables when she saw they were waiting for change. She would bring change from the till, and when they left money on the table, she would pocket it.

It was an awkward thing to approach your GM about. However, having witnessed it first hand, he had no choice.

Sara didn't agree with the assessment of the situation and was clearly surprised at the accusation. "But they gave it personally to me!" she pleaded to him. In the end, she agreed to return the crumpled five pound note, with a proviso. "I am not helping them out in that restaurant again."

Thankfully, she was as good as her word. She did rumble through the busy restaurant each morning for coffee though. It was on one of these sojourns that a guest asked Kali, one of the servers: "Is that the Hotel Manager?"

Kali nodded. "She's a bit rough!" the guest whispered.

It was well-noted. Today Sara was wearing black. She always wore a black shirt to highlight the ridiculous amount of dandruff flakes on her shoulders. But on this day she was also wearing black leather trousers and boots. It not only caught the eye, but when she positively marched down the laminate flooring of the restaurant aisle, it sent the cutlery on the tables bouncing up and down, creating a steely ringing noise throughout.

She just had no class. When Sara entered the lunch room, the staff cleared out. Her poor manners made it sickening to eat beside her. She talked with her mouth full and yelled over others as they chatted quietly. So it was with a sense of dread that she booked a Christmas party in the banquet suite for her entire family.

The room's capacity for a dinner was supposed to be sixty. Sara had sold eighty tickets to her family, with no discounted price. As I set the room, I sensed disaster was in the air. I could barely squeeze through the room of tightly-packed chairs when they were empty.

When the family arrived, my worst fears were confirmed: they were just like Sara. They guzzled down alcohol at the bar like prohibition was approaching as I opened the doors to the banquet suite. As she entered the room herself, Sara whispered in my ear: "Don't refund a penny!"

Steven Duncan, the Managing Director, always liked to pop by before each Christmas party night to ensure everything was under control. He stood with me at the service entrance and watched as the crowd climbed over tables and chairs to reach their seats.

Thoughtfully, he jingled some change in his pockets and summed it up perfectly. "Jesus Christ. It's like 'Night of the Living Dead' in there!" And with that he wished me good luck, and went on his way.

Before we could even get the starters out, complaints were ringing in my ears about the cramped seating. As the service staff tried to squeeze around the chairs, the Addams Family refused to lean in to help us reach the tables. They were getting their money's worth one way or the other.

By the time we got to the 'festive turkey' main course, at least two dozen had complained to me about the seating, the food, and the air conditioning in the room. Many simply got up and left. I was called through to reception where ten of them jumped me, demanding their money back.

During this argument, one of them ran through to the suite and pulled Sara away from her turkey dinner. A shouting match ensued. There were clearly some deep-seeded family matters that had not been resolved as a lot of name-calling and finger-pointing threatened to erupt into a punch-up.

By the time I got back to the festivities in the room, dessert had been served and the DJ was warming up. The sixty or so Living Dead who remained looked prepared to just cut their losses now and get on with getting pissed.

The DJ had the dance floor packed within a few songs and all seemed to be manageable again when he blew his amplifier. An almighty silence filled the air. "I normally bring a spare," he assured me, "but this time I didn't for some reason. I'll be back in an hour."

The silence was short-lived. Some just left in disgust. Unfortunately, the vast majority hounded me again, calling for Sara's head. When I told them she had already left the building, I was nearly pulled limb from limb. I was backed onto a staircase where I offered to put a bottle of wine on each of their tables until the DJ returned.

It was a miserable sight: the group of fifty or so now gorging themselves on free wine, yelling and complaining to each other about the festive family reunion. Eventually the yelling died down and they just sat about, listening to Perry Como's Christmas CD on an old boom box.

By the time the DJ did return, the party was already over. But my night was just beginning. Some of the group had also booked rooms in the hotel so they didn't have to worry about getting home.

Fifteen of them remained to slander Sara, the hotel, the Chef and my very good self as they demanded their money back. I would have loved to give it to them, but didn't have access to that kind of cash. So there I remained, behind the increasingly dimming safety of the reception desk, until two-thirty in the morning. At this point they agreed to come back tomorrow and see Sara herself; which they did.

Sara and the family representatives battled it out right in the lobby as guests checked in and out. At the end of another hour-long slagging match, Sara returned nothing. The

Living Dead then wrote to the Managing Director, who duly returned the money…and decided Sara's time was up.

Sara told me about her meeting with SD. "He sat me down and paced back and forth in front of me saying nothing. Then he just started at me, listing off hotels: 'The Sheraton. The Caley. The Balmoral…all hotels you could never be a GM at!'"

SD added his hotel on to the list. Sara announced she was going back to school to study astronomy. It made sense to me; her head was already in the clouds. However, she wasn't finished punishing SD quite yet. She came back to haunt the hotel group.

I discovered that the Assistant GM prior to me had left on bad terms and it was going to a tribunal for unfair dismissal. Now SD was in the unfortunate position of relying on the fruitcake he had just fired, to back him up on the witness stand.

They now had to put Sara up in the hotel and give her VIP treatment every time she was called in to meet with the lawyers, and eventually when she testified. Leon, the Hotel's solicitor told me: "We didn't know whether to put her on the stand or not. She's so unreliable we didn't know what she was going to say." Despite Sara, the Hotel won the case, but it was a nervy affair by all accounts.

While we waited to see who the next GM would be, SD had moved in to conduct his business from our hotel, while looking after the planning for the Group.

Nobody sat on the fence with Steven. You either loved him or you hated him; and vice versa. I already knew before his arrival that it was the people who worked closest to him that hated him…the GM's.

A few of them were scared of him; although I found this impossible. He was a cartoon-like figure and I couldn't help but laugh at him whenever I saw him. He was almost completely bald, and chubby. The ridiculous spring clips he insisted on wearing on his shirt sleeves reminded me of a cartoon: an editor hunched over a desk. At perhaps five feet tall only in heels, the spring clips would have been more suitable under his shoes.

I knew why the GM's disliked him of course. When Steven didn't like something…he overreacted slightly. "No, No, No, No, No, for the love of God! Laura! Why? Why didn't we fill the rooms last night? Almost every other hotel in the city did!" Picture the short, red-faced editor jumping up and down with steam coming out of his ears. That is SD cartoonified.

When he disagreed only mildly with someone, he would shake his head in his hands until he could summon the strength to correct them. This was when he took the time to articulate. This was special. I really enjoyed listening to him roll every 'r' for a full three seconds. It really dragged out the conversation and made his point hang in the air. Either that or he just liked the sound of his voice.

SD was also the ultimate micro-manager; no issue was too small for him to have to get involved in. He would call every hotel four times a day; and it was a sorry manager that wasn't ready with the info he wanted!

7:00am: "Hi Mike, did we sell out last night?"

"No Steven. Only sixty-three percent full last night."

Sharp intake of breath. "Oh no! Deary me." A few seconds of silence would elapse until he had recovered. "Any no-shows?"

"Two."

"Chargeable?"

"Yes."

"Alright then (deep sigh). What are we at tonight?"

"Sixty two percent…"

"Jeeeesus! Oh no, no, no! Mike! Okay, what are you selling at?"

"Seventy-five pounds."

"What! No, No. Come on Mike. We need to fill. Go down to fifty."

"Okay Steven."

12:00pm: "Hi Mike. Have you got the total revenue for last night then?"

"Eight thousand three hundred pounds."

Sharp intake of breath. "Oh jeeeez! (deep sigh) Alright. How's tonight looking?"

"Picking up a little. We're at seventy percent now."

"Good! Good job Mike." It was worth noting that neither of us had done anything to change the occupancy at this point. It was normal to fluctuate at least this much on any given day. "Okay, average rate?"

"Sixty three pounds."

"Sixty fucking WHAT? Mike, we can't afford to give them away. What are you thinking?"

"Steven, you told me to drop it to fifty pounds this morning."

"Mike, Mike, Mike. Look, eighty pounds or nothing. This is a four star hotel, not a hostel!"

3:00pm: "Hi Mike. How are we looking?"

"Still at seventy percent Steven. We're selling at sixty pounds to try to fill now."

Sharp intake of breath. "You're call Mike. I hope you're right."

7:00pm: "Occupancy?"

"Seventy-six percent."

"Fuuuuuck! Do whatever you can to get over eighty. Drop it to fifty pounds if you have to."

Steven was nothing if not indecisive. The problem was, whatever he was thinking just came out. He couldn't control himself in any situation, and his complete disregard for the unbelievably obvious was legendary.

HR received a lot of complaints from all levels of management regarding SD's behavior, but particularly about his behavior in meetings. Apart from his rants and outbursts, he showed a complete disrespect for others. His phone was never off, and every phone call was more important than what he was doing at the time.

In the middle of meetings, when his phone rang, the meeting suddenly stopped. SD picked up his phone and wandered in circles around the others at the table while everyone waited for this most important man. Not once did he ever excuse himself from the room. He just circled, waved his arms wildly, and shouted. Some tried to carry on the meeting conversation while SD yelled down the phone, but this was pointless. As soon as SD hung up he would say: "Sorry about that. Now, recap for me. What were we talking about?" He would re-argue any point that had been decided in his seeming absence, simply as a matter of principle.

Of his many magical moments, I feel fortunate to say I was present to witness his biggest blow-up ever. As we sat in a revenue meeting, the Reservations Manager phoned SD. The meeting halted, as usual. The rest of us waited for the usual outbursts and then SD's directions to the caller on how to bring the world under control again. On this occasion, it didn't come.

And the longer it didn't come, the more everyone looked at him. SD simply nodded and without even a goodbye, he hung up. And then it came. The phone landed near a plant pot in the corner; not in one piece either. SD ripped his glasses off so quickly that they caught in a spring clip on his arm and broke an arm off his specs.

Calming himself by grabbing the back of his chair, he stared at the Director of Sales, licking his lips. You could have heard a pin drop as he whispered at her: "What day is May 23rd?"

The SOD flipped through her diary. We all quietly checked our diaries. Looking up, she shrugged. "I don't have anything?"

"No. No you don't do you? Because if you did have a fucking Scotland Rugby International in Edinburgh in your diary (rolling every 'r' now), you would have remembered to block it off in the fucking system and jacked the rates up past sixty fucking pounds!"

There was a collective draw of breath. For once, SD had just cause.

It's Sales' job to broker the deals with large companies and offer them a 'group rate.' The size of their discount is related to the number of room nights the company uses during the year. The higher the usage; the cheaper the rate. Also in this contract is a clause stating that the hotel may apply 'blackout' dates, where the company gets no discount.

If the company books the rooms before they are told of the dates, the hotel has to honor that rate. So Sales and Reservations really have to have their finger on the pulse when any concerts, or say…rugby internationals are announced. Being the closest four star hotel to the stadium, all of the companies immediately tried to pick up the maximum number of rooms they were allowed at the discounted rate. The damage had been done by the time SD got the call.

And the news got worse! All hotels have an 'overbooking policy.' The hotel will sell more rooms than they have (if they can) by about ten percent because there are people who miss flights, or for some reason or other, just don't make it to the hotel. The credit cards of these 'no-shows' are still charged for the room. So by over-selling, the hotel can make more revenue than the one hundred percent occupancy would give them.

And if they all happen to show up, the front desk clerk just apologizes, and sends them to another hotel that they have already lined up…at a discounted rate for the hotel. There is indeed honor among thieves.

SD's problem here was multi-fold. First, as all the bookings came in a remarkably short time frame from many different agents, by the time reservations realized there was a problem, the hotel was already oversold by fifty percent.

To overbook by even ten percent is dangerous on a rugby weekend because there are never no-shows for this big an event. This brings up SD's second and third problems. Because all the other hotels in the city would be completely full already, there was nowhere to send the unlucky fifty percent to; so there was absolutely no chance of getting a discounted rate as a favor. Now SD would have to book people out that were paying us fifty pounds, to hotels that would be charging us over two hundred pounds a night.

Some hotels actually under-booked themselves on these big dates. Just in case they made a mistake with a reservation or two, they had flexibility. If they hadn't made an error, they could literally name their price from other hotels that had been careless.

As it happened, we just had to wait and see what happened on the day. The match was against Ireland. As all the Edinburgh hotels had been booked up solid for the weekend, the closest hotels we could find to book out the unlucky fifty percent to were in Dundee and Glasgow; both at least one hour away by car. Reservations tried to contact the guests before they arrived and send them straight to their hotel sixty or eighty miles away. As most of them could not be reached, there was general mayhem as some groups arrived to find that one of them had a room in Edinburgh, one in Dundee, and another in Glasgow. As they'd all booked separately, there was no way of knowing who was travelling as a party.

Because of this, compensation deals were brokered with the people that were inconvenienced. Some had taxis paid to and from Dundee and Glasgow every day so they could be around the festival atmosphere with their party. Almost all had their breakfast and dinners paid for too.

Over the course of the two days where the hotel was fully occupied, the room revenue was only seven thousand pounds. On a normal rugby weekend it would have been over twenty six thousand. The bill for the 'overbooked' ran to over twelve thousand pounds.

I wanted to ask Les, the Reservations Manager, how this whole affair could have happened, but he was never seen again.

As my hotel was the smallest in the group, and therefore the least profitable, SD did not spend a lot of time at our location. He popped round once a month to do a two-hour white-glove inspection with the GM and that was about it.

Luckily, he did not base himself at my hotel for long in the absence of a GM. Deciding he was too important for that, he demoted Laura, the GM of the larger sister hotel. She didn't seem to mind much. Laura was always positive and bubbly. I liked her; and she was good for my personal development.

As she spent most of her afternoons shopping in the town, or going for a massage, I was basically left to run the hotel myself. So when Laura fell pregnant shortly after her arrival, SD asked if I would assume control as the 'Acting General Manager.'

My tenure lasted one year. There were hiccups of course, but no disasters. In SD's words: "Nothing went up or down; it stayed level. And truth be told, I did expect things to slip a little." Because I wasn't given an Acting Assistant GM, I found it difficult to improve on what was already in place; and I certainly wasn't able to get out for shopping trips or massages.

The thing I enjoyed most about being GM was that you got to hear about every little complaint. To this day, I am absolutely amazed at some of the things people complain about. And they really are serious about it! As GM, it can either demolish your spirit, because you feel that nothing ever goes right; or you can have a laugh about them, and let it lift your spirits. I chose the latter.

The best complaint I ever had to respond to was about a duck. SD had a gimmick placed in every bathroom: a hotel logo'd plastic bath duck. It was a big hit, especially with stag groups. They would take the ducks out to night clubs and take photos of the ducks doing stupid things during the night. It seemed a perfect gimmick for them to introduce themselves to girls.

Most of our guests were business travelers however, who probably never floated their duck in the bath, or stuck it down a girl's top in a club. But the ducks always went home in their suitcases. These guests took them home for their kids, like the gentleman who wrote to me to complain about his flock of ducks. I read with increasing incredulity as the four page letter went on to describe how he had collected seven ducks and that not one floated upright in the bath. I tried it myself after reading the letter, and sure enough, they all tilted to one side.

The complainant described how he was 'bewildered at how such a poor quality duck can make its way into a four-star hotel.' He wrote of the 'great disappointment' his children and grandchildren experienced when the ducks did not float upright. At the end of the four pages, he finally cut to the chase. "I will not be returning to your hotel until this problem is rectified and we are suitably compensated."

I certainly wasn't about to give him a free stay for a tilting plastic duck. What would be next? Didn't like what was on TV? I did reply to apologize for the mental anguish it had caused two generations of his sensitive family, and to thank him for his feedback. I meant it too! No offer of compensation was made however, so if he did return, he certainly didn't make himself known. The four page letter stayed on my office wall as a reminder to me not to take things too seriously. Whenever I needed a laugh, I'd walk over and read the letter.

As I was sharing this complaint with Everett, the new GM of our sister hotel, he was ironically called away to deal with a cracker himself. A guest was at reception with a £450.00 phone charge that he claimed should have been a toll-free number. Everett apologized but stated that since he had no proof that it should be a toll-free number, he would have to be charged.

The guest went crazy. "The ad stated quite clearly that it was toll-free. You must have it programmed wrong in your phone system!"

"Show me the ad," Everett asked. The guest went quiet.

"I don't have it."

They argued back and forth for several minutes until the guest, realizing Everett wasn't backing down, stormed back to his room. He reappeared two minutes later with a men's magazine and flipped to the back pages. The guest seemed to lose his voice from this moment on. His face turned a strange shade of red, almost purple; either from rage or embarrassment…maybe both.

He pointed to the ad for a gay chatline and the number below that stated 'call toll-free.' Everett, his face turning a shade of red also, apologized profusely and refunded the amount from his bill. It seemed IT had programmed the phone incorrectly after all.

By far the worst part of my Acting GM role was having to deal with the owner's son. He was the designated architect for the hotel, and any decision regarding color scheme or design had to go through his company.

My problem was two-fold. First, it took them forever to make a decision. Second, when they did, it was invariably the wrong decision. After Sara had been sacked, SD spent a lot of money refurbishing the hotel to bring it up from three stars to four.

However, two years on, we were still dealing with ridiculous design issues. First of all, they decided that Queen sized beds would go in all the rooms. This would have been fine if all the rooms were the same size, but they weren't.

Some were much smaller than others. There were eight or nine rooms where the door met the bed when you walked in. You literally had to squeeze your knees between the bed and dresser to get to the far side of the room.

They had also replaced the carpeting at the entrance to the rooms with laminate flooring. This actually looked very nice; however the carpet was much thicker than the laminate, which meant that there was now a large gap under every door. As you walked down the corridors, you could now hear everything that was going on inside each room. It was not uncommon for me to find groups of guys giggling outside a door listening to people having sex.

The most ridiculous design concept of all however was putting the laminate flooring in the bathrooms. Within two weeks, two people had slipped when stepping out of the shower. One broke an arm; the other suffered a concussion.

The clever architect decided that something would have to be done, however they were waiting on legal advice from son number two, the group's lawyer of choice. The laminate flooring was still there two years and many accidents later, when I left.

As the end of Laura's maternity leave approached, SD was getting worried. He wasn't allowed to contact her, and she hadn't contacted anyone either. "Mike, these women are all the same. They say they don't want kids, and then as soon as they have one, they don't want to work again. I knew this was going to happen! Okay Mike listen, if Laura doesn't come back, I'm going to offer you the General Manager position on a full-time basis."

Laura had made quite a habit of being late though. SD had got my hopes up but I knew Laura, and Steven should have known better too. She had never been on time for a meeting since I'd known her. It would drive SD crazy when she strolled in fifteen minutes late, and then start chatting like it was pre-meeting coffee time. "Hi everyone, sorry I'm late. The traffic is crazy out there today. Oh Sandra, I like your hair!"

SD tried to shut her up as quickly as possible. "Everyone else made it here on time. Maybe you could leave a little earlier next time."

Sure enough, on the last day for Laura to contact someone, she did. When she did come back to work, it was as a sideshow. She was at the hotel even less than before; the baby didn't sleep well, she was teething, Laura was tired, etc. Every time SD came to see her, she was MIA. He was getting tired of it too, and came up with a plan.

The Group was building a new hotel right next to our sister hotel. Laura was 'promoted' to GM of this bigger and newer hotel. This was SD's plan to get her busy or get rid of her.

SD put the offer of full-time GM back on the table to me. This time I had to consider the consequences.

I knew if I took the permanent GM position, I would have to go in for 'the operation.' This is the one where the HR memory chip, with all the Management Skills and any other HR courses that got you to GM, are surgically removed. This is in accordance with the Fifth Law, which allows the GM to condemn others for the very things they do themselves…tenfold. As a bonus, they do this without memory or guilt.

I discussed the pros and cons with my wife Carla, who was now pregnant with daughter number two. It didn't seem right to us that I should have to give up all the skills that had got me to GM, and forget about Food and Beverage, my first love.

"I'm sorry Steven, I am really grateful for the offer, but we have decided to move to Canada."

SD brought in several contestants to interview for the GM job. They were a poor bunch in truth, so it wasn't hard to pick Kit Kat out of the mix. I still had two months before my move to Canada when Kit Kat came on board, which served as a handover period.

Kit Kat seemed a perfect replacement for Laura. He even kept his make-up and perfume in the same corner of the desk. This was apparently essential when called out to deal with guests. He would look at himself in the mirror, check his complexion, and give a quick two puffs of perfume on his neck before leaving the office.

Of course, if you were in the office with him at the time, he didn't need the mirror. He would ask you: "How do I look?"

Whenever Kit Kat had done something he thought was exceptional (which was often), he went around telling everyone about it. "That's my advice to both of you," he told Fiona and me one day. "Stay ahead of everyone. I am always one step ahead of everyone else."

It was this amazing narcissism that had prompted Fiona to comment: "If he were a chocolate bar, he'd eat himself!"

The name Kit Kat remained with him until the day when he fell one step behind everyone else. He should have perhaps been named after an ice cream rather than a chocolate bar though.

As with all events at Murrayfield stadium, the F&B staff were gearing up for a long and busy day. This time it was a 'walk for peace.' The march would be going straight past the hotel, culminating with a rally at the stadium.

Kit Kat took one look at my weekly beverage order as I prepared for the big day. "You must be joking. It'll take months to get rid of all that booze," he sneered in his Highland twang.

This was exactly the kind of arrogance that made everyone anticipate his cock-ups with great delight. "Oh really? Would you like to do the beverage order?" I replied.

Rather than admit he had no idea, Kit Kat took the clipboard from me and cut my order in exactly half. "I don't think people will be drinking at a peace march," he scoffed. "I checked the forecast and it's going to be hot that day. We'd make more money selling ice cream."

I didn't think he was serious, but the day before the march, three large freezers arrived and were stored in a banquet room. The one thousand ice cream bars arrived next. I had to hand it to him; it was a risk. He was either going to look like a genius or a moron.

On the big day, Kit Kat stood outside flogging the occasional ice cream at £2.50 a shot. Meanwhile, the bar ran out of beer and vodka before the march got within a mile of the hotel.

As the bar shut up shop, Kit Kat stuck a box of ice cream bars into everyone's arms and sent them packing into the 25C heat. "Come on guys, sell, sell!" he clapped as he cheered them on. Laughing as they went, they did their best, but knew it was a dead loss. Most of the ice cream melted in their arms, and Vicky finished top seller with seven. A total of forty three ice cream bars sold on the day. Better than I had expected, but 'moron' it was.

Normally, at the end of a long, hard Murrayfield event, we bought all the staff a drink. As there was nothing left in the bar to buy them, there are no prizes for guessing what Kit Kat gave them this day.

The following day, I raised the obvious question. "We need to move those freezers out of the banquet room. What are we going to do with all the ice cream?"

When Kit Kat was up, he was sky-high; but when he was down he was suicidal. He shot me a sad glance, clearly disgusted with himself. "I don't know." So much for his 'one step ahead' theory!

"What did Steven say?" I asked.

His jaw dropped. His eyes widened. But Kit Kat remained silent. "You didn't tell him!" I mouthed. We both knew SD would spot a two thousand pound expenditure with no return on the monthly balance sheet.

Kit Kat didn't give up right away though. The march was on the second day of the month, so he had twenty nine days to get rid of it all, before the balance sheet was due. He used ice cream for everything: 'dessert of the day' in the restaurant; staff rewards; even guest room amenities! All to no avail. At month's end there were still eight hundred and twenty nine ice cream bars on the books.

Kit Kat's ego finally melted a little bit. For months after I had moved to Canada, I was still getting e-mails from staff giving me the updated ice cream inventory count!

Moving countries can be difficult for managers, unless you are moving into a position that is already lined up. When you move, prospective new employers aren't always sure about the quality of the places you've worked at and your role there; and it can be difficult to contact people for references. Very often, you have to take a step back.

I didn't really feel I was taking a step back when I accepted a Food and Beverage Manager position however. On the contrary, it was a prestigious hotel and I was delighted to get back into Food and Beverage full-time.

Bitch-Nicole had been promoted to GM the week before she interviewed me. She had a double-barreled last name; but (unknown to her) the staff also gave her a double-barreled first name. The name had been given to her by the F&B staff in particular, because of the apparent ease with which she slashed their benefits package almost immediately. Many of them only found out about it when they got a bill from their Doctor or Dentist. As with most nicknames in the workplace, Bitch-Nicole's was as appropriate as it was unprofessional.

I could imagine that she would have had no problem agreeing to the 'GM operation,' had she been given a choice. However, Bitch-Nicole's parents, leaving nothing to chance, had set her up for success by having her heart removed at birth. This way, their little heifer would never have worry about learning any pointless Management Skills that she would only have to give up later. This gave her a decided cut-throat edge over the other GM candidates.

Once reaching the GM position, this heartless soul became a ruthless dictator; sacking everyone she distrusted. Bitch-Nicole was the master of motivation…Stalin-style. She found his technique was especially useful, as did Uncle Joe, when dealing with the Executive Committee. As she constantly passed on information that was supposed to be told 'in confidentiality,' the Executive Committee could trust nobody. Paranoia reigned supreme.

For Bitch-Nicole to be successful with this technique she had to appear forgetful. She also had to change her mind on every possible decision (usually several times). If anyone acted quickly on anything she had temporarily agreed to, they could expect to be brought to justice for not having the authority to commit the act. If they dallied, their agreement would soon be null and void, when she had changed her mind again. For this, one could also expect to be ridiculed at her first opportunity, publicly if at all possible, for not acting quickly enough.

Bitch-Nicole's exemplary motivational skills led to a split on the Executive Committee. Prince Alex the SOD and Kate the Snow Leopard clung tightly to Bitch-Nicole. Isaac in HR rocked the fence back and forth while the Puffer in Accounts cowered somewhere in the corner, awaiting the outcome. Chef and I were clearly alone on the outside.

Even allowing for her unpredictability, a lot had changed in the year since Bitch-Nicole had promoted me from F&B Manager to Director of F&B. It seems to be the destiny of the Food and Beverage Pilgrim: two steps forward and one step back.

Of course, Bitch-Nicole couldn't just get rid of me. She would have to plan out the sequence of events, just as she had done with the IT Guy, the Executive Housekeeping Manager and many, many others who had just vanished, unnoticed. There was nothing left for me to do but wait to see how she would play out the Symphony of a Sacking…

Overture

The story always begins with the General Manager allowing time off for a holiday. Don't be fooled when they feign delight at your holiday request form. They generally are delighted! As you prepare the handover for your team in the final hours before some well-earned rest, be prepared for the summons to the Dragon's Lair to learn the first part of their plot.

"I am going to move The Snow Leopard into F&B while you are away. I want to cross-train her in F&B. When she takes her holiday in a few months, you can cross-train in Front Office."

This prelude to events serves two purposes. First, it ruins your holiday. Second, the stress on your leave serves Stalin well; ensuring you are on edge and ill-prepared for the next steps when you return. However, the hope is that you may be looking forward to the holiday so much that you miss the signs.

In my case, I knew Bitch-Nicole had no intention of letting me look after F&B, never mind Front office! Very see-through; but the vanity of her power blinded her from the ridiculous obviousness of her lie. I took comfort in the fact that her smug smile made this seem a plausible explanation to her; or possibly she just didn't care. Either way, it would award me the small satisfaction of accepting my sentence without pleas for clemency, denying her a certain anticipated pleasure.

Act I

While the F&B Manager is away, the GM hands her puppet the list of instructions and 'recommendations' for them to be aware of, in case they are questioned. This list of recommendations is generally a GM's wish list: all the things they would like to see the F&B Manager accomplish (without any means or funds in order to achieve the projects).

When the F&B Manager returns from holiday, the Front Office Manager will have been sniffing around the department, telling the peasants how much better the world could be. The peasants, fooled into believing that their gulag-like working conditions may improve, are carefully quoted 'off the record.' Later, this will serve to de-motivate the F&B Manager further.

Within hours of my return, Bitch-Nicole de-briefed me on the happenings in my department: "Kate has made some exciting recommendations for F&B that I think we should discuss."

I took a look at the recommendations. The massive list came complete with Excel spreadsheets for each recommendation. I knew for a fact, from watching her struggle with my labor forecasts prior to my holiday that the Snow Leopard did not have the slightest idea how to read, never mind set up, an Excel spreadsheet! There could be no doubt that this was the handiwork of Bitch-Nicole herself.

"Well, I don't think any of these recommendations would work with our set-up, but I'll have a closer look at a couple of them," I smiled.

It's hard to say whether that was the resistance she wanted, to feel justified in her push; or if she was disappointed there wasn't more of a fight. Either way, I already knew it could have no effect on my fate; although I got the impression it was the latter because she tried to turn up the heat. "You know, everyone seemed much happier here while you were away."

Her comment didn't really bother me, because I knew for once, she was right…to an extent. The old adage was true: 'when the cat's away; mice will play.' It was no exaggeration to say that the entire hotel, with Chef and I in particular, had positively been on cloud nine while she had recently been on holiday.

I quickly considered my responses: "If by everyone you mean the Gang of Three, I have no doubt you're right." Too much venom! That was playing into her hand. Silence it was. The lack of response would not only disappoint her, it would unnerve her; however temporarily.

Act II

In order to remove any conspirators (who may inspire a final flare-up) from the scene of the crime, the GM and HR send their catalysts on a short break. This is also part-reward for a job well done.

If you are unsure what signs to look for; even if you are in a complete state of denial, this is the most tell-tale sign of all.

It was announced at a morning meeting a few days later that The Snow Leopard was suddenly taking advantage of a 'quiet week' to take a holiday. My alarm bells rang. Quiet week? I checked the hotel occupancy: there was neither peak nor valley. Incidentally, no cross-training was mentioned here.

I was off the following two days. On my second day, I called The Dick to see how things were going, as I always did (knowing there would be no handover for me on my return, when he would be off). In mid-conversation, The Dick informed me he had just been summoned to the Dragon's Lair, along with HR.

This was it then. It was all going to happen tomorrow. It was The Dick's day off; the Snow Leopard was away…and in a strange coincidence, Prince Alex would be away at a Sales conference.

"I'll call you back when I'm done," The Dick said.

It was the last time I ever spoke to him. I left several messages for him to call me back; but he didn't. Finally, I put my theory to the ultimate test: I called HR four times. When HR doesn't return your call; it's game over.

Crescendo

This is where the final insult is dealt in order to shock you and reduce your capacity to think. The hope is that this 'shock' makes you internalize your actions, blaming yourself. If it is done well, you leave quietly.

My case was slightly different. As I walked in the next day, I had already prepared myself for the final scene. As expected, it was at the end of my day when Bitch-Nicole called me through to the Lair for the last time. I noted that my casual awareness of HR's presence did not give her the satisfaction she had clearly desired. It was going to be small victories for the Director of F&B today; I enjoyed it.

Bitch-Nicole needn't have wasted everyone's time stating that she had three signed affidavits (no doubt from The Dick, Prince Alex and the Snow Leopard) all stating that 'everyone seemed happier' when I had been away. Hardly a crime against inhumanity; but she added that she felt I needed a fresh start too.

This is also crucial step in the procedure, especially (as in this case) where the F&B Manager has a crystal clear record as far as disciplinary hearings are concerned. If they can't make you resign, they have nothing. My options seemed pretty clear cut: freedom; or a miserable existence under Stalin's watchful eye.

I afforded myself a wry smile. I felt I needed a fresh GM, but I was not opposed to the option in front of me either. It was certainly no hardship escaping from her Gulag.

Then came the predictable final insult to heighten the impact of the last blow, and ensure I would jump at the chance of freedom. "Dick has some good ideas for F&B and I told him I'd like to hear them." I laughed outright this time. I knew the reason I was on the way out was because I couldn't control my Dick. Now the person who had asked me to get rid of him on so many occasions was going to get into bed with him? I didn't think so!

In order for The Dick to sign the affidavit condemning me, she would have had to make a deal with him. He would have been told that he would have an opportunity to put himself in pole position for the now-vacant F&B Manager's position. When he didn't get the job he would realize he had been used, and quit.

FINALE

"Now, we are going to go down the route of redundancy," she continued. "However; as you have been here for three years and have improved F&B significantly in that time, we would like to offer you the opportunity to resign. If you do, we will put 'laid off due to restructuring' on your Record of Employment. You'll get unemployment benefits."
Isaac nodded quietly in the corner as if this sounded like the opportunity of a lifetime to him; the uninterested observer.

This is the way it is always done. A deal the Government would love to know about. For resigning I was given a two-day reprieve, to hand over as much information to Bitch-

Nicole as possible; and make it appear it was by mutual consent. In return, the Government picked up the tab.

ENCORE

The final scene opened with a phone call: "Mike, where are you? The restaurant's packed! When will you be here?"

I was stunned. I didn't know what to say. I looked at my watch: 8:00am. "Five minutes." It seemed the height of arrogance to me that the GM who had just sacked me, could call and ask why I wasn't in early for my final day.

As I walked up the stairs for the last time, I could see the problem. There was Bitch-Nicole running around the restaurant in a panic. As I took in the scene, I could hear her asking everyone who passed her by: "Where is Mike? What time will he be here?"

EPILOGUE

According to Chef, The Dick slaved away night and day for eight weeks. Of course, Bitch-Nicole hired another female for the F&B Puppet position. Chef now owned the only set of testicles left on the Executive Committee. Isaac and The Puffer still attended, but they had been rendered impotent by the Gang of Three.

The Dick resigned on the spot when he was given the bad news; kicking, screaming and crying until the end. After he had wiped away his tears and the anger replaced the disappointment, two escorts walked him from the premises as he left under a cloud of obscenities. Unemployment benefits were no doubt waived on this occasion.

Chef afforded himself a giggle, taking in the scene from a safe distance. However, he too could hear the Orchestra warming up now…and prepared himself for the inevitable.

For myself, I decided I wanted to work in a 'pure' Food and Beverage environment. In the dog eat dog political world of hotels, staying put is not an option. Failure to strive for a promotion is akin to demanding a demotion. In my stride towards a second stint at the General Manager post, I hadn't even realized that I really didn't want it. I wanted nothing to do with contractors, sales people, maintenance issues or housekeeping problems.

It took me six months to realize how unhappy I'd been at The Plaza. In that time, I had moved to a large chain of box-built restaurants. No Human Resources; no Accounts; no Sales team; and no Front Office. Just Food and Beverage…sheer bliss!

Restaurants are not completely problem-free of course and this chain certainly had its share of challenges. However, the relaxed atmosphere and focus on purely food and beverage issues was a joy. Within a year I was promoted to General Manager.

Looking back now, I doubt if I could really appreciate and enjoy the 'pure' food and beverage business as much as I do, without having gone through the trials and tribulations of the hotel industry. It did not take me long to see that I finally had the best of both worlds. As General Manager, I was still concerned only with Food and Beverage. I had finally achieved my dream!

I had been pondering exactly this thought while making a cappuccino one morning. As I returned to the office, I sat back in my chair, fully relaxed; wondering if life could get any better. As I leaned forward to take my first sip, the familiar call came from the other end of the corridor: "Need help in the restaurant!"

It instantly took me back to Jean-Phillipe at the beginning of my journey: "We are all waiters in this business."

I grinned, slurping quickly at my cappuccino. "On my way!"

About the Author

Michael Kelly was born in Edinburgh, Scotland where he became a devoted follower of Hibernian Football Club and proud member of the Tartan Army. Since the age of nineteen, he has worked in four and five star hotels in Scotland and Canada. Holding a Diploma in Advanced Food Hygiene, Michael is a member of the Royal Environmental Health Institute of Scotland. He currently resides in Burnaby, British Columbia with his wife Carla, and their two daughters: Mhairi and Rhian.